# The Handbook of
# System-level Investing

# The Handbook of System-level Investing

Jon Lukomnik, Editor
William Burckart, Associate Editor

Library of Congress Cataloging-in-Publication Data

The Handbook of System-level Investing: How Experts Worth Trillions of Dollars are Rethinking Investing, Jon Lukomnik and William Burckart

Summary: A collection of essays about maximizing investment returns while minimizing risk, by assessing the interplay and interdependencies between their investments, the real economy, and the complex challenges of our environmental, social, and financial systems.

ISBN: 978-1-939282-59-0

Published by Miniver Press, LLC, McLean Virginia
Copyright 2026 Nell Minow

For information regarding permission, write to editor@miniverpress.com

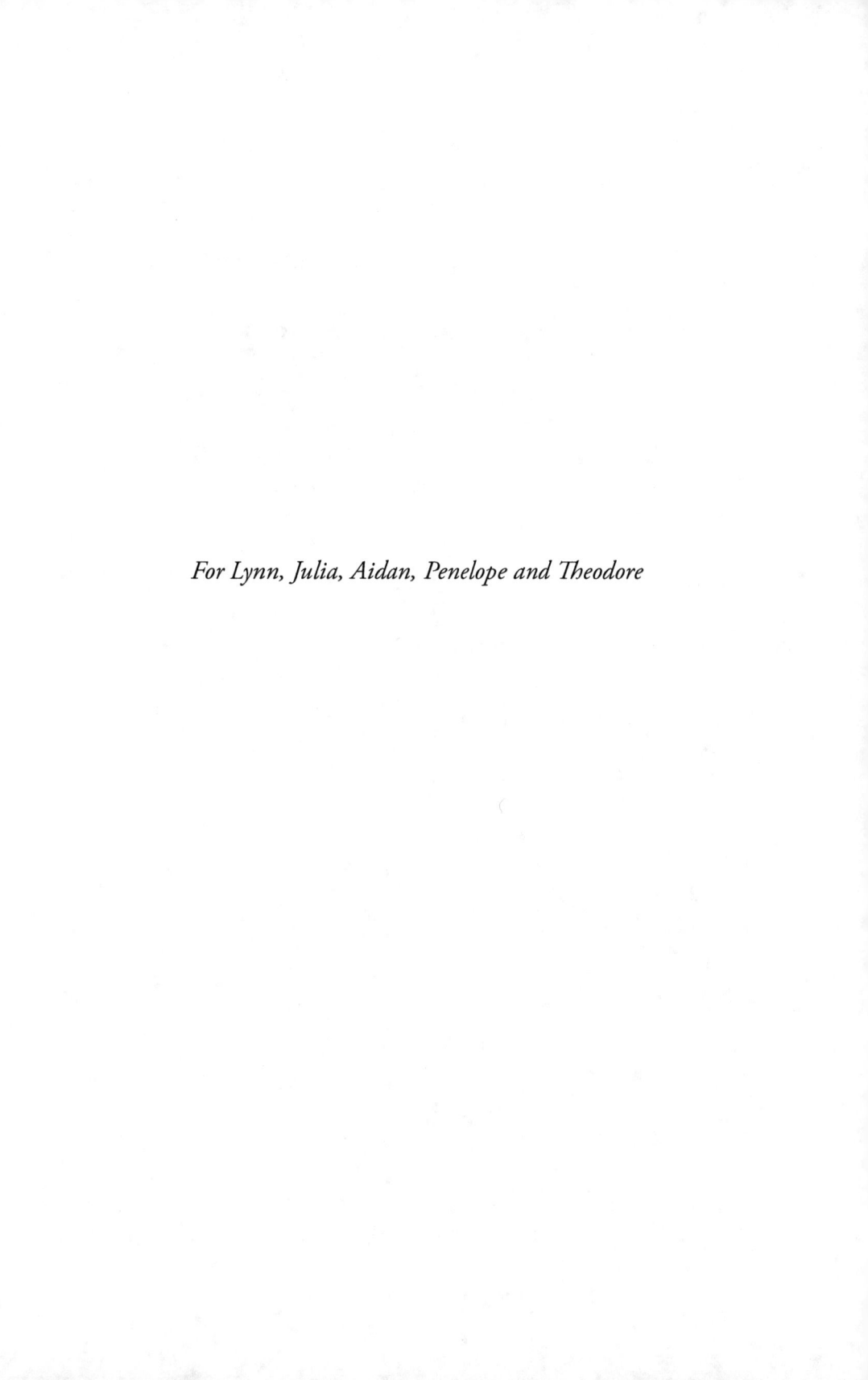

*For Lynn, Julia, Aidan, Penelope and Theodore*

# Acknowledgements

In the slightly more than the decade that we have been writing about system-level investing, the concept has grown from an emerging idea into a much-discussed, much-written-about, and increasingly practiced discipline. Its evolution has been a collective endeavor. While we hesitate to list all who have contributed – both because the community is large and because we fear inadvertently omitting someone – we want to underscore that we stand squarely on the shoulders of the predecessors and contemporaries who shaped this field. We continue to rely on the insights, research, and discoveries of many others. In particular, we wish to recognize two thinkers whose intellectual leadership has been foundational to each of us: James P. Hawley, Jon's co-author on *Moving Beyond Modern Portfolio Theory*, and Steven Lydenberg, William's co-author on *21st Century Investing*. Their work helped define the contours of system-level investing, and their ideas remain deeply woven into the theory and practice reflected throughout this *Handbook*.

There are also individuals and institutions whose direct support made this volume possible. We extend our thanks to the Tipping Point Fund on Impact Investing and especially to Fran Seegull and Jessie Duncan, whose belief in both the project and its unconventional funding and distribution strategy gave us the latitude to pursue it. We are equally grateful to the High Meadows Institute and Chris Pinney for their research support, and to Delilah Rothenberg, whose early thinking and collaboration were instrumental in shaping the *Handbook's* conceptual architecture. Finally, we owe a special debt to our publisher, the inimitable Nell Minow of Miniver Press. Her immediate grasp of what this *Handbook* aims to accomplish – and her willingness to champion a publishing model that promotes new ideas and advances the field – has reaffirmed our belief that publishing can be a true force for progress.

# Contents

# Foreword

## By Caroline Flammer[1]

*The Handbook of System-level Investing*, edited by institutional investing practitioners William Burckart and Jon Lukomnik – both Columbia University Sustainable Investing Research Initiative (SIRI) affiliates and School of International and Public Affairs (SIPA) faculty – is the much-awaited reference on system-level investing: a must-read for anyone seeking to understand and implement the next frontier of investing, one that makes financial practices fit for the 21st century.

Investing always evolves. The investing challenges of the 21st century are new, destabilizing and systemic. They involve complex, interconnected global issues that impact societies and economies. To maximize returns while minimizing risk, investors need to consider the interplay and interdependencies between their investments, the real economy, and the complex challenges of our environmental, social, and financial systems. System-level investing does just that.

Building on and going beyond traditional finance theory and sustainable investing practices, system-level investing recognizes the need for capital markets to be able to efficiently create investment opportunities from

---

[1] Caroline Flammer is the A. Barton Hepburn Professor of Economics, Columbia University.

a flourishing real economy, which in turn, depends on robust social, financial, and environmental systems. At the same time, investing influences those systems. The feedback loops are complex. System-level investors intentionally seek to manage their impacts on global systems, recognizing that mitigating systemic risks can reduce investment risk and enhance returns. Doing so, however, requires new investment strategies that directly address challenges such as climate change, biodiversity loss, racial and gender injustice, income inequality, and food and health systems fragility, among others.

This is difficult and new terrain for many investors. This *Handbook* will serve as a foundational guide for practitioners, academics, and educators alike and draws from the experiences of many of the leaders in the field. Both current and future generations of finance experts will want to learn about the cutting edge of finance and how to implement investment practices fit for the 21$^{st}$ century. This Handbook (along with Jon and William's earlier books on *Moving Beyond Modern Portfolio Theory* and *21$^{st}$ Century Investing: Redirecting Financial Strategies to Drive Systems Change*, respectively) will help you do so!

# Preface

BY STEPHEN B. HEINTZ[2]

In September 2014, the Rockefeller Brothers Fund (RBF) made a decision that would test both conviction and convention: to divest from fossil fuels and realign its endowment with its mission to advance a more just, sustainable, and peaceful world. At the time, it was a controversial step – even among peers committed to social purpose. Yet that choice became a proving ground for what *The Handbook on System-Level Investing* now seeks to capture: a disciplined, transparent, and value-driven approach to managing capital in a world defined by interconnected risks and interdependent outcomes.

When the RBF undertook this journey, it did not imagine that aligning investments with mission would require a re-examination of the very assumptions underpinning fiduciary duty. The past decade has shown, however, that the long-term viability of any portfolio depends on the health of the systems in which it operates – climate stability, social cohesion, democratic governance, and the integrity of markets themselves. In this light, fiduciary responsibility is not at odds with mission alignment, it is its natural expression.

---

[2] Stephen B. Heintz is president and CEO of the Rockefeller Brothers Fund.

This evolution reflects a larger movement, one that former RBF President Bill Dietel once described as a revolution "beyond grants, beyond foundations, beyond cash." Just as 20th-century philanthropy needed new tools and institutional forms to address the scale of emerging challenges, 21st-century investing requires new frameworks for influence that account for the systemic forces shaping both risk and return. System-level investing builds on that lineage of innovation, offering investors a way to channel financial, intellectual, and relational capital toward strengthening the resilience of the systems on which all enterprises and beneficiaries depend.

The RBF's own experience has demonstrated that this is not an act of charity but of prudence. Integrating sustainability factors, racial and gender equity lenses, impact considerations, and decarbonization priorities has enhanced the Fund's resilience and revealed new opportunities. Over the past decade, our endowment has remained financially robust – outperforming its benchmark with lower risk – while achieving 99.7 percent fossil-fuel-free status and deepening engagement with diverse managers and mission-aligned enterprises. Far from compromising returns, this integration has strengthened them, illustrating that market-based innovation and moral clarity can reinforce one another.

At the heart of this progress is partnership. The Fund's collaboration with its outsourced chief investment office, Cerity Partners OCIO, exemplifies a model of shared learning and adaptive strategy. They did not simply implement policy – they co-created an evolving framework responsive to new information and systemic change. Such relationships between asset owners, advisors, managers, government, and civil society mirror the interdependence of the systems investors seek to influence. Transparency and humility, rather than prescription, have guided this process, ensuring that the RBF's example informs peers without insisting upon replication. We are all learning as we go.

Today, institutional investors everywhere face a similar inflection point. Climate disruption, social inequity, and political instability are no longer externalities: they are structural determinants of market performance. Fiduciaries who fail to account for these systemic dynamics risk mispricing both opportunity and obligation. As debates over sustainability, diversity, and fiduciary duty intensify, it is worth remembering that stewardship of capital has always been about more than quarterly returns – it is about safeguarding the conditions that make prosperity possible.

The *Handbook on System-Level Investing* arises from that imperative. Developed by Jon Lukomnik and William Burckart, it gathers voices from across the global investment community to chart how investors can act as agents of systemic health. The contributors – leaders from pension funds, asset managers, foundations, and policy institutions – offer practical frameworks and case studies for integrating systems thinking into investment strategy, governance, and stewardship. Their work builds on the same ethos that guided the RBF's transformation: curiosity, courage, and a willingness to learn in public.

As Dietel observed about an earlier wave of philanthropic innovation, "The task before the revolutionaries is sobering." The same can be said here. System-level investing demands patience, collaboration, and a reorientation of metrics toward long-term system performance. Yet its promise is profound: the possibility that capital, deployed wisely and transparently, can become an instrument not only of wealth creation but of systemic repair and resilience.

This *Handbook* is both a reflection of what has been learned and an invitation to what lies ahead. It affirms that the alignment of financial and societal purpose is not a luxury – it is a fiduciary necessity.

# Introduction

Chapter 1:

# Why, What, Who, Where & How: Introduction to the Handbook of System-level Investing

By Jon Lukomnik and William Burckart[3]

## Why?

Investing evolves when its foundational tools no longer match the realities investors face. We have reached that point again. For almost 75 years, investing largely has meant following the dictates of Modern Portfolio Theory (MPT), first espoused by Harry Markowitz in 1952.[4] MPT, with its emphasis on diversification, remains the best tool for extracting the optimal portfolio from the extant capital markets because it mitigates the idiosyncratic risk of different securities, styles, and asset classes. Diversification, benchmark-relative performance, and, more recently, ESG integration, provided investors with a reliable set of tools for navigating

---

[3] Jon Lukomnik is Editor of this Handbook. He is co-author, with James P. Hawley, of *Moving Beyond Modern Portfolio Theory: Investing that Matters*. William Burckart is Associate Editor of this Handbook. He is co-author, with Steve Lydenberg of *21st Century Investing: Redirecting Financial Strategies to Drive Systems Change*.

[4] Harry Markowitz, "Portfolio Selection", *Journal of Finance*, Vol. 7 No. 1 (March 1952).

markets. Those tools worked well when material risks were issuer-specific, sector-specific, or factors that could be diversified, hedged, and priced.

But today, the most consequential risks are outside the portfolio. Climate instability, deepening economic inequality, geopolitical fractures, the deterioration of information integrity, and stresses within the financial system's own infrastructure do not affect only one security or one asset class: they alter the conditions under which markets function. Those risks to the environmental, social and financial systems underpinning our economy create systematic, or non-diversifiable, risk.[5] Investors haven't discussed that risk much – or didn't until system-level investing gained some interest in the last ten years – because MPT assumes that the general price level of the markets (effectively what investors call beta) is exogenous. But that silence about beta does not address its salience: Systematic, non-diversifiable risk determines 75 to 94 percent of the variability of your returns. By contrast, security selection and portfolio construction, the things an investor can control through trading (and the focus of MPT), only drive 6 to 25 percent of the variability in returns.[6]

Until recently, investors lacked both the theory and a practical field guide for addressing those systemic risks and the resultant impacts on the financial markets. When our two books on system-level investing were published in 2021 – within a month of each other – we set out to fill that gap. Both *Moving Beyond Modern Portfolio Theory: Investing that Matters*, co-authored by Lukomnik and James P. Hawley, and *21st Century Investing: Redirecting Financial Strategies to Drive Systems Change*, co-authored by Burckart and Steve Lydenberg, drew on the data and the lived experience of practitioners who had already begun to recognize the limits of relying exclusively on MPT-era tools. Our argument, then as now, was straightforward: If the health of environmental, social, and financial

---

[5] William Burckart and Steve Lydenberg, *21st Century Investing: Redirecting Financial Strategies to Drive Systems Change* (Berrett-Koehler: 2021)
[6] Jon Lukomnik and James P. Hawley, *Moving Beyond Modern Portfolio Theory: Investing That Matters,* (Routledge: 2021)

systems drives investor outcomes, prudent investors must account for and influence the conditions that sustain system health.

The field has accelerated in the five years since those books were released. A growing number of asset owners and managers – from pension funds, insurers, and endowments to asset managers and investment consultants – increasingly adapt their investment beliefs and policies, governance structures, capital allocation practices, stewardship strategies, and data models to address risks and opportunities that they cannot diversify away. That is a huge paradigm shift. Mitigating systemic risks by acting both within and outside the capital markets is new. It's complex. It's difficult. And it's dynamic over time.

Much of the work those system-level investors have done has been innovative, sometimes experimental, and often ahead of what the industry had the language to describe. It has also been dispersed across geographies, asset classes, and organizational types. As a result, the information and skill sets have been fragmented.

That, in a nutshell, is the "why" of this *Handbook*.

## What?

Being a system-level investor means trying to mitigate real-world systemic risks that cause non-diversifiable risk in the capital markets. That, in turn, requires investors to go further than the well-trod MPT path. Sometimes system-level investors feel they are bushwhacking through an unfamiliar landscape. But paths beyond MPT have started to become signposted. This *Handbook* represents the first attempt to map that emerging landscape. It is not intended to introduce a new ideology, nor to discard the substantial value of MPT. Instead, it builds on the logic of MPT-based diversified, long-term investing models. What system-level investing does is extend investing from the trading terminal to examine real-world conditions that determine whether capital markets can sustain the returns required by beneficial investors. System-level investing asks investors to look beyond security-level analysis and see the whole map: the norms, rules, incentives, information flows, and feedback loops that underpin market behavior.

In so doing, we are very aware that handbooks have special obligations to readers. A handbook is a manual to a field of practice. As such, it should shorten the learning curve, even while respecting complexity. It should offer breadth and depth without unnecessary weight. It should provide authority without jargon or mystique.

This *Handbook* integrates the familiar logic of diversified, long-term investing with a clear-eyed understanding of how real-world systems behave – and how investor actions, individually and collectively, shape those systems over time. It equips investors to manage not only prices and probabilities but also the structural conditions (including norms, rules, incentives, information flows, and feedback loops) that determine whether those prices and probabilities will support long-term value creation.

## Who?

*Who are the contributors?*

Handbooks should be authoritative. The contributors to this *Handbook* are that. As of the time of this writing, they manage or advise on more than $5.5 trillion in aggregate assets. More importantly, they include some of the best thinkers in investing, and they have graciously agreed to share their experiences. They speak candidly about breakthroughs and blind alleys, about what translated smoothly into practice and what required rethinking, about the difference between good intentions and measurable influence. Seen together, the contributions in these pages make it clear that system-level investing is not a departure from finance but an evolution of it. The goal is to learn from their specific journeys. What worked and what turned out to be a dead end. What shortcuts were discovered and what turned out to take longer than expected. What was easy and what was hard. What was expected that didn't happen, and what wasn't expected that did.

*Who should read this Handbook?*

If you're an investor, this *Handbook* is for you. Wherever you are in your system-level investing learning curve – from newly curious to skilled practitioner – this *Handbook* has tips, lessons and sometimes just stories for you. It will accelerate your system-level knowledge by reading about the experiences of others.

# Where?

As University Pension Plan Ontario (a contributor to this *Handbook*) explains in its statement of investment beliefs, "Value and risk are created in the real world. They are priced and harvested in the capital markets."[7]

The corollary to that statement is that mitigating systemic risk or taking advantage of the opportunities such risks create requires action in the real world. And that requires new tools and a new mindset.

Here's an analogy. When the impressionist painters first went outside to paint in the 19th century, painters had used paint for millennia and easels for centuries. But the impressionists needed to adapt to the new environment. Paints needed to be in transportable tubes, not the animal bladders and open containers used previously, and reformulated to stand up to the elements. Easels, which had been bulky, heavy pieces of furniture, needed redesigning for easy packing and carrying.

Similarly, moving beyond diversifying idiosyncratic risks on a trading desk computer screen to mitigating risks in the wider world means investors also

---

[7] https://myupp.ca/wp-content/uploads/2022/07/UPP-investment-beliefs.pdf. Accessed September 28, 2025.

need new tools and new skills. And just as the impressionists understood the impact of light and air in a new way once they left their studios, system-level investors gain newfound appreciation for the feedback loops between their investments and the financial, social and environmental systems, and understanding of how the various systems interact.

# How?

If systematic risk determines more than 75 percent of the variability in your return, what can you do about it? Here is the heart of the *Handbook* and its *raison d'etre*. If new paths are being blazed, where do they lead? Which are quick and easy, and which require specialized training, equipment and a huge amount of exertion?

Most investors don't leap straight to system-level practice; they enter through practical on-ramps that extend familiar tools toward system health. The most common – and often used in combination – are:[8]

- *Long-Term Value Creation.* Re-orienting analysis, mandates, and governance to multi-year value, investing in both issuers and assets that address evolving opportunities and risks over time.

- *Impact Investing.* Deploying capital with explicit, intentional social and environmental objectives alongside financial return, supported by purpose-built measurement.

- *Negative / Exclusionary Screening (including reweighting).* Reducing or removing exposure to activities with unacceptable harms – or reweighting indices – to lower systemic risk footprints while maintaining broad market exposure.

---

[8] William Burckart, Steve Lydenberg, and Jessica Ziegler, "Tipping Points 2016: Summary of 50 Asset Owners' and Managers' Approaches to Investing in Global Systems" (New York: The Investment Integration Project and IRRC Institute, 2016)

- *Investment Stewardship*. Adding an ownership discipline – engagement, voting, and escalation – progressively aimed at market-wide norms, standards, and policy that shape issuer behavior.

- *ESG Integration*. Systematically incorporating environmental, social and governance factors into financial analysis of an individual issuer. Even when applied only at the security level (not portfolio or system level), it builds the habit of tracing risk and value creation back to the wider world.

- *Universal Ownership*. Recognizing that diversified portfolios internalize economy-wide externalities – and that managing those externalities is material to returns. Moreover, the more diversified, and the longer the time horizon, the more material.

Taken together, these pathways provide concrete entry points – and momentum – for adopting a broader system-level approach. They also vary by investor type, size, and mandate, underscoring a central theme of this *Handbook*: System-level investing is not a wholesale reinvention, but a disciplined evolution of existing practices toward influencing the conditions that drive long-term value.

Whichever on-ramp you use, we suggest that all paths lead to three levels of system-level investing:

1. The selection of appropriate systemic risks upon which to focus.
2. The decision about what makes a system healthy.
3. The tools and techniques system-level investors use to mitigate systemic risk.

"Systemic risk" sounds simultaneously ominous and bloodless. Can those two words include every situation that may diminish returns, no matter how minor that diminution or how remote the potential? Does a risk need to pose a clear and present danger to a portfolio today to be considered? How does an investor select which risk(s) matter?

We suggest that a systemic risk qualifies for investor focus if it satisfies these four criteria: consensus, relevance, effectiveness, and magnitude:[9]

- Requiring *consensus* around the salience of a risk helps ensure that investors focus resources on issues of genuine systemic importance rather than individual "pet" concerns. To prevent narrowly conceived or self-interested priorities from driving the action, a systemic risk should be widely examined and recognized as materially significant. Such consensus can be demonstrated through validation by experts, academics, and practitioners, or by formal acknowledgment from authoritative bodies – such as inclusion among the United Nations Sustainable Development Goals.

- For a risk to be *relevant*, it must have a reasonable likelihood of materially affecting an investor's portfolio returns across asset classes. Investing is challenging enough without diverting attention to issues that lack meaningful financial consequence. A key step in assessing relevance is to articulate the transition mechanism – the pathway through which a systemic risk translates into financial impact. For instance, climate change affects returns through both physical and transition risks; extreme economic inequality undermines economic growth and increases recession frequency and depth; antimicrobial resistance in bacteria leads to excess mortality and economic disruption. By making these causal pathways explicit, investors can distinguish between broad systemic risks and those of limited relevance, ensuring focus on issues that pose a credible threat to financial performance. Without a probable link to portfolio outcomes, designing mitigation strategies would be unwarranted.

- A core assumption of this *Handbook* is that investors can mitigate systemic risks in the real world, even if they cannot diversify them away in the capital markets. The corollary is that investors must also be capable of acting effectively. If there is no plausible path for an

---

[9] Steve Lydenberg, "Systems-Level Considerations and the Long-Term Investor: Definitions, Examples, and Actions" (New York: The Investment Integration Project, 2017)

investor to influence or reduce a systemic risk, the issue fails the *effectiveness* test. System-level investors are not omnipotent – they must have credible means to drive change, or risk expending resources without meaningful impact. For example, while investors can calculate the probability of an asteroid strike causing material damage, they have no viable levers to mitigate that risk – hence, no rational basis to design investment strategies around it. In a more down-to-earth example, different investors have different abilities based on size, influence, culture, geography, etc. Effective system-level investors adjust their efforts based on their unique skills and resources.

• Think of *magnitude* as the degree of uncertainty surrounding the scale of an issue's long-term impact on investment returns in the absence of mitigation. Considering magnitude helps investors focus on systemic risks with the potential to cause significant and enduring financial disruption – and to design responses aimed at reducing that uncertainty. For example, if unmitigated, climate change is projected to reduce returns for large UK pension funds by as much as 30 percent by 2050. [10] While no forecast is certain, the consistency and credibility of such estimates – especially when supported by multiple studies and the broad consensus recognizing climate change as a systemic risk – make the magnitude of its potential financial impact material.

Having qualified a systemic risk as worth focusing on, the paths lead to understanding how to mitigate those risks. If the problem is systemic – a denigration of an environmental, social or financial systems – then the solution is also systemic – improving system health. But what does that mean?

Healthy systems are adaptable, clear, connected and directionally aligned: [11]

---

[10] Ortech financial, "Climate Risk Assessment – Top 30 UK pension funds," November 2024.
[11] William Burckart, Steve Lydenberg, and Jessica Ziegler, "Measuring Effectiveness: Roadmap for Assessing System-level and SDG Investing" (New York: The Investment Integration Project, 2018)

- *Adaptability* enables a system to respond to shocks and evolve over time. That is more than resilience. While resilience is important, it implies a return to the status quo ante. But the real world keeps changing; systems evolve. Adaptability combines both resilience and evolution.

- *Clarity* means the information within a system flows coherently and is accessible and reliable. Think of a system like a river. If the water flow is aligned, it is navigable. If there are eddies and whirlpools, or gaps such as waterfalls, then navigation becomes impossible. Improving the clarity of a system works similarly. Clarity enables investors to comprehend how the system creates or destroys value.

- *Connectivity* reflects the quality of interconnection among key system participants and across system dimensions. Strong connectivity addresses gaps, blind spots, and underserved components that weaken system function, and reduces fragmentation among interdependent but siloed actors. By strengthening these linkages, connectivity enables positive feedback loops that improve system health and resilience.

- *Directionality* lines up incentives, standards, rules and behavior so the system tends towards health, not entropy. Investors who intentionally shape market norms and corporate practices – for instance by codifying expected corporate governance standards – are practicing directionality.

Once system-level investors have qualified a systemic risk as a mitigation target, and understood the mitigation necessary to improve system health, they use a set of tools and techniques, some of which are familiar mainstream investing practices and some are newer:[12]

---

[12] William Burckart, Melissa Eng, Jessica Ziegler, and Monique Aiken, "(Re)Calibrating Feedback Loops: Guidance for Asset Owners and Institutional Investors Assessing the Influence of System-level Investing" (New York: The Investment Integration Project, 2023)

- *Investment Enhancement* happens when investors adapt familiar tools used for traditional portfolio management to the purpose of systemic risk mitigation. For example, purely MPT-focused investors engage with companies to increase enterprise value, but system-level investors choose their engagement target(s) based on the systemic risk they want to mitigate (e.g. engaging with pharmaceutical and health care companies about the opioid crisis, or about the abuse of antibiotics that leads to increased antimicrobial resistant bacteria).

- *Field Building* includes enlarging collective wisdom, creating new tools and shaping standards (of behavior, disclosure, investments) to improve investors' ability to mitigate systemic risks. For example, industry associations pool resources for research, and private sector entrepreneurs create new tools that merge AI and multi-variate models to examine climate and other systemic risk impacts.

- *Opportunity Generation* is effectively the inverse of systemic risk. Investors who study systemic risks often see investment opportunities in mitigating those risks. Investors concerned about extreme levels of inequality understand the power (and risk/return potential) of microloans. Those who understand underinvested populations often choose to invest through non-traditional emerging managers. Investors concerned about climate change invest in electrification projects, battery technology, alternative energy, resilient infrastructure, etc.

\* \* \*

While some may want to read the *Handbook* from cover to cover – particularly those who are leading the evolution of an investing organization towards system-level practices – others may want to dip in and out of the *Handbook* based on a specific subject. That is, of course, the unique quality of a *Handbook*. Each chapter is authored by investors and advisors who have lived through implementing system-level investment programs.

11

The case studies are authentic. And fascinating. While each investor's experiences are different, there are some universal takeaways.[13]

Towards that end, here is a very brief synopsis of the topics you will find in this *Handbook*.

## Section I:

How System-level Investing Comes to Life – Three-Part Case Study of PFZW / PGGM

*Chapter 2: How to Get Started*. Jaap van Dam was there at the beginning. He recalls how and why, starting with a blank sheet of paper, PZFW, the second largest Dutch pension plan, and its investment manager, PGGM, have become exemplars of system-level investing.

*Chapter 3: From Two-dimensional to Three-dimensional Investing*. Geraldine Leegwater and Colin Tissen describe PGGM's investment program from the inside, and answer a few key questions: How does the €261 billion pension manager create public market investment portfolios that fit its three-dimensional (risk/return/impact) mandate? What changes has PGGM made to its investment process, organizational structure, daily working routines and culture? And what were the results?

*Chapter 4: A Real Economy Approach to Integrated Investing and Portfolio Management*. Dirk Schoenmaker and Willem Schramade provide the academic theory behind how PGGM builds its investment portfolio. As they note, selecting securities and other investments to build a portfolio that generates good financial results while enabling good societal outcomes is far from a trivial problem. They provide a solution.

---

[13] The purpose of the Handbook is to provide exemplars of system-level investing and to illustrate tools and analyses that investors may find useful. Nothing herein should be considered legal or investment advice. Information is provided "as is" and may be incomplete or out of date. No warranties are made as to accuracy or completeness.

## Section II:

## Getting It Right: One Size Fits One

*Chapter 5: Different Organizations, Different Leverage Points.* As Head of U.S. Stewardship and Sustainable Investments at LGIM America (now L&G Asset Management), John Hoeppner relied on structured engagements appropriate for a global asset manager. Now, at Builders Vision, he emphasizes deploying flexible capital in a targeted approach to catalyze innovation and shift value chains. As he notes, effective system-level investing means leveraging the unique skill sets, resources and culture of each specific investor, not adopting a standardized color-by-the-numbers approach.

*Chapter 6: System-level Investing for Asset Managers.* BNP Paribas Asset Management's Jane Ambachtsheer, Sarah Annan, and Adam Kanzer explain why one of the world's largest asset managers is firmly on-board as a system-level investor, and how they engage – and what they've accomplished – through a series of case studies. From saving horseshoe crabs as part of their biodiversity efforts to combatting forced and child labor, they discuss how and why to use collaborative engagement, when and how to escalate, and why acting on systemic risk is necessary, but not a panacea.

*Chapter 7: How To Organize an Investment Department as a System-level Investor.* Barbara Zvan, Aaron Bennett and Brian Minns of University Pension Plan Ontario faced a unique challenge: how to create a multi-billion-dollar investment office out of thin air during a pandemic. The goal was to bridge the gap between system-level philosophy and the day-to-day functioning of the investment team. The solution: integrating system-level investing into governance, culture and compensation. Everything from top-level investment beliefs to reporting, from how they hire to the language they use, helps embed system-level investing at both a structural and a granular level.

*Chapter 8: Where To Focus: Identifying Systemic Risks and Setting Goals.* Carole Laible and Steve Lydenberg of Domini Impact Investments thought they had a simple task: Create goals for the management of forest assets. What they found is that systems are complicated, complex and sometimes confounding. Subsystems abound, and the goals for one subsystem might conflict with the goal of another. As they write, resolving those conflicts "turned out to have complications." This is the story of that challenge, detours encountered on the road to its resolution, and lessons learned along the way.

*Chapter 9: Measuring Success: Evaluation and Measurement.* Emilie Goodall notes three different, and sometimes conflicting, reasons to evaluate and measure an investor's system-level investing efforts: to learn to understand what works (or doesn't) in mitigating systemic risk; to improve by refining efforts and allocating resources; and to prove by showing that those efforts contribute to success. She builds on her experiences at asset manager Fidelity International to suggest some best practices.

# Section III:

# Tools and Techniques for System-level Investing

*Chapter 10: Investment Belief Statements.* Saksham Malhotra of Australian superannuation fund HESTA shows how a clear set of investment beliefs can serve as a fund's true north – linking purpose, governance, and day-to-day investment practice. For HESTA, these beliefs articulate how fiduciary duty connects to the health of the systems on which members' long-term returns depend. Malhotra explains how the fund's belief framework shapes asset allocation, stewardship, and policy advocacy, while translating systemic issues like climate change, gender equity, and housing affordability into actionable investment strategies. The result: a coherent, organization-wide approach that embeds system-level thinking into investment decisions, culture, and performance.

*Chapter 11: Engagement and Systemic Stewardship.* Jake Barnett of Wespath and Patrick Peura of Allianz, former co-leads of the Net-Zero Asset Owner Alliance's Engagement Track, trace how a global coalition of asset owners reimagined stewardship for a systems era. Confronting the limits of company-by-company engagement, they show how the NZAOA shifted focus toward underused levers – asset-manager oversight, proxy voting, and policy alignment – to create smarter, more systemic forms of influence. Their work produced a series of practitioner-tested best practices for climate voting, policy engagement, and net-zero alignment that connect stewardship with real-economy change. The result is a blueprint for evolving engagement from a transactional dialogue into a coordinated, principle-based force for systemic transformation.

*Chapter 12: How To Work with Your Consultant on System-level Issues.* Max Messervy demystifies the investment consulting business and explains how asset owners can productively engage consultants on system-level investing without running afoul of fiduciary, governance, or commercial realities. Drawing on experience across pensions, insurers, endowments, and sovereign institutions, he shows how consulting business models, incentive structures, and "house views" shape what advice is possible—and when. Messervy offers practical guidance on contracting, scoping, and sequencing engagements; when to rely on retainers versus project work; how to assess a consultant's readiness for system-level investing; and when specialist advisors may be required. The chapter is a pragmatic roadmap for turning consultant relationships into effective partners in advancing system-level objectives.

*Chapter 13: Policy as Table Stakes.* Corey Klemmer, former Policy Director at the U.S. Securities and Exchange Commission, argues that system-level investors cannot achieve their goals without engaging with the legal and regulatory "plumbing" that shapes financial markets. Drawing from her experience at the SEC, she reveals how administrative law, judicial review, and political polarization have reshaped the policy landscape – and why effective investors must understand and influence it. Klemmer offers practical guidance on how to engage regulators, craft persuasive comment letters, and build coalitions that counter entrenched interests. Her message is clear: For investors seeking to strengthen the systems that underpin market health, policy engagement is not optional – it's foundational.

*Chapter 14: Capital Market Assumptions and System-level Investing.* Scott Kalb and Paul O'Brien show how Capital Market Assumptions (CMAs), one of the most fundamental tools in traditional finance, can become a lever for system-level change. By climate-adjusting CMAs, they demonstrate how allocators can translate the physical and transition risks of climate change into tangible return and risk projections, aligning fiduciary duty with planetary reality. Their analysis reveals that most CMAs remain backward-looking, underestimating the financial impact of systemic risks and overstating future returns. They offer a framework for integrating system-level risks into portfolio construction – turning CMAs from static forecasts into instruments for resilience and real-economy alignment.

*Chapter 15: Guardrails and Standard-shaping.* Nippon Life's Takeshi Kimura introduces two of the most powerful levers available to system-level investors: internal guardrails that discipline investment practice and external standard-shaping that raises norms across markets. Drawing on global examples – from Nippon Life's Transition Finance Framework to emerging efforts like the Taskforce on Inequality and Social-related Financial Disclosures – he shows how guardrails prevent sustainability arbitrage and guide portfolios toward long-term system health, while standard-shaping transforms those same principles into market rules. Kimura explores the tension between global consistency and local flexibility, the persistent free-rider problem, and the need for pragmatic balance between self-governance and collective action. The result is a practical roadmap for how investors can institutionalize their values and turn private discipline into public impact.

## Section IV:

## System-level Governance and Accountability

*Chapter 16: Applying Fiduciary Duties to System-level Investing.* Legal scholars Susan Gary, Keith Johnson, and Tiffany Reeves explain why system-level investing is not only permissible under fiduciary law but, in many cases, required by it. Drawing on U.S. trust and pension law, they trace how fiduciary duty has evolved alongside financial theory – from the legal list era to modern portfolio theory – and show why prudence today must account for systemic risks such as climate change and inequality. The authors make a compelling legal and practical case that system-level investing represents the next evolution in prudent, long-term fiduciary practice. While they focus on the U.S., their analysis – highlighting that the dynamic nature of fiduciary duty, including the duty to investigate relevant facts, and the obligations of care, loyalty, and impartiality across generations – is applicable in many jurisdictions.

*Chapter 17: Data and Information Flow for System-level Investors.* U.K. investment consultant Roger Urwin explores how data – long treated as an operational input – has become a strategic asset for system-level investors seeking to translate sustainability complexity into decision-useful intelligence. He charts the "data journey" from raw ESG inputs to actionable insights, highlighting how interoperability, quality, and context shape investment outcomes. Urwin introduces the emerging "Human Intelligence × Artificial Intelligence stack," blending human and artificial intelligence to improve foresight and decision speed, and examines how investors, data specialists, and technology providers are re-engineering the information ecosystem to serve systemic goals. His message is both pragmatic and visionary: in the era of system-level investing, the fusion of data, narrative, and technology will determine which investors thrive.

*Chapter 18: CalSTRS Case Study: How to Explain Why You Do What You Do.* The California State Teachers' Retirement System treats communication as a strategic discipline rather than either compliance or superficial public relations. In this way, the second-largest U.S. public pension fund uses governance-anchored communication to turn system-level investing from abstraction into practice. By linking investment beliefs to policy, and policy to transparent action, CalSTRS builds legitimacy with members, policymakers, and markets alike. Pre-emptive transparency, evidence-based storytelling, and consistent fiduciary framing depoliticize debates and sustain trust in contested environments. The result is a model for communication as infrastructure – making complex systemic strategies legible, credible, and repeatable across audiences and cycles.

Use this book as a manual: Clarify beliefs, align mandates and engagement with system goals, participate in standard-and policy-setting, allocate intentionally, benchmark your influence and integrate system-aware metrics into governance and reporting. That's how investors move from beliefs to blueprints to constructed investment programs. And from portfolios that ignore the existing systems to portfolios that sustain them, thereby creating future investing prosperity.

Enjoy the *Handbook.*

# Section I:

# How System-level Investing Comes to Life.
# Three-part Case Study of PFZW / PGGM

Chapter 2:

# How to Get Started:
# The case of PFZW / PGGM

By Jaap van Dam[14]

## Introduction

In the aftermath of the Great Financial Crisis (GFC), in 2011, the Netherlands' second-largest pension fund, PFZW, felt, amongst others, that its societal "License to Operate" was deeply under pressure. This led to a long transformational journey which resulted in the "Investment Framework 2013 – 2020" and "Investment Strategy 2020." Looking back, this was the moment that the fund explicitly started to consider itself as a system-level investor.

This case study describes the journey in which PFZW / PGGM has integrated (elements of) system-level investing into its DNA in the 2010's. In a certain sense, it can be considered as the "prequel" to the next chapter, written by Geraldine Leegwater and Colin Tissen of PGGM, PFZW's asset manager.

---

[14] Jaap van Dam is Strategic Advisor and Board Member for Global Asset Owners and Former Chief Strategist PGGM

As I was very closely involved, I will use first person to clearly indicate that this is a case study from the inside and that I do not pretend it to be objective. And it is also to emphasize the fact that I have found that there is no objective best way to manage transformational processes: There definitely are do's and don'ts, and there definitely are necessary conditions to increase the probability of success, but a transformational journey heavily relies on the key players. In many senses, it is an emergent journey that requires sensitivity and agility to arrive at good outcomes.

## PFZW and PGGM

PFZW is the compulsory collective industry pension plan for the workers in the Dutch health care industry, with more than 2.9 million (year-end 2024) predominantly female participants. At the time, it was a Defined Benefit fund, though it is transitioning to a collective Defined Contribution structure by 2028. Fund assets amount to €259 billion, placing PFZW somewhere in the top 20 pension funds by size globally.

The PFZW Board consists of employer and employee representatives, with an independent Chair. PGGM is PFZW's pension service organization, responsible for, among other things, risk management, fiduciary advice on investment policy, and the actual management of all investments, both internal and external to PGGM.

## The Problem We Were Trying to Solve

The global financial crisis (GFC) of 2007-2008 hit financial institutions and pension funds, including PFZW, hard – not only in significant negative returns and a deep dent in the solvency of the fund, but also because the societal trust in pension funds in The Netherlands sunk. In other words, our societal license to operate was at stake. This led PFZW's Board to reflect on the following:

- Is the "efficient markets" paradigm still relevant for us? Although PFZW invested largely in line with efficient markets principles – the dominant investment paradigm – it sustained significant losses, in terms of returns and solvency ratio, less than a decade after the dot-com crisis of 2000–2002.

- Looking ahead, it appears that both the long-term risk capital we provide and the returns we need to earn on it have become scarcer. How do we cope with this problem?

- The implied license to operate of traditional defined benefit (DB) pension plans can no longer be taken for granted. Societal trust in pension arrangements is at a very low level. How do we cope with this?

- Although we are recognized as one of the most sustainable (or re-sponsible) pension plans in the world, movement toward sustain-ability in the real economy seems to be much more pronounced and salient. How can we contribute more to creating a sustainable world?

While the GFC was the catalyst, we had other reasons for initiating the project. First, PZFW and PGGM had been one organization until 2008. As an emerging, if young, entity, PFZW developed an identity at a certain distance from its service provider PGGM. As the asset owner, PFZW believed it should formulate and own the principles for investing.

Second, the GFC prompted questions about PFZW's role in the "real econo-my" that encompassed a broader scope than traditional investment questions: For example, does our asset portfolio include investments or investment categories that are harmful to the economy in general, or to parts of the financial sector in particular? As a large asset owner with a long horizon, should PFZW not contribute to the economic and sustainable well-being of its members or society at large instead of being agnostic to them?

Third, we had questions about pension board governance, control and competence. Do Boards really have control of both investment policy and its implementation? Who is really at the helm of the fund? Can the Board cope with the complexity of the investments? Finally, the separation between pension plan and service organization substantially lengthened the investment value chain and brought in many new faces looking for a common framework and language to tackle the investment problem.

As you can see in the description above, the "systems" view of the word pops up in a number of different ways:

- How can we cope with potentially scarce returns?
- How can we contribute more to creating a sustainable world?
- Do we hold investments that are harmful to the economy?
- As a large asset owner with a long horizon, should PFZW not contribute to the economic and sustainable well-being of its members or society at large instead of being agnostic to them?

## Conceiving the Solution: The "White Sheet of Paper" Project

The PFZW Board felt that having a strong set of principles would get everybody in the chain moving in the same direction and speaking the same language. These factors together brought the "White Sheet of Paper" (WSOP) project into being in late 2011. It was born when Jean Frijns and I looked each other in the eye during a long and ineffective PFZW investment committee meeting over the enormous stack of paper on the table that asked for decisions but lacked a common framework through which to make this decision.

What is important to remark and remember is that at the time of the project, we were entering, to a large extent, uncharted territory. At the time, *system-level investing* did not mean anything to anybody. Important concepts now shaping the thinking of many asset owners, like *universal ownership*, *impact* or *double materiality* were not common at the time of this project. The investment world had a strong financial-only focus

24

(or even paradigm) then. It was only slowly warming to the idea that "non-financial factors" like E, S and G, might play a role in shaping risk and returns of individual investments – in other words, the lens was still strictly outside-in. The investment portfolio was the central object and the idea that there might be a more systemic lens and a two-way relationship between pension fund investing and the wider economy/capital markets/systems did not exist.

Once tabled, the WSOP project had broad support within the PFZW Board. Board members devoted considerable time to the project over the course of its several phases, which lasted 18 months. Six Board members, predominantly members of the Investment Committee, but not investment specialists, were willing and able to spend one day per week or more on the project. They proved to be its driving force, both inspiring the broader PFZW Board and directing the PGGM organization.

To provoke fresh thinking, the project adopted an "outside-in" approach, meaning that the committed Board members took upon themselves to gain access to the best investment thinking in the world. The central question to be answered was stated as follows: "How can we invest in a way (1) suited to the financial ambition of our plan, (2) in which sustainability is fully integrated, and (3) that is well understood and controllable by the board?"

These three larger questions were in turn broken down into a "pyramid" of 27 ($3 \times 3 \times 3$) more detailed questions. This $3 \times 3 \times 3$ pyramid was the central beacon in the design of the project. For example, if we zoom in on the "suited to the financial ambition of our plan" pillar, the three questions in the second layer were: "what are our investment beliefs?," "where will we get the returns we need?" and "how will we stay within our risk-appetite?" And on the most granular third level, the questions under "where will we get the returns we need?" unfolded as: "which risks will be adequately rewarded?," "how material are these sources of return?" and "how do we organize ourselves to harvest these sources of return?"

Under the "in which sustainability is fully integrated" pillar, one of the next three questions was "what is our role as an asset owner?," which unfolded at the most granular level as "what is our role in the value chain?," "how can we contribute to a better world?" and "what about investing more in our own country or in our own sector, healthcare?"

Based on the top three questions mentioned above, we divided the project into three pillars, each of which took 4-5 months to complete. The whole process, which culminated in the Investment Framework, was geared toward answering these three primary questions. Note that there was no reference to the current approach. The questions did not ask "how can we improve?", or "how can we do better?" In that sense, the project was transformational by design.

Each pillar developed a distinct rhythm, which helped the process. Phase 1, the "divergent phase," geared toward opening minds and getting fresh thinking outside-in. Phase 2, the "convergent phase;" involved Board members deciding how the information from the outside world would transform into the Investment Framework. Phases 1 and 2 each for all three the pillars ended with a large, interactive Board session lasting 3-4 hours. A few PGGM staff members would be in the room during these sessions, mostly in the background, to ensure that PGGM understood the Board's thinking. Preparation for these full Board meetings consisted of the following steps:

- Collecting and discussing relevant, accessible literature on the key topics in the pyramid. PGGM staff collected and summarized this literature.

- Interviewing experts. For each of the three question areas, we invited ten external experts on the topic at hand to participate. For example, the six involved Board members interviewed peer investors, strategic advisors such as Keith Ambachtsheer[15], and original investment

---

[15] Keith Ambachtsheer is Director Emeritus of the International Centre for Pension Management at the Rotman School of Management, University of Toronto.

thinkers such as Antti Ilmanen[16]. PGGM staff then wrote up these interviews for the Board.

- Asking Board members to fill out "workbooks" containing statements on the topics at hand. Their ratings of these statements, which ranged from "like" to "dislike," were gathered and processed to produce very clear input as a starting point for discussion.

- Inviting a number of "contrarian thinkers" to address the full PFZW Board. These speakers were asked for their explicit opinions about what PFZW should keep doing, what it should change, and what it should stop doing on the topic under review, which led to very intense and thought-provoking discussions. During these exchanges, the project team took great care to document all the potential outcomes.

It is important to note that the senior management of the investment function of PGGM did not have a formal role in the process. This was done to avoid the typical bias to current practice.

The outcomes of interviews were written up, and each exchange led to a document summarizing the discussions. Three separate "pillar documents," one for each of the core questions, were created out of these exchanges, which formed the basis for the final document that created the Investment Framework. We brought all materials together in a 518-page book (that still has a prominent place in my bookcase).

## The Outcome: The Strategic Investment Framework

The outcomes of the process were a document called the Strategic Investment Framework 2013 – 2020; a board that felt empowered to take an ownership role for the investments of the fund; and a shared language

---

[16] Antti Ilmanen is Principal and Global Co-head of the Portfolio Solutions Group at AQR Capital Management.

between board/PFZW and Investment Organization/PGGM. With the benefit of 10 years of hindsight, I add to that a fourth outcome: an irrevocable change in the DNA of PFZW and PGGM. In short, an enormous transformational change.

The Strategic Investment Framework held 16 principles with a clear but high-level explanation around them. Here are the five principles that contributed most to the development and integration of the systems perspective of PFZW vis a vis investments:

1. We assume our social responsibility by contributing tangibly to a sustainable, viable world.

2. A sustainable, viable world is necessary to generate sufficient returns over the long term.

3. Innovative investments are necessary to continue to achieve our ambition in the future.

4. A focused portfolio of investments of which we have a thorough knowledge and that fits well with our identity can contribute effectively to achieving the ambition.

5. Complexity is used only if appropriate for the achievement of PFZW's pension ambition.

The first two principles are the most important here. Principle #1, "*we assume our social responsibility by contributing tangibly to a sustainable, viable world*," clearly indicates that PFZW embraces a broader responsibility than financial return generation only on behalf of its members. There is a clear element of what is now called "double materiality", in which the systems perspective takes shape: the system will generate and influence our portfolio and investment outcomes, but we can, want and need to play a role in the system. As PGGM's then CEO, Else Bos would say: "*We will use the steering power of capital.*" As a top 20 global pension fund, this was a realistic statement. The entire board was convinced that this principle was shared by PFZW's members.

Principle #2, "*A sustainable, viable world is necessary to generate sufficient returns over the long term,*" is a statement of enlightened self-interest. It clearly says that if the ingredients (such as capital, labor, natural resources) of financial returns and the financial system are not maintained well, long-term return generation is at risk. The system-level lens is clear: By playing a role in the system, we can contribute to protecting our members from systemic risks and the systematic risks in the capital markets they would engender. In other words, PFZW says clearly, we do not want to "freeride" on the system or cause negative externalities; we will play our part in keeping return generation sustainable.

These two principles clearly are an expression of PFZW's mission. Of course, the big next question then is: how and where to put these principles into action?

## From Principles to Implementation: Investment Plan 2015 – 2020

Immediately after the approval by the board of the investment framework, we at PGGM started working on the Strategic Investment Plan 2015 – 2020 so as to translate the framework-of-principles into a plan-of-action. In this plan we formulated some bold, "moonshot" objectives. These objectives were meant to be bold Big Hairy Goals that would force PGGM into transformational change when it came time to take significant steps in the newly formulated direction, most of all, acting on climate change and investing in solutions. (I did not know the concept of Transformational Change then, so this was an intuitive step). We did not really know if our objectives were realistic. For example, when it came to the carbon footprint, it was not possible to measure this reasonably well at the time – but we decided to do it and see where we got; and, very importantly, we decided to solve the challenges along the way. These were the two most significant objectives that led us into the world of system-level investing quoted from the Strategic Plan 2015 – 2020:

1. ***Quadruple the Positive Sustainability Contribution***
   *We are leveraging the steering power of capital. By investing in solutions within the portfolio wherever possible, PFZW's positive contribution to the selected themes – climate pollution & emissions, water scarcity, food security, and health – will be significantly increased.*

2. ***Halve the Portfolio's Negative Footprint***
   *Where possible, the negative footprint on the selected sustainability themes will be halved. We are adopting a phased approach. Our first focus is on halving the $CO_2$ emissions of the public equity portfolio.*

The objectives of the plan were ambitious, and the five-year horizon worked very well as a framework for step-by-step implementation. By and large, the objectives were realized, and, as a result, PFZW and PGGM inspired other asset owners to go on a comparable path.

## Lessons Learned

I have formulated the lessons from my own experience in a way in which I hope they will be valuable for other organizations that go on a transformational or systemic journey:

1. **Start at the right moment.** We started at an existential moment: the deep wounds after the Great Financial Crisis and the birth of PFZW. This was probably the best possible moment we could have chosen. So, if the moment presents itself, use it and jump in! This is not necessarily the famous "burning platform"; it can be a change in the composition of the board or the executive, or a shared dream between key players. The opposite is also true: When the moment is not there, think twice before jumping into a project that aims for transformational change.

2. **There has to be critical mass in key people, and their thinking needs to be aligned.** We embarked on a journey that was fully supported by the Chair of the Board, the Chair of the Investment Committee and the CEO of the Investment Department. They immediately saw the logic and jumped on board, willing to spend both their own time and to apply significant resources to the project. Also, they shared a strategic mindset that was open to significant change and moving into uncharted territory.

3. **Strongly diverge at first. Cast a wide net.** We strongly empowered the board members to go on a journey in the outside world to find answers to our questions. They interviewed a broad group of both investment leaders and broader societal stakeholders and listened with an open mind. This enormously enriched the thinking and the quality of the conversation. I would go even further: I think it is impossible to create this kind of lasting change by only looking internally. Then your view will come from <u>what</u> you do, not what you <u>could</u> do.

4. **Redefine the problem from engineering to a much broader "what is our role in society" problem.** We wanted to solve deep investment questions but created a far richer context in which we could couple the investment challenges directly to the question of our role in the wider system of society. This made sure that the outcome of the process would not just be another investment strategy.

5. **Find a good balance between the "designers" and the "executors," or the professionals.** Kees Dorst[17] says "leaving the problem with engineers may be solving for the wrong stuff." In the context of pension fund investing, this is a deep truth. Investors are typically trained as a kind of engineers to solve very specific problems that are not necessarily the problems of the board or the fund. They "generate alpha" or "diversify the portfolio" or another specific task.

---

[17] Kees Dorst is Professor of Transdisciplinary Innovation at the University of Technology Sydney's TD School and an expert in design.

The understanding by the investors of the board problem is often limited. In the WSOP we solved this by keeping the investors at a certain distance during most of the project and putting the board members in the front seat. This was liberating, and I am convinced that the outcomes of the project could never have been found with an engineering approach.

6. **Use the right language for the right people and repeat and repeat.** High Level Principles need continuous explanation and visible application to keep them alive. The text with principles that was enthusiastically and fully embraced by the board proved difficult to understand and apply by the investment organization and the people in it. It may be that you need different versions for different audiences. We did not fully realize this. The consequence of this was that some of the principles in practice got an interpretation that was a reduced and impoverished form of the original.

## Takeaways

1. **The Board must fully subscribe.** In my view, it is impossible to be a significant system-level investor without the full support and understanding of the board, not only of the principles and the thinking, but also of potential reputational consequences (positive and negative) and potential return consequences. The latter should be realistic and not defined away in an optimistic belief about the outcomes.

2. **Own the principles and apply them continuously.** Somebody needs to be the owner of the principles, keep them alive, make sure that the interpretation can evolve over time etc. Boards by their nature change constantly, which makes it difficult for them to develop real continuity in owning things like the Investment Framework.

3. **Start small, in an area that feels natural, experiment and learn. Then scale up.** In the journey towards system-level investing, you may be able to find pockets in your portfolio or teams that have a natural fit with system-level investing: For example, the real estate team may be very much focused on reducing the energy use of the buildings because this improves the letting potential and thereby the expected returns. From that starting point, increasing the focus on energy efficiency and footprint reduction is a natural one.

4. **Do not overfocus on measurement.** The investments business is obsessed with measurement, to an extent that investment organizations will not move on system-level investing if they cannot measure the impact. This is in my mind the wrong order of things. If the people doing the system-level investing have the right culture, they will "know it when they see it." My advice: Create understanding, knowledge and motion, then try to measure your contribution.

# Conclusion

I have looked back at the White Sheet of Paper project with the benefit of a good decade of hindsight. And I have, in a quite personal way, formulated lessons learned from a transformative journey to system-level investing. I hope the insights will be relevant for finance practitioners that seek to embark on a similar path to system-level investing.

## Chapter 3:

# From 2D to 3D Investing

By Geraldine Leegwater and Colin Tissen[18]

At PGGM, we have made a fundamental shift toward three-dimensional (3D) investing, which adds sustainability to the traditional two dimensions of risk and return. This approach requires us to balance financial returns, risks, and sustainability across our €250 billion portfolio, with the aim of delivering a good pension for the members of our client PFZW, the pension fund for the social and welfare sector in the Netherlands.

To support this shift, we have introduced a new investment policy that focuses on contributing to societal transitions and managing systemic risks. We dissolved our dedicated Responsible Investment department and embedded sustainability across the entire organization. We established a new Total Portfolio Management team to oversee portfolio-wide decisions, integrated sustainability KPIs into variable remuneration, and began working in multi-disciplinary teams to foster a culture of collaboration and shared responsibility.

---

[18] Geraldine Leegwater is CEO Investment Management, PGGM. Colin Tissen is Sustainability Lead Mandate Management, PGGM

As long-term investors, we hold a fiduciary duty to help fulfil PFZW's pension ambitions. With an investment horizon of over 40 years for a starting nurse in a hospital, long-term developments in environmental, social, and financial systems will shape the pensions of PFZW's participants. This horizon compels us to identify risks that we believe are not yet fully priced in – especially systemic risks.

Addressing these risks requires societal transitions. We aim to contribute to such transitions by investing in companies that enable them, limiting our exposure to those that hinder them, and engaging in stewardship. Building a 3D portfolio is not about only investing in 'sustainable' or 'green' companies; it is about investing in companies that have the potential to become sustainable over time and those that are essential parts of the value chain of technologies we need to make transitions happen. It also includes companies that may not have a strong negative or positive effect on sustainability but are needed to create a well-diversified and representative portfolio.

Building such a portfolio is easier said than done and comes with challenges. This chapter outlines practical steps to implement 3D investing, highlights the obstacles we encountered, and shares key insights from our transition. We focus on three aspects: the investment policy, the organizational design, and the organizational culture. The chapter concludes with our lessons learned.

## 3D Investment Policy: Understanding the Problem

PGGM manages global investments across a wide range of asset classes. Including, for example, public and private equity, direct infrastructure investments, public and private real estate, and credit risk sharing. This diversified exposure means we are connected to many different sectors, geographies, and financial instruments. While this breadth offers opportunities, it also increases our vulnerability to systematic risks that cut across markets and asset types.

For example, climate change is a planetary risk that includes acute events (e.g. heatwaves, floods) and chronic developments (e.g. melting ice sheets). PGGM is not exposed to all planetary risks, as we do not invest in all global assets. However, some planetary risks translate into economic impacts (e.g. asset devaluation) and financial market risks (e.g. asset price volatility) that do affect PGGM. These are systematic risks that are difficult or impossible to diversify. Reducing planetary risks is primarily the responsibility of governments and policymakers. Investors, however, have a role in mitigating financial market risks – a subset of planetary risks.

## The Solution: A New Investment Policy

Sustainability has long been part of PGGM's investment approach. For instance, we helped build a platform with other asset managers and owners that links business activities to the UN Sustainable Development Goals (SDGs). This taxonomy lets us measure how well companies align with the SDGs and helps us steer part of our portfolio in that direction. In addition, even before launching our 3D investment strategy, we had already set goals to reduce the financed emissions of our portfolio.

SDG alignment and carbon emissions are useful proxies for how sustainable a company is today. But having a sustainable portfolio does not automatically reduce our systematic risks. We can exclude a high-emission company from our portfolio, but that company will continue polluting – and those emissions still contribute to climate risks that affect our investments. It is hard for investors to directly contribute to reducing systemic risks, but stewardship offers the best chance to make a meaningful impact.[19] Hence, it might be more beneficial to remain invested in the high-emission company and engage the company to set emission reduction targets.

---

[19] Can Sustainable Investing Save the World? Reviewing the Mechanisms of Investor Impact - Julian F. Kölbel, Florian Heeb, Falko Paetzold, Timo Busch, 2020

To better manage systemic risks, we have shifted our approach to 3D investing. We now focus more on forward-looking indicators – ones that show whether an investment supports or aligns with a broader transition and we apply a 'Know What You Own' (KWYO) principle. This principle means that, for each investment, we want to be able to explain why we invested based on the dimensions of return, risk, and sustainability.

In our PFZW/PGGM 3D investing framework, we have defined four (partially overlapping) categories of investments: neutrals, improvers, positive alignment investments, and impact investments (Figure 1).

*Figure 1: PFZW/PGGM 3D Investing Framework*

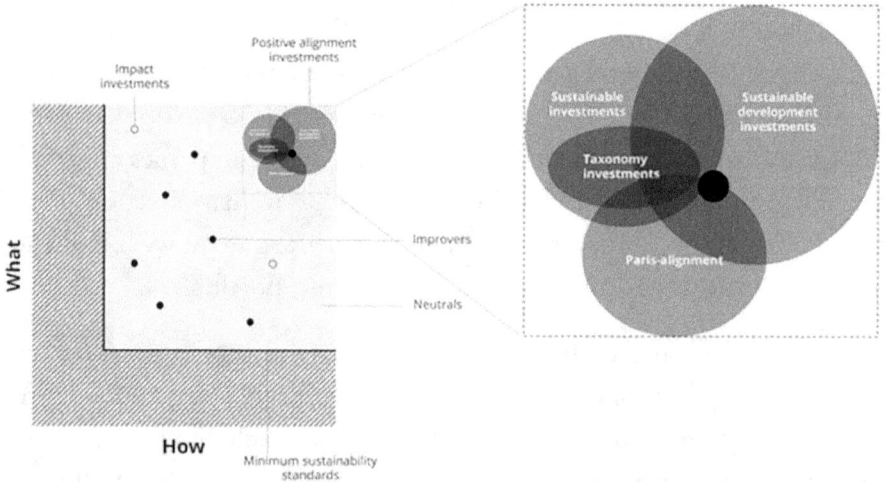

"Neutrals" are companies that meet PFZW's minimum sustainability standards but do not show clear positive sustainability characteristics. These minimum standards cover risk management (like mining companies without water policies), participant preferences (such as tobacco producers), and ethical concerns (like companies at high risk of violating international norms). Neutrals help us maintain a diversified portfolio.

Another part of the portfolio consists of "positive alignment investments." These are companies or funds that either offer SDG-aligned or Taxonomy-aligned products and services or are actively working to cut their carbon emissions in line with the Paris Agreement. We also invest in "improvers" that are not sustainable now but are working towards improving their environmental and social sustainability over time. In addition, a small part of the portfolio will consist of "impact investments" as defined by the Global Impact Invest Network (GIIN): Investments made with the intention to generate positive, measurable social and environmental impact *alongside a financial return.*

The forward-looking, transition approach needed to contribute to addressing systemic risks is incorporated into this approach. For example:

- Improvers are an important part of the framework. By investing in and engaging with improvers, we can grow the share of positively aligned investments in our portfolio over time.

- We set targets on the Paris alignment of the portfolio. This means financing companies that are actively reducing their emissions. If they hit their targets, our portfolio emissions should fall over time. We support companies in their progress through engagement.

- A small portion of our portfolio is dedicated to impact investing in PFZW's three focus areas: Climate, Nature & Biodiversity, and Health in the Netherlands. One example is our new NL Health impact strategy with the aim of visibly contributing to the healthcare and welfare transition in the Netherlands. We do this, for example, by investing in innovative medical technology, residential and care homes, and affordable housing for healthcare professionals.

- We have added systemic engagement to our stewardship efforts. This means engaging not just with individual companies, but with sector organizations, regulators, and other asset managers. It also includes field building and being active in collaborative initiatives. For example:

- We are active members of Climate Action 100+ and Nature Action 100.

- We co-developed the Sustainable Development Investment Asset Owner Platform (SDI-AOP) taxonomy to determine the SDG alignment of company activities.

- We contributed to funding the expansion of the Carbon Risk Real Estate Monitor (CRREM) alongside other investors.

Additionally, we evaluate asset managers based on how well their engagement and voting practices align with PGGM's and PFZW's investment beliefs, and we factor this into our manager selection process.

- Using this approach, we believe we can contribute to lowering both systemic (i.e. risk to systems, such as climate change) and systematic (i.e. non-diversifiable financial) risks, though the degree and method of influence vary by asset class. For example, in public markets, we focus on investee and systemic stewardship – engaging with companies, industry groups, and policymakers, and filing shareholder resolutions. In private markets, such as infrastructure and private real estate, we often hold larger stakes and can exert direct strategic influence. In alternative credit, our Credit Risk Sharing team partners with major banks globally to take on a portion of the credit risk in their loan portfolios through synthetic securitization, offering unique engagement opportunities.

In short, 3D investing is about balancing financial returns, investment risks, and sustainability. It does not mean only investing in sustainable companies – that might create concentration, regional, and sector risks. Instead, we aim to support transitions and manage transition risks through capital allocation and active stewardship, all while keeping our portfolio diversified. Over time, we believe this will help drive sustainability across the broader investment universe.

## Case Study – The Public Equity Portfolio in 3D Investing

Redesigning the public equity portfolio meant making intentional choices: which investments can deliver strong returns, stay within risk limits, and improve sustainability? We started by setting clear targets and constraints, including liquidity needs and risk budgets. Then, we asked both internal and external managers to develop model portfolios, helping us explore possibilities and trade-offs.

We ultimately chose a mix of two complementary strategies: fundamental and systematic. Fundamental managers conduct in-depth company research, which is essential for understanding sustainability – not just through data, but through interpretation. However, this approach is limited in scale. To ensure diversification, we combine it with systematic strategies that use quantitative models to assess the full investment universe across all three dimensions.

We moved away from passive investing because of our KWYO principle. Fundamental managers provide a KWYO document for each portfolio position, while systematic managers must be able to deliver such documents on request, within 48 hours. In these documents, managers provide a low, medium, or high conviction for each dimension and explain how they arrived at these beliefs. For example, they provide information about growth potential, the company's management of sustainability risks, and engagement objectives.

Previously, we tracked a broad index with thousands of companies, applying exclusions and sustainability tilts. Now, the benchmark serves as a reference point – not the starting point. This shift to "conscious investing" reduced our holdings from 3,500 to about 800 companies. Although we transitioned to a more active approach, management fees are still very low – largely due to the size of our mandates.

Table 1 provides a comparison between the previous equity portfolio, the new 3D portfolio, and the FTSE All World index. The new portfolio carries slightly more active risk, with tracking error rising from 1.0 to 1.2 percent. But it also delivers measurable sustainability improvements: Paris alignment increased from 23 to 30 percent, the SDG alignment from 19 to 21 percent, and the $CO_2$-intensity on a revenue basis decreased from 86 to 73 mtCO$_2$e/mlnUSD.[20] In comparison, the FTSE All World index has a Paris alignment percentage of 18 percent, SDG alignment of 12 percent, and a $CO_2$-intensity of 249. In addition, one of our equity managers now runs a dedicated improvers strategy, targeting at least 50 percent of capital in companies with expected sustainability progress.

*Table 1: Characteristics of the new 3D Equity, the old 2D Equity, and the FTSE AW index. Based on June 2025 (3D Equity, FTSE AW) and March 2025 (2D Equity) data.*

| METRIC | 3D EQUITY | 2D EQUITY | FTSE AW INDEX |
|---|---|---|---|
| #SECURITIES | ~800 | ~3,500 | ~4,000 |
| TRACKING ERROR | 1.2% | 1.0% | 0.0% |
| SDG ALIGNMENT | 21.4% | 18.9% | 11.7% |
| PARIS ALIGNMENT | 29.5% | 22.5% | 17.7% |
| CO2-INTENSITY | 73.2 | 85.9 | 249.0 |

Finally, our manager selection process evolved to reflect the 3D approach. We now prioritize asset managers who combine strong financial performance with sustainability expertise and robust stewardship practices across

---

[20] To determine SDG alignment, we use the taxonomy of the SDI-AOP (SDI Classification) and data from Entis. For each company we invest in, the alignment is based on the percentage of revenues from products and services that align with one or more of the SDGs. Paris alignment is based on the Net Zero Investment Framework of the IIGCC (Net Zero Investment Framework) and measures the percentage of invested capital in companies that are aligning, aligned, or achieving net zero.

the firm. By embedding stewardship into manager selection, we aim to raise the bar across the financial sector – an essential step in system-level investing.

## Organizational Design

We also changed the organizational design to better fit the 3D strategy. Our organization had been built for a 2D perspective and adding more transition – and sustainability themes to the investment portfolio reached the limits of our capacity to design, implement and manage this in the investment portfolio. The reasons were threefold:

1. Addressing systemic risk requires specific expertise and thinking along integrated industries and supply chains. It also requires integrated thinking across asset classes instead of each asset class tackling the issue in isolation.

2. The investment portfolio of PFZW previously was cut into more than twenty separate investment portfolios, all with their own investment guidelines. However, topics related to systemic risks do not follow the lines of separate investment mandates. Incorporating these into the investment portfolio requires a total portfolio approach, which was missing in our organization.

3. PGGM used to have a dedicated Responsible Investment (RI) department. Adding sustainability tasks to the investment process through this department reached its limits. We faced the risk that the RI department started to take care of almost all investment activities that included a sustainability element. For example, sustainability engagement, analyzing and implementing sustainability legislation, vendor analysis, and exclusion lists. This led to sustainability knowledge being concentrated in that department.

These reasons made us decide to redesign our investment process into a new investment organization, which enabled us to address these issues. The new investment process is designed from the perspective of realizing the pension ambitions of the asset owner, PFZW and incorporates all three dimensions in every step of the investment process.

## Case Study – New Organizational Design and Investment Process

The investment process now distinguishes between four layers.

1. The Strategic Investment Policy includes the strategic asset allocation, investment cases outlining investment plans and conditions for mandates, and the sustainability policy.

2. Total Portfolio Management (TPM) is the implementation of the investment policy. The TPM team is responsible for writing mandates for each investment category and incorporating 3D objectives in each mandate.

3. Mandate Management (MM) is responsible for managing the seven investment mandates of PFZW. This includes the portfolio design and day-to-day management of the mandates, manager selection, and developing sub-mandates.

4. The internal and external management of sub-mandates constitutes the fourth layer.

## 2D Organisational Design

## 3D Organisational Design

**Strategic Investment Policy**

**Strategic Investment Policy**

**Total Portfolio Management**

**Mandates**

**Mandate Management**

The new organizational design helps to better manage systemic risks in several ways:

- Products are not designed in isolation but in multidisciplinary teams with colleagues responsible for assorted products. Not only does this address systemic risk top down from an integrated portfolio perspective, it also brings top-down and bottom-up perspectives together. As a result, the guardrails of a product deeper into the investment portfolio always fall within the guardrails of the parent product.

- PFZW assigned a total portfolio mandate to PGGM. The TPM department implements, manages, and monitors the total portfolio mandate, which includes all activities related to the top-level management of the portfolio. Activities include delivering on the required risk, return, sustainability characteristics of the total portfolio, rebalancing, currency management, dividing overall sustainability targets into relevant targets for 3D investment mandates, and overseeing systemic risk and stewardship on overarching themes in the portfolio.

- We dissolved the Responsible Investment team and incorporated their variety of activities into the relevant departments. For example, managing the investment universe based on PFZW's minimum sustainability standards is part of the total portfolio management mandate. Overseeing and implementing sustainable legislation is part of the legal department, and stewardship is part of the investment teams and TPM. In addition, we introduced a new research team doing both economic and sustainability research. The research team also facilitates research on topics that are relevant across different asset classes. This approach of moving away from a separate RI team ensures that knowledge on all three dimensions is developed within each part of the organization.

The result is a new investment process, a new organizational structure and a new way or working, which should enable us to deliver long-term investment results for PFZW.

## Organizational Culture: Changing Our Behavior

A change in the investment policy and an adjusted organization structure will not automatically change behavior, though both are minimum necessary requirements. From the launch of the joint PFZW-PGGM Strategy 2030, of which 3D investing is one of the goals, we confirmed that our employees are the most important asset in our organization. The paradigm shift from 2D to 3D will only happen if we all manage to enlarge our thinking beyond modern portfolio theory. Our organizational transformation should go along with changing our way of thinking and behaving.

The full integration of risk, return and sustainability in the investment portfolio and investment process is more than adding additional sustainability to a traditional investment portfolio that is optimized alongside risk and return. Solving this three-dimensional puzzle while only keeping traditional Modern Portfolio Theory in mind, might create confusion. The book *Moving Beyond Modern Portfolio Theory* from Jon Lukomnik and James Hawley describes how the underlying assumptions of MPT are limited and the reality in financial markets is different compared to the traditional theoretical approach.

Most investment professionals in our organization, like elsewhere, grew up with MPT. Incorporating systemic risks, real-world transition themes, and long-term value creation into our more traditional way of thinking requires a new approach. Especially after the financial crisis of 2008, the focus was on with financial risks in financial markets. Systemic risks to our society can become financial risks to investors but were traditionally not integrated sufficiently in our thinking.

Moreover, addressing systemic risks requires a total portfolio approach as these risks do not follow the traditional investment guidelines of an investment mandate. This total portfolio mentality was missing in our organization as employees were rewarded on the results of sub-mandates.

Lastly, to keep up with the speed of development in analyzing systemic risks followed by designing implementable policies requires a multidisciplinary approach. Not only to improve the lead time till implementation, but also because potential 3D investment policies should not be designed in isolation in a strategy department, but together with the analysts and portfolio managers. Especially because there is greenfield thinking and investing involved.

The case study below outlines how we addressed the organizational culture in our new 3D strategy.

## Case Study – A New Way of Working

From the start of our new strategy, we created a so-called People Model. This model has a dedicated team focusing on all aspects related to our most important asset – our employees. The team focuses on the development needs regarding knowledge, competencies, and behavioral skills. In all areas, dedicated programs were designed:

- *Leading 2030*: Our strategy implies a major transformation on the "what" and the "how" in our organization. This requires leadership that is equipped to fulfil this task. Our Leading 2030 program, tailored to our specific needs during the transformation, aims to help our leadership team with this. It started with the personal purpose of all leaders and the connection of their purpose to Strategy 2030. It followed with filling in the development needs for all leaders to enable them to contribute to the goals of our strategy.
- Working in *multidisciplinary teams* (MDTs): Our new way of working will move towards co-creation in MDTs. This requires a different way of working compared to a waterfall approach, where the issues at hand were addressed one after another. Working in MDTs is not easy. Employees in different teams have distinct views and incentives.

To foster collaboration, each MDT will contain one member that has the additional role of observing and discussing the behavior in the team. This might seem like overdoing it, but in our focus on content-driven discussion we tend to forget to reflect on whether we are collaborating efficiently and whether every team member feels comfortable joining the discussion.

- *Organizational values*: Via a bottom-up process involving all employees, we chose three new values for our organization. These values are teamwork, trust, and innovation. After the launch of these values, we reflected on which behavior is of added value in realizing our goals and which behavior we should leave behind. Building the new investment portfolio requires more teamwork as we move from managing separate asset management mandates towards a total portfolio approach. The new investment process is built on trust as we move away from decision making in many committees towards assigning responsibilities to individuals. Innovation is the driving factor behind building the new investment portfolio.

Next, we translated the new values into "helping" and "blocking" behaviors. For example, helping behaviors include asking for and giving feedback, being curious and open to other perspectives, and taking shared ownership. This contrasts the blocking behaviors of siloed thinking, lack of trust, and avoiding tough conversations.

- New values and helping behaviors should be put into action. Therefore, employees were asked to come up with ideas to promote them. These ideas include a cross-team shuffle day, where employees spend a couple of hours shadowing colleagues they do not usually work with, and 'feedback fuel cards' that employees can use to exchange one-on-one feedback over free coffee.
- *3D investment academy:* This to-be-developed academy consists of learning paths for different type of (investment) roles within the organization. A learning path will include, for example, courses to

acquire the desired knowledge. We aim to build long-term relationships with universities to facilitate this.

- *Compensation:* We shifted our compensation approach from being based solely on the returns of the asset management mandate to being tied to performance across both financial returns and sustainability goals within the total investment portfolio.

The above-mentioned initiatives all contribute to realizing our strategy. But change is a challenge and changing individual, let alone collective, behavior is unruly. It requires endless training and perseverance. This part of the implementation of our move from 2D to 3D investing is the hardest to achieve and will require an extended period of joint development.

## Lessons Learned and Conclusion

We are in the middle of a fascinating journey, learning and adapting every day. In this final section, we share some of the main challenges and our lessons learned.

Some of the challenges we face are:

- There is uncertainty about the scale of systemic risks and how significantly they impact our portfolio. While we can assess the potential effects of various climate scenarios on portfolio value, we cannot predict which scenario will occur. Additionally, translating these scenarios into economic losses at the company and portfolio levels involves numerous assumptions, which may lead to either overestimation or underestimation of the impacts. For instance, reaching climate tipping points could greatly intensify economic consequences, but these are difficult to model in our climate risk assessments.

- It is challenging to demonstrate the extent to which PGGM's stewardship and investment activities have caused real-world changes.

Although we can measure correlations, establishing causation is not possible because it would require knowing the outcome of a hypothetical scenario – what would have happened without our investment or engagement?

- Data on how much companies are exposed to environmental and social risks – and how much they contribute to those risks – is still evolving. However, more data solutions are becoming available. For example, some providers now map company asset locations and compare them to key biodiversity or protected areas.

- Driving behavioral changes within an organization can be difficult. As with any transformational change, it can be challenging for employees to adapt. Furthermore, 3D investing involves topics that may fall outside employees' current areas of expertise. Therefore, it is important to support employees in expanding their knowledge and skills, and to foster a shared understanding of systemic risks and investment policy. One way to achieve this is by involving employees in the co-creation of policies.

We continuously work to address these and other challenges. For example, we are currently reviewing various methods for measuring both transition and physical climate risks that affect our portfolio to refine our approach. In parallel, we are building a strong network of academic institutions, asset managers and owners, think tanks, and other organizations. This network enables us to stay informed about new developments and to share our own experiences to support others in their progress.

Considering our commitment to sharing experiences, we conclude with a few lessons learned, focusing on the three aspects discussed in this chapter: the investment policy, organizational design, and organizational culture.

*Investment Policy: Managing systematic risks requires the integration of risk, return, and sustainability within each invested asset class.*

Much of the academic empirical research and the discussion papers within the investment community on topics such as responsible investing

51

and managing systematic risks are focused on public equity investments. However, PGGM invests across a broad range of asset classes, and only approximately 25 percent of our exposure is in public equity.

Systematic risks affect all asset classes, so it does not make sense to adjust our investment and engagement approach for only a portion of the portfolio. One of the key lessons we have learned is that we must move beyond the public equity perspective and consider which 3D investment strategies are most appropriate for each asset class in which we invest.

For example, how do we engage with General Partners on integrating sustainability into their deal sourcing and due diligence? And how can we pursue more direct impact investments in private markets? We have observed that many impact investment opportunities related to the energy transition exhibit a risk-return profile that lies somewhere between infrastructure and private equity. In response, we established a dedicated Climate and Energy Transition Solutions mandate, positioned at the intersection of these two asset classes.

Finally, we aim to gradually transition to a Total Portfolio Approach. A substantial portion of our performance will be determined by our asset allocation decisions between asset classes, rather than capital allocation within them. Over time, this new approach will enhance our ability to adjust asset class allocations based on a comprehensive assessment of risk, return, and sustainability.

*Organizational Design: Knowledge on sustainability should be built across the organization, rather than being concentrated in one department.*

The complete integration of sustainability into the investment portfolio requires full integration of sustainability into the investment process, instead of keeping sustainability-related activities in a separate department. Integrated thinking requires that the expertise related to risk, return and sustainability is not kept in separate departments but comes together in each individual step of the investment process and related departments.

_Organizational Culture_: _Working in multi-disciplinary teams fosters the collaboration that is needed to move beyond modern portfolio theory._

Shortening the "time to market" of investment issues can be achieved by moving from a waterfall approach, where different steps in the investment process are followed sequentially, towards an approach where multi-disciplinary teams work together in going through the different stages of the investment process

In conclusion, we believe our 3D strategy contributes to mitigating systemic risks across the portfolio. We integrate forward-looking sustainability indicators into investment decisions, exercise active stewardship to influence outcomes, and invest in innovative solutions that address systemic challenges. Internally, we foster success through a collaborative, cross-functional approach that breaks down silos and ensures a total portfolio perspective in the development of new strategies and mandates. Ultimately, our goal is to enhance the portfolio's risk profile, financial performance, and sustainability.

Chapter 4:

# A Real Economy Approach to Integrated Investing and Portfolio Management

By Dirk Schoenmaker and Willem Schramade[21]

Universal asset owners such as pension funds play a crucial capital allocation role in the real economy. With their investment choices, they can make or break the future of individual companies, real estate deals and infrastructure projects. Their choices affect the pathways of countries' and sectors' future economic and societal performance. And this relation is a two-way street: asset owners are not only important in achieving and maintaining flourishing economies, but their long-term performance also depends on having flourishing economies in the future. In a symbiotic relationship, pension funds can pay a good pension in a thriving, livable world exactly because their investments have contributed to that thriving, livable world.

---

[21] Dirk Schoenmaker is Professor of Banking and Finance at the Rotterdam School of Management, Erasmus Universiteit Rotterdam and a Research Fellow at the Centre for Economic Policy Research. Willem Schramade is Professor of Finance at Nyenrode Business University.

We started thinking about the link between investments and the real economy in our work at pension funds and asset managers. Despite all the sustainability frameworks, ESG datasets, and other efforts, we felt we weren't really investing in a way that recognizes and strengthens this symbiotic relationship. Even worse, this crucial point was consistently missed over the last half century of financial engineering. Financial markets were treated as places where asset owners came to optimize the expected risk-return of their portfolios while having close to zero agency. Modern portfolio theory and its asset pricing models, such as the Capital Asset Pricing Model (CAPM) and Arbitrage Pricing Theory (APT), treat Environmental, Social and Governance (ESG) risks (and much that happens in the wider world outside the capital markets) as exogenous. They reduce risk to the statistics of what happens to be easily measurable: historical returns. Sophisticated econometrics translates those historical returns in factor exposures, providing a good cover for what is essentially an extremely narrow view of risk. Tragically, most financial market participants have come to believe and accept that view, or they at least behave as if they do. In contrast, system-level investing treats social and environmental disturbances as endogenous systemic risks that cascade in the economy and related capital markets. It explicitly recognizes that investment choices today matter for the economy and society of tomorrow.

But how can we make this recognition practical? This is far from trivial. After all, it implies a break from current practices: different goals and different assumptions about our agency with respect to risk, returns, societal impacts, and their interdependencies. This represents a major challenge: How do we bring the symbiotic relationship between pension funds and society to life in an investment strategy? How do we select securities and other investments to build a portfolio that generates good financial results while enabling good societal outcomes as well? We have first-hand experience with designing solutions to these challenges for pension funds (e.g. Pension Fund for Healthcare and Wellbeing – PFZW) and asset managers (e.g. Robeco, Schroders).

This chapter presents a real economy approach to integrated investing that aims to answer two fundamental questions:

1. To what extent do companies contribute to a healthy future economy?
2. How can investors build an integrated portfolio – using forward-looking indicators on companies – to attain such a future economy?

The first step is to assess companies on their creation of integrated value, which combines financial, social and environmental value. We developed the integrated value framework from the recognition that the long-term value of a company is not only determined by its financial performance but also by its ability to solve societal problems.[22] The innovation on earlier concepts like social license to operate is that we are able to include all three components (financial, social and environmental) in a company's valuation. Ideally, company management steers on integrated value (i.e. not only aims for financial value creation but also for societal value creation). In the second step, investors can use these financial, social and environmental indicators to build a diversified portfolio. Investors can do so by selecting to allocate capital to a mix of positive impact companies, impact-neutral companies and negative impact companies that can and want to improve. The underlying belief is that universal asset owners can in this way create long-term value and thus play their part in steering the future economy on a healthy path.

The main challenge is mental. Can we shift mindsets from financial-only value to integrated value? And do we dare to use these forward-looking indicators for social and environmental impact to build integrated portfolios? The good news is that we can still employ modern portfolio theory for building diversified and integrated portfolios. The only change is that we move from 2D (risk-return) investing to 3D (risk-return-impact) investing, as Dutch pension fund manager PGGM is doing for PFZW.

---

[22] Schoenmaker and Schramade (2023), *Corporate Finance for Long-Term Value*, Springer.

This chapter is organized as follows. The next section takes a step back and discusses the problem of chasing the wrong goal. We then proceed by presenting solutions at two levels: first at the company level, then at the portfolio level. We finish with lessons learned and some generalized takeaways.

## The Problem: From Shifting Goals to Shifting Approaches

Society is facing serious social and environmental challenges. To guide the transition towards a sustainable and inclusive economy, the United Nations has developed the Sustainable Development Goals (SDGs). These goals are set at the levels of the economy, society and the environment (see Figure 1). The classical division of labor is that the government takes care of social and environmental externalities and companies focus on economic production.[23] However, the notion that addressing externalities is exclusively a task and responsibility for government, is increasingly being questioned.[24] While production has grown at an average rate of about three percent over the last decades (World Bank), progress on social and ecological goals is falling behind and most of the UN SDGs will not be met by 2030. Hart and Zingales argue that externalities cannot be fully separated from production decisions.[25] In the case of non-separable activities, profit and damage are inextricably connected for technological reasons. Companies thus face a choice in the degree of sustainability in their business model.

In corporate governance, principals set the objective of the company. Investors (in tandem with other stakeholders) can choose to include social and environmental interests in the company's goal function. In fact, this is

---

[23] Jensen (2002), "Value maximization, stakeholder theory, and the corporate objective function," *Business Ethics Quarterly*, 12(2).

[24] Stoelhorst and Vishwanathan, (2024), "Beyond primacy: A stakeholder theory of corporate governance," *Academy of Management Review*, 49(1).

[25] Hart and Zingales (2017), "Companies should maximize shareholder welfare not market value," *Journal of Law, Finance, and Accounting*, 2(2).

quite common outside the US. Moreover, a recent insight is that universal asset owners have an incentive to include these interests, as their long-term performance depends on the future state of the economy.[26]

Let's explain the intuition behind this argument with Figure 1, which shows that economies and societies can be seen as embedded parts of the environment. A livable planet is a precondition or foundation for human-kind to thrive. Next, we need a cohesive and inclusive society to organize production and consumption in order to ensure enduring prosperity for all. In their seminal book *Why Nations Fail*, Daren Acemoglu and James A. Robinson show that political institutions that promote inclusiveness generate prosperity. Inclusiveness allows everyone to participate in economic opportunities.

## Figure 1: Interlinkages Between Economic, Social and Environmental Systems

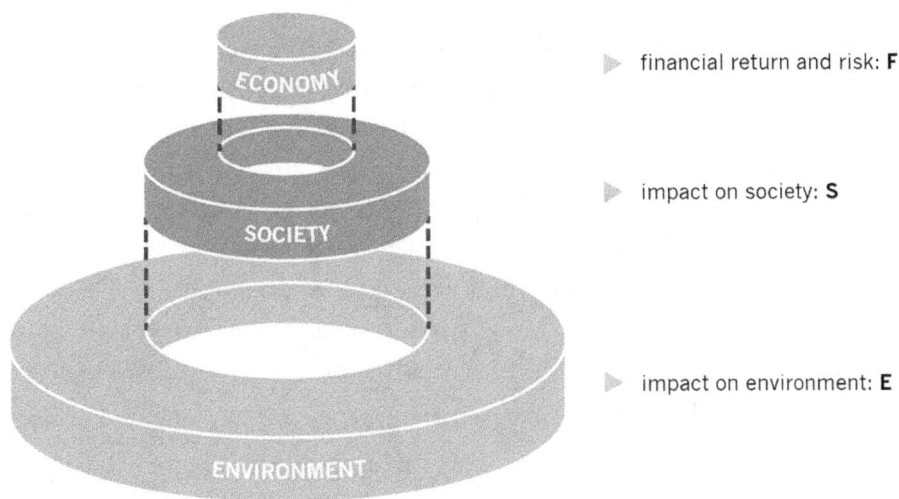

- financial return and risk: **F**
- impact on society: **S**
- impact on environment: **E**

---

[26] Quigley (2025), "Universal Ownership in Practice: A Practical Guide for Asset Owners," Available at SSRN.

Figure 1 shows that societies need to set goals at all three levels to ensure a flourishing economy in the future. The problem is that the majority of current investment approaches continue to pursue only financial value, often in a way that comes at the expense of social and environmental value. Table 1 summarizes the main sustainable investment approaches.

## Table 1: Sustainable Investment Approaches

| Investment approach | Risk | Goal | Role of social and ecological issues |
| --- | --- | --- | --- |
| ESG integration | Exogenous | Financial value | Risk factor to financial returns |
| System-level investing | Endogenous | Financial value | Indirect goal: means by which to ensure financial returns |
| Integrated investing | Endogenous | Integrated value | Part of the goal function |

Whereas ESG integration looks at social and environmental risks affecting financial returns (treating ESG risk to systems, rather than the particular enterprise, as exogenous), system-level investing looks at companies affecting economic, social and environmental systems (treating systemic risks as endogenous), thereby improving expected long-term financial returns.[27] System-level investing is a very welcome improvement on leading asset pricing models, which treat risk as exogenous. The system-level perspective acknowledges the need for healthy systems for financial reasons, but in its application by many investors the goal still seems to be that of maximizing financial value.

In line with the SDGs, integrated value combines financial, social and environmental value.[28] To achieve long-term value creation, companies

---

[27] Lukomnik and Hawley (2021), *Moving beyond modern portfolio theory: Investing that matters*, Routledge.
[28] Schoenmaker and Schramade (2023), *Corporate Finance for Long-Term Value*, Springer.

(and their investors) need to perform at all three levels. In that way, they can futureproof their business model for a sustainable economy. This may imply that some companies have to give up short-term financial return to invest in social and environmental solutions. System-level investing and integrated investing are complimentary in their plea for healthy social and environmental systems. The route is different: System-level investing takes an indirect route towards social and ecological issues (with long-term financial returns as end-goal), whereas integrated investing adopts a direct route towards addressing social and ecological issues. However, integrated investment still recognizes that institutional investors need a strongly positive financial return to meet their beneficiaries' requirements. And both approaches need to balance short-term and long-term results. As a result, system-level investing and integrated investing can result in similar priorities and portfolios.

Let's illustrate the dilemma between short-term and long-term with our case study of Inditex (below). As a fast fashion company, Inditex may move to slow fashion with, for example, a rental model for their clothing, resulting in less turnover in collections. This reduces cash flows in the short term but puts Inditex to the forefront (achieving long-term financial return) if and when social and environmental externalities are internalized in the fashion industry.

## Solutions Based on Integrated Value

The real economy approach starts with companies operating in the real economy. We build on our new integrated value measure that aids companies in futureproofing their business models. The social and environmental value components reflect societal impact. Universal asset owners can then rank companies on impact and build a diversified portfolio with positive impact companies, impact-neutral companies and negative impact companies that can and want to improve their impact.

# Company-Level Solution:
## Futureproofing Business Models

Sustainability challenges put the economy in transition. On the environmental side, climate change and biodiversity loss are asking for new solutions. On the social front, social inequalities and poor labor practices in the supply chain are under pressure. Companies need to adapt to these transitions by changing (i.e. futureproofing) their business model.[29]

Sustainability transitions can thus have a major impact on company valuation. The traditional view holds that stock prices reflect rational expectations of future cash flows. But transitions are only partially priced in and therefore not very visible in market-based valuation ratios, as the number of analysts paying attention to sustainability factors is still limited and subject to learning.[30] Moreover, there is evidence that markets historically over-discount future cash flows, providing evidence of short-termism.[31] Future transitions and externalities are thus not adequately quantified or captured in the structure of existing valuation methods.

To capture these effects, company valuation can be broadened from narrow financial valuation to broad integrated valuation. We have developed the concept of integrated value $IV_i$ of company $i$, that combines financial value $FV$, social value $SV$, and environmental value $EV$:[32]

$$IV_i = FV_i + SV_i + EV_i \qquad (1)$$

Recent advances in impact accounting and valuation enable companies to measure social and environmental effects and monetize these via welfare-

---

[29] Kurznack, Schoenmaker and Schramade (2021), "A model of long-term value creation," *Journal of Sustainable Finance & Investment*.

[30] Lo (2017), *Adaptive markets: Financial evolution at the speed of light*, Princeton University Press.

[31] Davies, Haldane, Nielsen, and Pezzini (2014), "Measuring the costs of short-termism," *Journal of Financial Stability*, 12

[32] Schoenmaker and Schramade (2023), *Corporate Finance for Long-Term Value*, Springer.

based pricing techniques. Chapter 11 of our textbook *Corporate for Long-Term Value* contains a company case-study of the integrated valuation of Inditex. The fast fashion industry faces major social and environmental challenges, such as pollution and the exploitation of workers. Since the industry is characterized by high levels of outsourcing, those challenges tend to be hidden down the supply chain.

This case-study shows how the social and environmental value can be calculated in four steps:

1. **Materiality assessment** – determine important social and environmental factors;
2. **Quantification** – express these factors in their own units Q;
3. **Monetization** – express these factors in money with shadow prices SP; and
4. **Valuation** – discount value flows (Q*SP) to achieve SV and EV.

Table 2 shows the integrated value calculation for Inditex. The integrated value of €42 billion is about half of its financial value of €79 billion. The positive social value is driven by consumer surplus, employment wellbeing and corporate taxes. The negative social value is caused by poor labor conditions and underpayment in Asian garment factories. The negative environmental value is based on environmental pollution caused by how suppliers grow cotton, garment production, burning of out-of-fashion collections and transport from Asia to Europe and North America. While these numbers are very rough estimates, they do give a clear indication of the health (or lack thereof) of Inditex's business model.

## Table 2. Components of Integrated Value for Inditex (Euro billions, 2021)

| INTEGRATED VALUE CALCULATION (EQUAL WEIGHTS) | VALUE (EURO BILLIONS) |
|---|---|
| FINANCIAL VALUE (ENTERPRISE VALUE) | 79 |
| POSITIVE SOCIAL VALUE | 283 |
| NEGATIVE SOCIAL VALUE | -137 |
| NEGATIVE ENVIRONMENTAL VALUE | -183 |
| INTEGRATED VALUE | 42 |

*Source: Schoenmaker and Schramade (2023),*
*Corporate Finance for Long-Term Value, Chapter 11*

Integrated value is the basis for a new relative valuation model, called the futureproofing ratio.[33] The futureproofing ratio is defined as the ratio of integrated value $IV$ to financial value $FV$:

*Futureproofing ratio=IV/FV* (2)

The futureproofing ratio measures the net social and environmental externalities in relation to financial value. To better understand the working of the futureproofing ratio, it is useful to disentangle the net externalities in positive social and environmental value ($SV +, EV +$) and negative social and environmental value ($SV ^-, EV ^-$). Both can be expressed in ratios versus FV as well.

The transition opportunity ratio is defined as positive social and environmental value ($SV +, EV +$) divided by financial value $FV$.

*Transition opportunity ratio=(SV + EV +)/FV* (3)

---

[33] Marijnissen, Schoenmaker and Schramade (2025), "Futureproofing companies & valuation ratio," Available at SSRN.

The positive social and environmental externalities represent transition opportunities for the company, which come into the money when transition shocks happen that cause the positive externalities to be internalized. As discussed before, positive social and environmental value can be a source of long-term value creation.

Likewise, the transition risk ratio is defined as negative social and environmental value ($SV^-$, $EV^-$) divided by financial value $FV$:

*Transition risk ratio=*$(|SV^- + EV^-|)/FV$ (4)

Transition risk assesses a company's vulnerability to transition shocks. The monetized negative social and environmental externalities are an indicator for transition risk, as the company faces high costs when these externalities are internalized. Climate-related financial risk exposures, for example, are on the rise.[34] More than 100 climate lawsuits have been filed per year globally since 2015.

To cast the transition risk ratio as a positive quotient, we take the absolute value of $SV^-$ and $EV^-$ in equation (4). Using equation (1), we can link the three ratios as follows:

*Futureproofing ratio=1+transition opportunity ratio-transition risk ratio* (5)

These ratios allow us to switch our perspective on risk from a backward-looking perspective based on historical stock data to a forward-looking transition risk perspective. Table 3 summarizes the ratios for Inditex. The futureproofing ratio is 0.58, which is below one. The transition risks exceed the transition opportunities putting Inditex's business model at risk.

---

[34] Wetzer, Stuart-Smith and Dibley (2024), "Climate risk assessments must engage with the law," *Science*, 383(6679).

## Table 3. Futureproofing Ratio of Inditex (2021)

| Ratio | Formula | Value |
|---|---|---|
| TRANSITION OPPORTUNITY RATIO | $\dfrac{SV^+ EV^+}{FV}$ | 3.58 |
| TRANSITION RISK RATIO | $\dfrac{\lvert SV^- + EV^- \rvert}{FV}$ | 4.05 |
| FUTUREPROOFING RATIO | $\dfrac{IV}{FV}$ | 0.53 |

The futureproofing ratio measures the extent to which a company is prepared for future internalization shocks. A ratio larger than one indicates that a company is relatively well prepared for future internalization shocks and contributes to building the future economy. By contrast, a ratio below one suggests that a company is less able to absorb transition shocks and thus less prepared for the future economy. Further down the range, a ratio below zero means the negative social and ecological value is larger than the company's financial value, indicating a highly unsustainable business model and a potential inability to withstand significant transition shocks. The value of these latter companies can decline rapidly, turning them into "stranded assets."[35]

To show proof of concept, we evaluated 23 companies on the AEX (Dutch) index based on the integrated value methodology.[36] This means calculating the financial, social, and ecological value that each company generates and ranking these companies according to their futureproofing ratio. Figure 2 plots the futureproofing ratios of the AEX companies. Companies are ranked in four buckets according to their futureproofing ratio: leader (>2); upper middle (1-2); lower middle (0-1); laggard (<0). Companies, that are outside the middle range (0-2), are highlighted with a bigger bullet depending on their distance from the neutral futureproofing ratio of one.

[35] Caldecott, Clark, Koskelo, Mulholland, and Hickey (2021), "Stranded assets: environmental drivers, societal challenges, and supervisory responses," *Annual Review of Environment and Resources*, 46(1).

[36] Marijnissen, Schoenmaker and Schramade (2025), "Futureproofing companies & valuation ratios," available at SSRN.

It is our hope that this Index will influence the way companies think about creating value for the long-term. The next sub-section discusses how investors can use this methodology to build an integrated portfolio.

## Figure 2. Futureproofing Ratio Ranking of AEX Companies

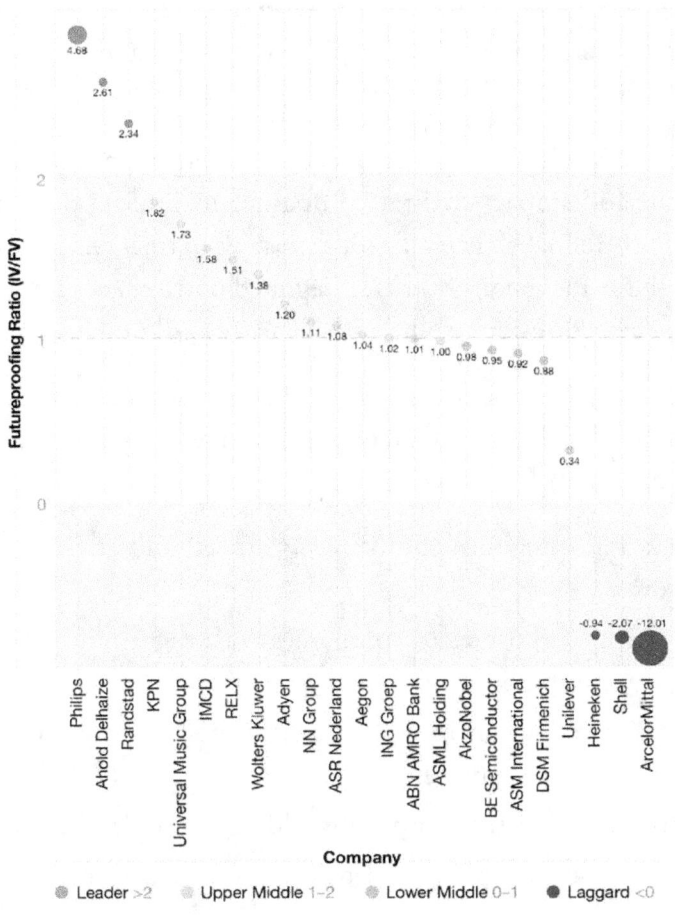

*Source: Marijnissen, Schoenmaker and Schramade (2025), 'Futureproofing companies & valuation ratios'.*

# Portfolio Level Solution: Building an Integrated Portfolio

Universal asset owners can use the integrated value measure to build an integrated portfolio. We distinguish three phases in building such an integrated portfolio. The first phase is about impact (i.e. the social and environmental value components of the integrated value measure). Universal asset owners determine company impact and decide how to steer on impact by selecting positive impact companies and negative impact companies that can and want to improve.

The second phase is about portfolio risk management. Universal asset owners can add impact-neutral companies to build a diversified and integrated portfolio, balancing factor exposures to their desired weights. In the third phase, they monitor their integrated portfolio continuously with a view to create long-term value and act as steward of long-term capital.

To be practical, we present a five-step approach with the first three steps as part of phase one and the final two steps as part of phase two and phase three respectively:

1. Rank and categorize companies on social and environmental exposures;
2. Investigate exposures to companies with high transition risks and high transition opportunities;
3. Selective reduction in high transition risks and increase in high transition opportunities;
4. Optimize risk-return-impact by adding impact-neutral companies;
5. Continuous portfolio monitoring to act as stewards of long-term capital.

*Step 1: Rank and Categorize Social and Environmental Exposures*

The first step is to rank potential investee companies by their net impact or net externalities. This net impact is calculated with the integrated value measure. Figure 3 shows conceptually how to do the ranking.

## Figure 3. Ranking Companies by Net Externalities

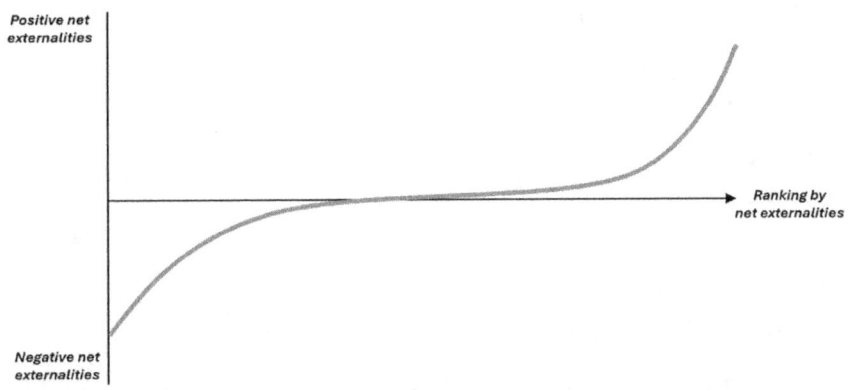

Next, Figure 4 shows how to move capital in two ways: (1) reducing negative externalities; and (2) pushing companies across the horizontal axis to improve their net impact. Ideally, asset owners move capital or investment within companies that want to improve their impact. Alternatively, asset owners move capital across companies to those that want to improve their impact.

## Figure 4. Moving Capital Within and Across Companies

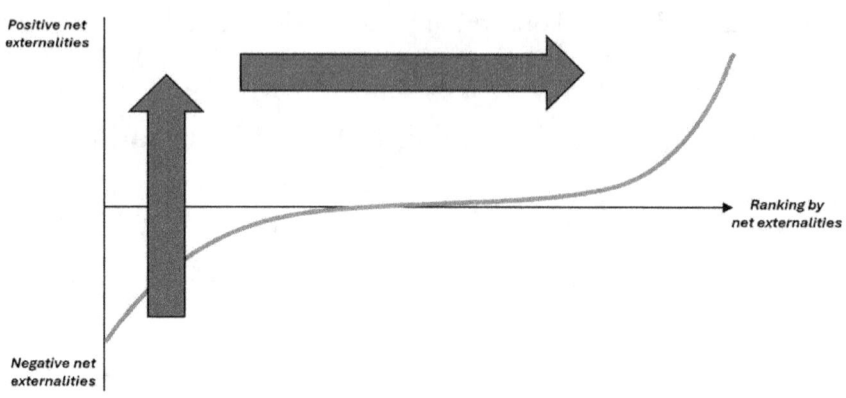

*Step 2: Investigate Exposures to High Transition Risk*

To make things concrete, we simulate an illustrative universe of 100 companies. The overall parameter settings for the simulation are inspired by our AEX Futureproof Index. Figure 5 plots our simulated companies ranked on their futureproofing ratio (FR) and Figure 6 ranked on their transition risk ratio (TRR).

## Figure 5. Investment Universe Ranked on Futureproofing Ratio (FR)

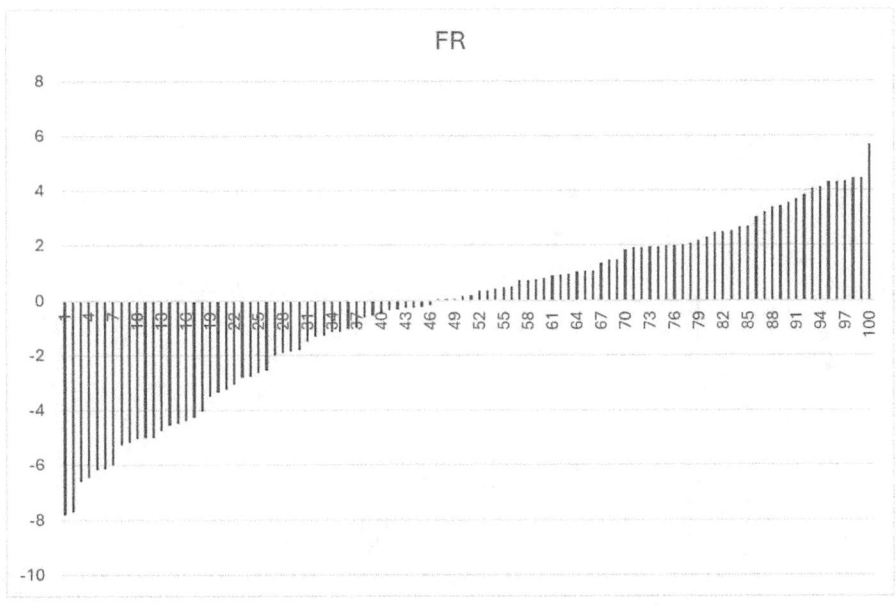

## Figure 6. Investment Universe Ranked on Transition Risk Ratios (TRR)

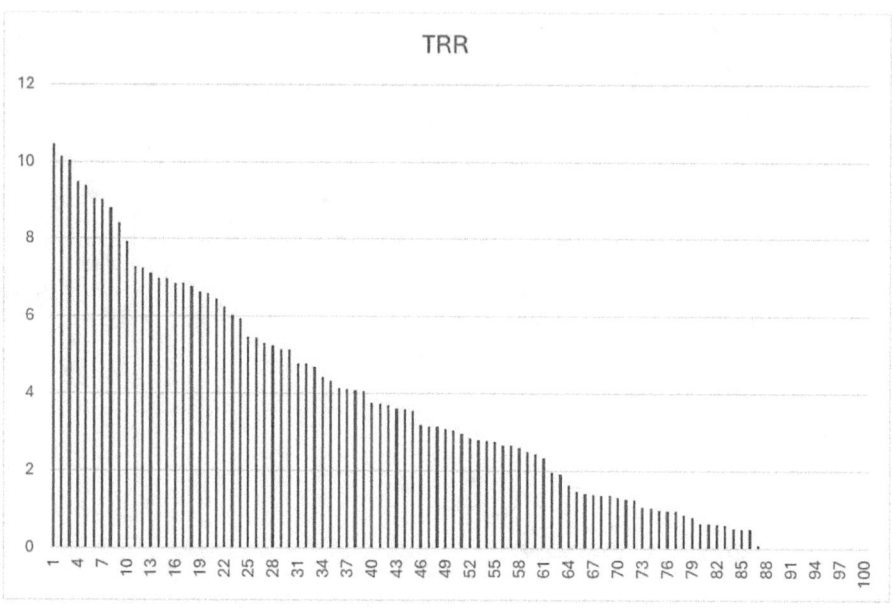

*The final step is to plot the FR against the TRR in Figure 7.*

## Figure 7. Futureproofing Ratio (FR) Against Transition Risk Ratios (TRR)

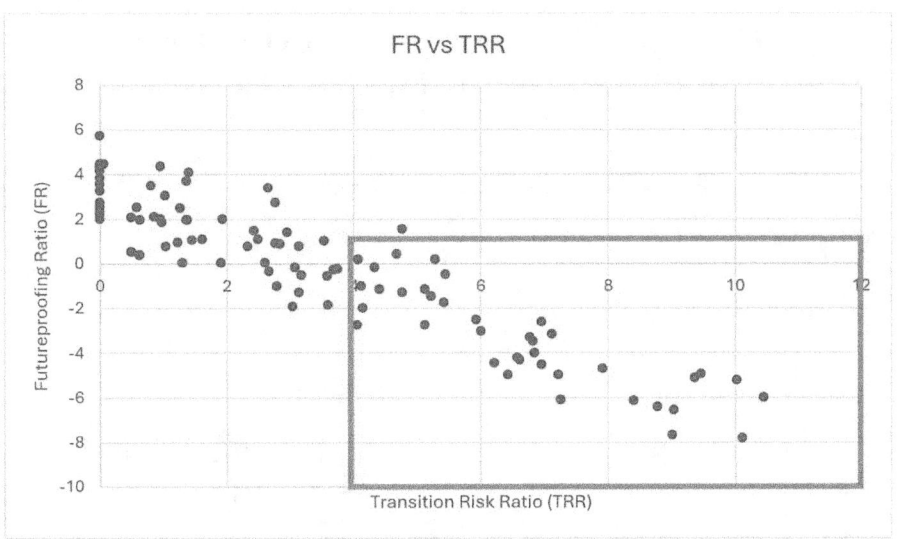

The bottom-right companies in Figure 7 are high risk. Asset owners can define strict cut-off (binary) rules for high-risk companies or apply multiple shades when determining a list of high-risk companies. These high-risk companies are worth further investigation. The key question is which companies are better positioned than their ratios suggest? Asset owners' analysts can analyze companies' transition pathways, both in an absolute way and relative versus the sector.

Applying this thinking to the Inditex case, we find that Inditex is currently in the bottom right of Figure 7 with a FR of 0.53 and a TRR of 4.05 (see Table 3). Figure 8 shows our estimates of Inditex' value flows at the company's current trajectory. This is unsustainable: The company's improvement efforts are nullified by its volume growth, and its negative social and environmental value flows continue to be very large in 2030 and 2050. This is at odds with a company and an economy within social and planetary boundaries. This is unlikely to be tolerated by society, and hence the company's license to operate will be at risk. Responsible management means that this should be fixed. But how?

## Figure 8: Inditex's Value Profile Over Time – Current Trajectory

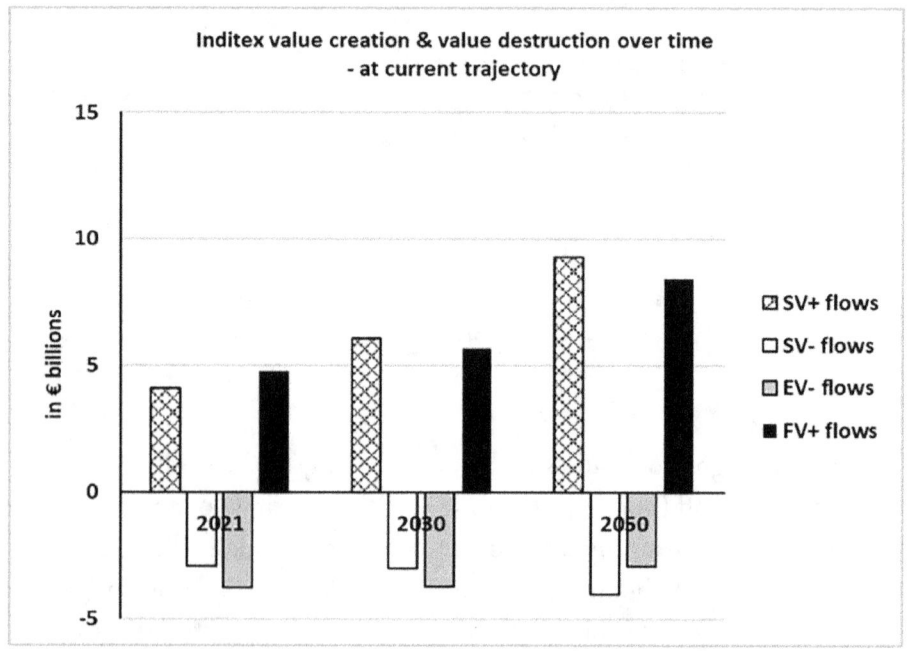

*Source: Schoenmaker and Schramade (2023),*
*Corporate Finance for Long-Term Value, Chapter 11.*

We modeled an alternative pathway that does eliminate the negative externalities (see Figure 9), but it requires significant business model change. That business model change would include, for example, lower frequency of new collections; responsible supply chain management with decent pay for suppliers and suppliers' employees; experiments – and subsequent scaling – of rental clothing and circular production.

## Figure 9: Inditex's Value Profile Over Time – Ambitious Trajectory

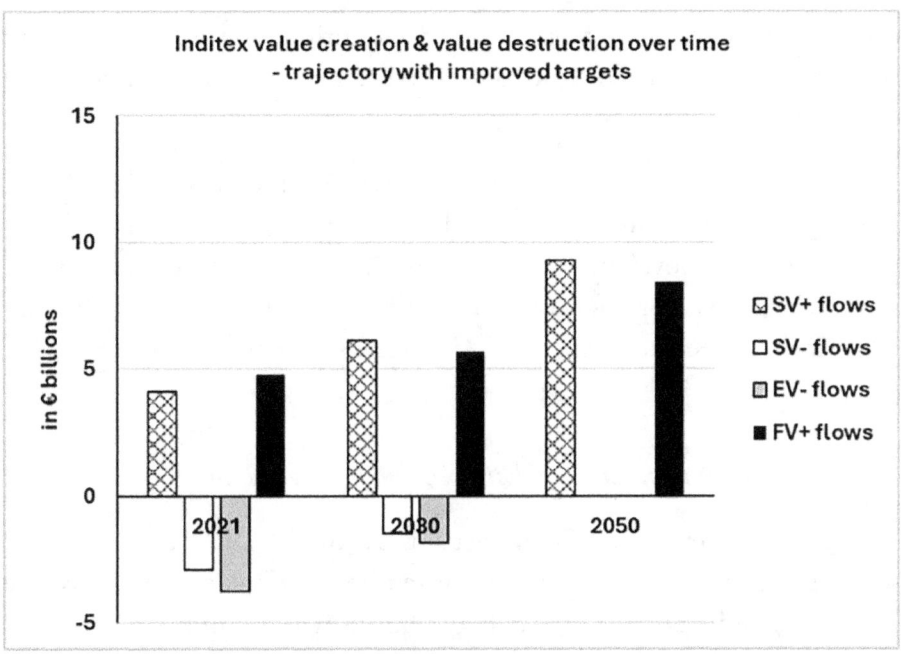

*Source: Schoenmaker and Schramade (2023), Corporate Finance for Long-Term Value, Chapter 11.*

So, the analyst must judge whether Inditex is willing to explore and act on these alternative pathways. If positive, the company may be included in the asset owner's portfolio (step 3) with active monitoring and engagement (step 5).

Of course, analysts can also plot FRs against Transition Opportunity Ratios (TOR) to identify companies that asset owners want to invest more in.

*Step 3: Selective Reduction in Exposures to High Transition Risk*

Following the transition risk analysis in Step 2, asset owners need to decide which transition risk exposures are acceptable and which aren't. How many exposures can you have with sufficient attention? For which company is it worthwhile to become a committed shareholder that supports the company on its pathway?

Based on this further analysis, asset owners determine the shortlist of high transition risk exposures to keep (and help improve) and the longer list of companies to remove (and potentially of new companies to add). Again, asset owners can accordingly make a shortlist of high transition opportunity companies to keep and expand their holdings in these companies.

*The link between firm-level analysis and system-level influence*

The first three steps are about impact at the firm-level but when applied at scale, they contribute to significant system-level influence. Let's illustrate how this could work with the energy transition as example.

In Step 1, companies are ranked according to their carbon impact (expected future carbon emissions). In Step 2, companies are analyzed on their risks and opportunities. In Step 3, investment choices are made on companies to avoid (high risk; no potential/willingness to improve) and companies to select (transition prepared, or working on transition). The five most affected sectors in the energy transition are 1. energy companies; 2. energy utilities – both on the supply side; and on the demand side 3. transport; 4. manufacturing; and 5. real estate (heating).

On the supply side, an integrated investor could select energy companies and utilities that include renewables in their mix or plan to transition to renewables. On the demand side, this might include car companies with serious capacity to produce electric vehicles, or are willing to build up this capacity. The same applies to low-carbon manufacturing and energy-efficient real estate. These choices, if and when made by several large universal asset owners, would accelerate the transition from fossil fuels to renewables.

The analysis and selection at company-level in Steps 1 to 3 could thus lead to system-level influence. The methodology for assessing company-level integrated value and futureproofing ratios helps to shift system dynamics on the social and environmental front. The integrated portfolio approach contributes to shaping system conditions, by promoting positive impact companies, improving negative impact-companies and avoiding laggards.

*Step 4: Optimize Risk-Return-Impact*

Whereas the first three steps focus on social and environmental system risks, we now turn to portfolio risk management to diversify idiosyncratic risk and balance sector and factor exposures. After selecting companies with positive impact and companies with negative impact that can and want to improve in Step 3, asset owners decide which impact-neutral companies to add to build out a balanced portfolio. Impact-neutral companies are those in the mid-range with a FR between 0.6 and 1.4 in Figure 5. If there are not enough impact-neutral companies within this range, the range (in particular the lower limit) may need to be widened by selecting negative-impact companies, starting from the least negative.

A balanced portfolio is diversified over factors, sectors and countries. This is standard portfolio management. The aim is to build a portfolio that has similar risk-return characteristics as the market. Similar but not identical, which means that the active asset owner has a tracking error against a capital-weighted market index.

The result is a more concentrated portfolio with higher stakes in fewer companies, that you know (know what you own principle) and, of course, can support in steering towards (more) positive impact – and thereby also futureproof the economy. This is the real economy approach towards integrated investing.

There are more formal approaches towards building 3D portfolios optimizing among the three components:

$$\max \alpha\mu + \gamma\theta - \beta\sigma^{\wedge 2} \tag{6}$$

Where an investor maximizes return $\mu$ of the investment portfolio by means of factor $\alpha$, and minimise risk (measured as variance $\sigma^2$) by means of factor $\beta$ The portfolio impact is denoted as $\theta$, and optimized by means of factor $\gamma$.[37] Impact is now incorporated in the goal function. However, this optimizing approach reduces impact to the summary factor $\gamma$. As explained, we believe that it is not really possible to collapse a company's business model and real word impact into a single statistic.

A pressing question is how much companies a large universal asset owner needs for a properly diversified portfolio. There are two main portfolio risks. On the one hand, asset owners do not want to miss out on positive market developments (FOMO). On the other hand, they want to reduce their exposure to negative market developments (stranded assets). On the first (FOMO), Brøgger, Koëter and Van Dijk find that a portfolio with 500 to 1000 companies provides a large, global investor ample diversification against idiosyncratic risk.[38] On the second (stranded assets), asset owners need to investigate transitions and the transition preparedness of individual companies. Traditional car companies are at risk of becoming a stranded asset in the transition to electric driving. The risk of stranded assets increases with the number of companies in the portfolio. So, the optimal number of companies probably lies somewhere below the 500 to 1000 companies of Brøgger et al (2025).

---

[37] See, for example, Blitz, Chen, Howard, and Lohre (2024), "3D Investing: Jointly Optimizing Return, Risk, and Sustainability," *Financial Analysts Journal*, 80(3); and Roor, Schoenmaker, and Maas (2025), "Integrating Transitions and Impact Measurement in SAA," *Journal of Portfolio Management*, 51(9).

[38] Brøgger, Koëter and Van Dijk (2025), "FOMO in Equity Markets? Concentration Risk in (Sustainable) Investing," available at SSRN.

*Step 5: Monitoring Portfolio Performance and Acting as Steward*

The final step is monitoring portfolio performance. Are companies realizing profit and impact? Are adjustments needed due to a changing environment? It is important that universal asset owners act as stewards of long-term capital. That means supporting companies in good and bad times and steering them on their impact journey through engagement.

But when companies renege on their impact commitments and thus put the long-term relationship at risk, this may be a reason for divestment. This is clearly a tool of last resort. Stewardship means working together on long-term value creation and thereby futureproofing the economy.

## Lessons Learned and Takeaways

We have been working over the past ten years developing the integrated value measure for companies and propagating more concentrated portfolios with companies that you know.

Along this journey, we learned some lessons:

- Use forward-looking risk indicators, not backward-looking data. It is difficult to drive change via the rear-view mirror.
- Look at business models if you really want to learn about your portfolio companies (this is fundamental investing, but not with alpha as the goal). ESG ratings or other summary statistics, which are used in the many asset pricing models, are too superficial and thus not sufficient.
- Focus on material social and environmental issues and don't forget about companies' competitive position (real economy approach).
- Most importantly, get started, even if data are not perfect. We did that with our AEX Futureproof Index, which was illuminating and fun to construct.

We also have some generalized takeaways:

- Capital allocation is at the core of the financial system. Integrated investing aims to allocate capital on positive, or improving, social and environmental impact. This is the power of finance.

- Integrated investing really starts to work if universal asset owners collectively reduce negative social and environmental impact at the same time. There is also a need to engage with negative impact companies that can and want to improve. Again, the power of finance.

- The last and most important takeaway is the need to change mindsets from "market only" to "integrated" investing.

Integrated investing is a powerful way to apply system-level investing. It enables us to assess integrated value and futureproofing ratios at company level. The ultimate aim of this forward-looking assessment, rooted in the real economy, is to shift system dynamics on the social and environmental front. This real economy approach contributes to shaping system conditions, by promoting positive impact companies, improving negative impact-companies and avoiding laggards.

**Section II:**

# Getting It Right – One Size Fits One

Chapter 5:

# Different Organizations, Different Leverage Points

### By John Hoeppner[39]

## Introduction: The Systemic Mandate – A Fiduciary Imperative

The premise of system-level investing rests on the belief of financial inter-connectedness: environmental and social externalities – including climate degradation, public health crises, and resource scarcity – create un-diversifiable risk in the capital markets that diminish long-term financial portfolio value. For institutional investors, addressing these macro threats is increasingly recognized as a fiduciary imperative, in addition to being the right thing to do. The operational challenge, however, is bridging the gap between this long-term necessity and the capital market's reliance on short-term financial incentives.

My professional journey has provided a unique perspective on this challenge, having implemented advanced stewardship strategies within two

---

[39] John Hoeppner is Head of Investment Stewardship at Builders Vision. He was previously Head of US Stewardship and Sustainable Investments at LGIM America.

distinct organizations – L&G Asset Management (formerly LGIM), a global asset manager, and Builders Vision, a $15 Billion family office founded by Lukas Walton which uses grants and investments to accelerate promising solutions in three sectors: food & agriculture, energy and oceans. The key insight is that effective system-level investing is not about a single, standardized approach. From L&G Asset Management's large index asset manager perspective, utilizing the sheer scale and consistency of a universal owner to enforce higher minimum standards drove results. From Builders Vision's vantage point, deploying flexible capital and the thematic agility of a highly targeted approach to catalyze innovation and shift value chains is showing promise. Both approaches require organizational leaders willing to champion the effort, articulate a strategy and take actions.

This chapter synthesizes the challenges, solutions, and lessons learned from deploying two distinct stewardship approaches to advance system-level investing.

## Leveraging Scale and Transparency as a Universal Owner (L&G Asset Management)

Legal & General Group PLC (L&G), the parent company of L&G Asset Management is a 180-year-old, FTSE listed financial services firm managing a global pool of approximately $1.4 trillion in assets.[40] Given its significant retirement client base and index fund businesses, L&G is fairly categorized as a universal owner – a designation it readily embraces.[41] For a firm with this approach, mitigating systemic risk is synonymous with preserving client value in its funds and generating long-term value for L&G shareholders.

---

[40] https://group.legalandgeneral.com/en/about-us/our-businesses/asset-management. Accessed November 21, 2025

[41] https://am.landg.com/en-uk/institutional/responsible-investing/active-ownership/. Accessed November 21, 2025

For six years I was part of a global investment stewardship team within L&G Asset Management – a group of over 20 investment professionals speaking 15 different languages and sitting across three offices. There, I was tasked with advocating for global minimum standards such as emissions disclosures, nature policies, and governance practices – each carefully related to L&G's views on how to decrease risk to portfolio companies and markets. I led the U.S. team, which met with U.S. companies and our investment clients.

The sheer scale and scope presented natural challenges for the team.

- **Prioritization**: how to prioritize systemic themes across a global diversified portfolio?
- **Standardization**: how to apply standardized expectations across diverse sectors, company sizes, and markets?
- **Measurement**: how to measure the effectiveness of investment stewardship activities? How to measure the client benefits of changing systemic risk?
- **Conflicts of Interest**: how to manage conflicts of interest inherent in corporate engagement?

The foundation for overcoming these challenges was a clear team purpose. "To protect client assets through raising market standards and best practices."[42] This statement, shared internally and externally, guided decisions and debates. Most large asset managers approach every corporate engagement case by case. We took an approach that attempted to change market-wide performance. We attempted to approach this goal with humility and the mindset of incremental progress.

---

[42] ibid.

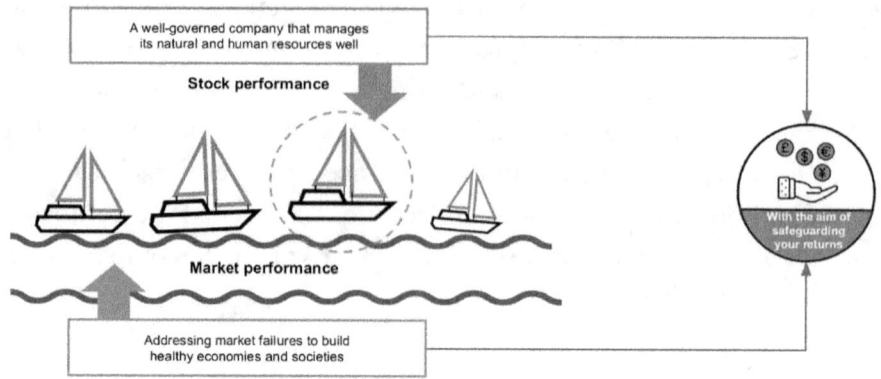

A well-governed company that manages its natural and human resources well

**Stock performance**

**Market performance**

Addressing market failures to build healthy economies and societies

With the aim of safeguarding your returns

*Source: Legal and General Asset Management*

The team attempted regular thematic prioritization – which at the time resulted in defined "Super Themes" (Climate, Nature, People, Health, Governance, Digitization). The goal was to prioritize the themes most financially material to clients – but that is easier said than done, as each of these system risks can drastically impact portfolio value based on assumptions, time periods and scenarios. On roughly an annual basis, there was an honest assessment of potential scale and probability of projected financial impact, but that assessment is ultimately an estimate.

Prioritization was also focused on where L&G believed its unique influence could change corporate or market actions, which meant there was an openness to engage on novel issues such as anti-microbial resistance, living wage, climate lobbying, and methane measurement.[43] [44] [45] The International Sustainability Standards Board (ISSB) was one guiding framework, but its definition of what is material is primarily related to

---

[43] https://blog.landg.com/categories/esg-and-long-term-themes/antimicrobial-resistance-could-be-the-next-pandemic--heres-what-were-doing-about-it2/. Accessed November 21, 2025.

[44] https://am.landg.com/asset/4a6c63/globalassets/lgim_document-library/capabilities/north-america-principles-on-executive-pay-lgim.pdf// Accessed November 21, 2025.

[45] https://am.landg.com/asset/4a40f9/globalassets/lgim_document-library/climate-impact-pledge/cro_climate-impact-pledge_2025.pdf. Accessed November 21, 2025.

company enterprise value and not the risk to the systems that any specific company or companies impact(s).

To drive maximum system-level impact, L&G Asset Management used an approach which sent a market signal – highly transparent, clearly detailing expectations and views of minimum standards and best practice.[46] This meant the views were picked up directly by companies, corporate advisors, proxy advisors, activists, peer investors, regulators, press and clients.

Companies disliked this prescriptive, one-size-fits-all approach, believing they were all unique. For example, there were clear views on carbon emission disclosures, green revenue, water risk, deforestation, diversity, human rights policies, and a range of governance items. Beyond clear signaling of the standards, L&G Asset Management reinforced their views by directly engaging with companies, linking performance to proxy voting decisions, and offering investment strategies which tilted, by overweights or underweights, companies based on these same underlying indicators. This guidance was so transparent that companies could self-serve and understand L&G's views and look across their competitors and suppliers using disclosure tools. Examples of this effort can be seen in the LGIM ESG Score and the Climate Impact Pledge.[47] [48] By creating standardized and structured views, L&G Asset Management was able to measure market wide shifts – and tracked change over time. For example, in the 2025 Climate Impact Pledge report, 74.6 percent of companies met minimum expectations on climate policy advocacy (up from 70 percent the prior year).[49] For deforestation there is a similar year over year uptick in 'Adequate or Strong Policies'.[50]

---

[46] https://am.landg.com/en-uk/institutional/responsible-investing/investment-stewardship/. Accessed November 21, 2025.

[47] https://esgscores.landg.com/. Accessed November 21, 2025

[48] https://climatepledge.landg.com/. Accessed November 21, 2025

[49] https://am.landg.com/asset/4a40f9/globalassets/lgim/_document-library/climate-impact-pledge/cro_climate-impact-pledge_2025.pdf. Accessed November 21, 2025

[50] ibid. Accessed November 21, 2025

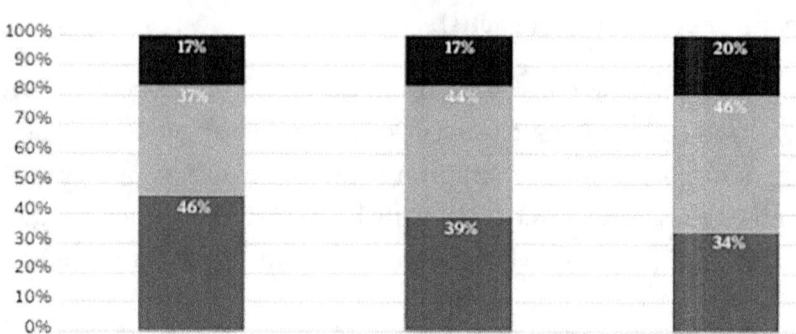

Breakdown of companies by strength of deforestation policy (2023-2025)

■ Adequate or Strong policy   ▪ Weak policy/General statement   ▪ No policy

Source: L&G, as at April 2025. The bar chart shows the % of companies with no deforestation policy, a weak deforestation policy and an adequate or strong policy between 2023 and 2025, as defined by Sustainalytics. Companies that have no deforestation policy may receive a vote against. For illustrative purposes only.

As I reflect on my experience with L&G Asset Management, I came away with two salient observations:

1. A transparent, universal ownership approach to system-level investing is directly exposed to politicalization critiques. Systemic risks, by their very nature, are complex, take time to manifest, are difficult to measure, include multiple actors, involve complex trade-offs with competing interests, and usually impact consumers, non-financially valued externalities, and policy. The financial projects related to the impact of macro themes can and should always be debated, but once an investor takes a clear view, they become a target for stakeholders that have different views (and likely conflicted interests). Given this tension, it is essential that asset managers take views well-founded in evidence, take the time to explain where the assumptions are and how the financial impact could materialize. Ultimately their clients need to support these views rather than disengage.

2. Asset owners (particularly in the US), and their underlying beneficiaries, must demand clear stewardship purpose and actions from their asset managers, especially those running large index strategies.

Asset managers are legally obliged to act on investors' behalf and will make thousands of tiny decisions like how to vote, what topics to ask companies about, and what policies to make public. By not speaking up on systemic issues, asset managers will make decisions that are safe and legal but not necessarily in their clients' true, long-term best interest.

I believe currently very few institutional asset owners in the U.S. are explicit or even interested in the system-level investment approaches of their asset managers. I recall the time I met with an executive of a large public pension fund who expressed zero interest in a distinct climate-related corporate engagement approach. This was despite the state's severe exposure to physical climate risk. Ironically, two years following the meeting, the state had a catastrophic climate event that financially and physically impacted many of the pension fund's clients.

## Case Study: Leveraging Agility and Flexible Capital (Builders Vision)

Builders Vision (BV), a family office founded by Lukas Walton, operates with a thematic, impact-oriented mandate focusing on three system-level sectors: food & agriculture, energy, and oceans[51]. Its innovative approach to investing flexible capital includes teams that deploy grants, direct investments, and fund investments. The team is designed for agility with a goal of building and scaling new market solutions. My role as Head of Investment Stewardship is a newly created position that seeks to align public companies' business activities to create market resilience across these three essential sectors.

The overarching stewardship challenge BV faces is how can a capital pool that is small relative to the total public markets (though large for an

---

[51] https://www.buildersvision.com/. Accessed November 21, 2025.

organization of our nature) use its public equity and fixed income exposure to support the system-level shifts across food & agriculture, energy, and oceans. To be more specific – what proxy voting strategy maximizes impact? How should index exposure be tilted to reinforce market signals? Where is our involvement in corporate engagement a game changer?

The anchor of BV's approach to system-level investing starts with a 2050 outcome, then we identified thematic 'system frictions' that may prevent us from reaching those goals. Then we determine where BV is best suited to tackle those system frictions with the tools we have. Some of these outcomes are explicitly economically oriented and others are about different stakeholders. For example, in the Oceans System outcomes displayed below, there are two near-term outcomes that exemplify this: "blue products and solutions effectively address a range of customer needs, spurring further ocean-focused innovation" and "the policy and regulatory frameworks governing oceans better support the health and resilience of ocean ecosystems."[52] Detailing the entire system-level outcomes to target and measure helps our multi-disciplinary team of investors and philanthropists understand the interdependence of the various stakeholders and evaluate if gains for one outcome are coming at the cost of another.

---

[52] https://www.buildersvision.com/news-and-media-coverage/builders-vision-releases-2023-impact-report. Accessed November 21, 2025.

| Long-Term Outcomes | Near-Term Outcomes |
|---|---|
| By 2050, we aim for a world in which: | By 2030, Builders Vision and its partners intend to contribute to shifts in the Oceans ecosystem that will pave the way toward our vision, including: |
| → Ocean resources are sustainably utilized in the blue economy to promote healthy oceans and economic prosperity.<br><br>→ Ocean ecosystems are resilient and balanced, and ocean resources are abundant and healthy.<br><br>→ Oceans meaningfully contribute to climate resilience and global emissions reduction targets.<br><br>→ Policies, policy enforcement, and policymaker knowledge support the blue economy and promote ocean health. | 1. Key stakeholders (investors, funders, researchers, general public, etc.) recognize oceans as a market-driven solution to climate change.<br><br>2. The policy and regulatory frameworks governing oceans better support the health and resilience of ocean ecosystems.<br><br>3. Key stakeholders (policymakers, scientists, insurance providers, etc.) have increased access to better quality data about the oceans.<br><br>4. More people are equipped with the skills and experience needed for jobs that promote the health and resiliency of oceans.<br><br>5. Blue products and solutions effectively address a range of customer needs, spurring further ocean-focused innovation.<br><br>6. Ocean investments are shown to be profitable, catalyzing investment into the ecosystem from a range of sources.<br><br>7. Oceans are healthier and more resilient. |

Based on our organizational goals and our public markets exposure, we established a stewardship vision that has two components: public companies develop products and supply chains which advance our priority system outcomes (Solutions) and public companies establish guardrails for sustainability related market failures (Risks).

This means our goal is to champion growth and revenue-based solutions such as traceable seafood, sustainable aquaculture, plastic alternatives, regenerative agriculture, renewable energy, low-carbon cement and support companies and markets reducing the practice of externalizing systemic risks.

From an implementation perspective, one of the first steps was to analyze how our public markets managers were approaching the stewardship activities we valued. Each asset manager partner was assessed across four categories:

- **Influence** – Size, investment style (active / fundamental / index / quant), access to management, industry thought leadership; *the general theory is the larger and stronger executive relationships, the more influence.*

- **Stewardship Program Strength** – Team size, integration of team with investments, number of engagements, escalation strategy, sponsoring and voting of shareholder proposals, collaborations, regulatory environment, unique campaigns, quality of reporting; *the general theory is the more comprehensive a program the more effective it can be – many managers just go through the motions so discerning true impact / effectiveness is difficult.*

- **Builders Vision Alignment** – Purpose, ambition, existing priorities; *the general theory is that asset managers' stewardship agendas vary and may or may not be aligned with the change BV seeks.*

- **Collaboration Potential** – Capacity, willingness to interact with clients and genuinely consider feedback; *the general theory is those managers willing to listen and engage with BV are better partners.*

This assessment created groupings of managers that helped the team determine which managers are most strategically aligned with BV and most likely to have market influence and impact.

This analysis also uncovered various approaches to proxy voting – roughly two thirds of our managers had custom proxy voting policies and one third used proxy advisors' policies. We made the intentional decision for at least the first few years not to attempt to pull the proxy voting back in house to BV, but rather to highlight differences of opinion and analyze the decisions and assumptions with the ultimate goal to learn and try and influence the asset managers' voting approach. This is a work in progress.

From an index strategy perspective, one of the core approaches leverages the FTSE TPI (climate transition) Index series. We like the combination of FTSE's index design expertise and TPI's forward-looking data and analyses of how companies manage their climate transition. Additionally, components of the TPI score are used in direct and collaborative engagements of many other investors. This means there is structured corporate engagement reinforcing the same data gaps and transition approaches that tilt the index and that companies are getting consistent feedback.

On multiple occasions we have been approached by thoughtful asset managers who have offered to create custom index approaches for BV which would further emphasize data related to one of our sector's outcomes. While we greatly appreciate the creativity and care of these approaches, ultimately, we are less interested in a custom approach and more interested in major financial institutions using those same indicators in their own business practices, in whatever way that could be appropriate for them. These could include new products, different loan profiles, enhanced corporate client relations, research, etc. This kind of system-level consideration – one that could catalyze broader action or additional capital – would be highly motivating for BV, as it generates both greater impact and financial value than BV's capital alone could achieve.

In BV's early efforts with direct corporate engagement, we are encouraged with the access and genuine exchanges we have had with large public companies. It appears that public companies are open to candid dialogue related to our systems goals – specifically because we have extensive experience with market building philanthropy, disruptive early-stage investing, and co-invest with corporate venture capital teams. These experiences and forms of capital appear to signal that we have gained an experience and point of view to be taken seriously.

Lastly, BV has increasingly focused on its convening power to help build the field. BV creates forums for peer exchanges with the goal to attract more capital towards sustainable solutions. For example, BV hosts conferences to convene General Counsels of family offices and foundations to share approaches and learnings to help legal teams drive impact within their organizations.[53] During NYC Climate Week, BV brought together investors and business partners around key BV's sectors – food & agriculture, energy, and oceans – and finance themes to showcase progress being made through innovative financing models, actionable investment opportunities and successful corporate programs.[54]

There are a few lessons learned from our first year of testing a new stewardship strategy:

- Agility allows BV to take calculated risks on solutions deemed "too hard" or "too slow" by large mainstream public market managers (e.g. pursuing green cement as a focus).

- Our multi-tool structure (grant, direct, fund) ensures that when system frictions are identified (e.g. the need for policy to level the playing field for diverse crops), the appropriate capital tool or advocacy strategy can be applied to remove the blocker, securing the path for market-rate returns.

- BV's influence transcends the size of its capital commitment. Our expertise, strategic advice, and connectivity to influential networks in addition to our assets under management are showing promise in our pursuit of system outcomes.

---

[53] https://www.buildersvision.com/news-and-media-coverage/advising-for-change-2023-recap-how-legal-teams-can-drive-impact. Accessed November 21, 2025.
[54] https://www.buildersvision.com/blog-posts/from-urgency-to-action-catalyzing-markets-at-climate-week-nyc-2025. Accessed November 21, 2025.

## Takeaways

System-level investing is messy. It starts with developing (or borrowing) a framework to understand how interconnected investments are with the rest of the world. The acknowledgement that actions as investors impact the entire system (economic, environmental, social) is the necessary starting point for all investors, regardless of size.

In my experience, this reflective process can feel vague for finance executives even if the directional nature seems obvious. Given this complexity, system-level investing needs to be supported by the highest level of executive and board leadership to ensure organizational buy-in. As the examples of L&G Asset Management and Builders Vision reveal, while the tactical playbook may differ based on the size and flexibility of capital, the requirement for strategic, top-down conviction remains universal.

Chapter 6:

# System-level Investing
# for Asset Managers

By Jane Ambachtsheer, Sarah Annan,
CFA and Adam Kanzer[55]

## Introduction

Recent years have seen the increase of geopolitical conflicts, extreme weather events, threats to social stability and technological risks. The World Economic Forum's Global Risk reports have mapped these trends, highlighting environmental, technological, geopolitical, and societal risks as among the most severe over both the short- (2 years) and long-term (10 years) in its 2025 report.[56] The picture painted is of a world facing multiple, intersecting, systemic risks which can be seen as "un-diversifiable threats

---

[55] Jane Ambachtsheer is Global Head of Sustainability at BNP Paribas Asset Management and an Honorary Research Fellow at Oxford University's Smith School. Sarah Annan, CFA is Senior ESG Specialist at BNP Paribas Asset Management. Adam Kanzer is Head of Stewardship, Americas, at BNP Paribas Asset Management. Any views expressed in this chapters are those of the authors as of the date of publication, are based on available information, and are subject to change without notice.
[56] The Global Risks Report 2025, World Economic forum, https://reports.weforum.org/docs/WEF_Global_Risks_Report_2025.pdf

that can disrupt entire markets or economic systems through complex interconnections, potentially triggering chain reactions across multiple sectors and undermining overall market growth."[57] Increasingly, we hear reference to the "polycrisis," emphasizing how these risks intersect and strengthen each other.[58]

As a global investor diversified across asset classes, regions, and sectors, BNP Paribas Asset Management's "universal owner" mindset recognizes that corporate externalities may generate profits for one company or industry while diminishing value for many others, or in the future – risks that cannot be diversified away. Diversification, however, is not the sole instrument available to us for risk mitigation. We may also engage with companies and governments as part of our strategy. We aim to help shape a more resilient and sustainable future because we believe the economic model that will best serve investors in the long term is one focused on low-carbon energy production, healthy ecosystems, and equality of opportunity.

### Connecting systemic risk to system-level stewardship

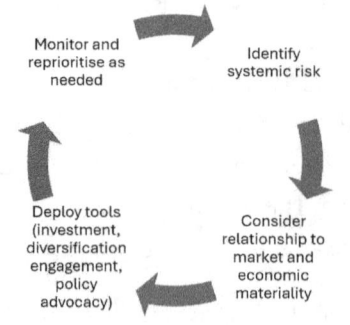

*Source: BNPP AM - October 2025*

---

[57] UKSIF (2025), Systemic risks: A framework for portfolio resilience, https://uksif.org/wp-content/uploads/2025/05/Systemic-risks-a-framework-for-portfolio-resilience.pdf
[58] Helleiner, Eric (2024). "Economic Globalization's Polycrisis," International Studies Quarterly. 68 (2) sqae024, https://doi.org/10.1093%2Fisq%2Fsqae024.

From the narrow perspective of investment returns, addressing systemic risk is not simply about seeking better returns for our clients – it is about preserving the systems we need to deliver those returns over the coming decades. Systemic risks "affect the performance of markets that underpin all investments."[59] If a ship is taking on water, it no longer matters how fast its going, or in what direction. Restoring the integrity of the hull is paramount.

## Addressing System-Level Risk in Asset Management

Systemic risk is an endemic feature of the global capital markets, due to the breadth and interconnected nature of modern markets and, arguably, a lack of sufficient guardrails. Given the prevalence of systemic risks, we choose to integrate systemic risk management as a core part of our strategy. As an asset manager serving a broad client base, including insurers and pension funds with very long-term horizons, we believe we are responsible for understanding how our investments may impact systemic risks, how systemic risks may impact our investments, and what we can do to mitigate them.

When developing our approach, we sought to identify the critical preconditions for a sustainable and inclusive economic system, recognizing that we depend upon a stable climate, a healthy biosphere, and an inclusive economy to deliver value to clients. [60] Identifying the key threats to the systems we rely on is a necessary first step toward mitigating those risks:

- Climate risks: Transition risks driven by regulation and physical risks from climate change have widespread impacts, propagating

---

[59] UKSIF (2025), Systemic risks: A framework for portfolio resilience – UKSIF, https://uksif.org/systemic-risks-a-framework-for-portfolio-resilience/

[60] BNP Paribas Asset management (2024). Our Global Sustainability Strategy – Updated and on course, https://www.bnpparibas-am.com/en-us/institutional/forward-thinking/our-global-sustainability-strategy-updated-and-on-course/

through supply chains, financial networks, and economies. There is no market, economy or company that does not sit within the Earth's climate system, ensuring that shocks can cascade across assets and sectors, requiring collective focus from investors and regulators.[61]

- Nature loss-related risks: Biodiversity loss, resource depletion, and ecosystem degradation threaten economic and financial system stability, undermining the natural capital that economies depend on, causing potential systemic shocks to multiple sectors[62]. As we paraphrased the Dasgupta Review on the Economics of Biodiversity in Sustainable By Nature: Our Biodiversity Roadmap,[63] "the human economy is embedded within the biosphere." The World Economic Forum estimates that up to half of global GDP is at risk by nature loss and the sixth mass extinction event. [64]

- Inequality: Inequality threatens market stability and long-term growth by enabling unequal access to opportunities, which widens the wealth gap, undermines social mobility, cohesion and stability.[65]

- Interconnected systemic risks: Climate change, biodiversity loss, and inequality are not isolated challenges; they are deeply interconnected systemic risks that reinforce and exacerbate one another. The impacts of each can amplify the others, creating feedback loops that threaten the stability and resilience of economies, societies, and natural systems.

---

[61] Bolton, P., & Kacperczyk, M. (2021). Do investors care about carbon risk? Journal of Financial Economics, 142(2), 517-549.

[62] Scholtens, B. (2017). Why finance should care about ecology. Trends in Ecology & Evolution, 32(7), 500-505.

[63] BNP Paribas Asset Management (2021). Sustainable by nature our Biodiversity roadmap, https://docfinder.bnpparibas-am.com/api/files/940B42EF-AFFF-4C89-8C32-D9BFBA72BF24

[64] https://www.weforum.org/press/2020/01/half-of-world-s-gdp-moderately-or-highly-dependent-on-nature-says-new-report/

[65] BNP Paribas Asset Management (2024). Levelling Up: Our Roadmap for Addressing Inequality, https://docfinder.bnpparibas-am.com/api/files/0db88173-c83d-43f5-a72e-f9c72ecf3f54

Each of these preconditions, or pillars, of a stable economic system are being destabilized by a range of drivers, including some that originate from within the capital markets, namely the externalities generated by publicly listed companies, private companies, and other invested assets.

Effective systemic risk management requires a reorientation of approaches. Risk management focused solely on risks to individual issuers will not translate to a reduction of systemic risk.

However, our disclosure regimes, as well as our concepts of "materiality", tend to focus almost exclusively on risks to individual issuers. But "materiality" is a flexible concept, designed to hone-in on what is most important. This is implicitly context-dependent. When addressing a systemic risk, the health of the system that is being degraded is most important.

A company's impacts on nature, for example, will not always create foreseeable risk to that company, but may exacerbate the systemic risk of nature loss, which affects most companies. The complexity and severity of this systemic risk is entirely lost by placing enterprise value – as opposed to biosphere integrity - at the center of concern. By further way of example, Scope 3 greenhouse gas (GHG) emissions constitute the bulk of total global GHG emissions. The analysis to translate an individual company's Scope 3 emissions into risk to the emitting company, however, is complex and dependent upon numerous assumptions and uncertainties outside the company's control. Many companies will therefore conclude that their Scope 3 emissions are 'not material' and certainly not a threat to enterprise value. Broadly diversified investors, however, need this information to effectively understand and aim to mitigate the systemic risk of climate change, regardless of how emissions might impact individual emitters. Impacts on nature can be even more difficult to evaluate at the level of a single company but may pose investor relevant risks at the sector, country, or portfolio level.

In short, the sum of the parts to an individual company does not add up to the whole of impact to a portfolio: litigation and regulatory fines, the cost of consumer boycotts, the cost to retrofit factories or insure coastal properties are only partial reflections of the actual drivers of system instability (e.g. GHG emissions, exploitation of species, deforestation), but they become the sole focus of investor attention if viewed solely from an individual enterprise value viewpoint.

In addition to a directional reorientation of attention (from so-called 'outside-in' risks (idiosyncratic) to 'inside-out' risks ('externalities', 'impacts' or 'contributors to systemic risk'), a conceptual reorientation is needed as well. For example, traditional risk modeling techniques tell us that the highest impact events are also the least likely to occur. These are often labeled 'fat tail' events, referring to their position on the bell curve. However, systemic threats such as ecosystem collapse cannot be modelled using the same tools we use to predict random events. Ecosystem collapse is already happening, initiated and driven by human activity. It is proceeding according to biological processes and complex interactions between species, not by the laws of economics or statistical analysis. In statistical language, it is "path dependent" and we are already a fair way down the path.

## Stewardship as a Key Tool to Address Systemic Risk

Portfolio management strategies are inherently limited in their ability to address non-diversifiable risks, including climate change, biodiversity loss or inflation. The systematic risk in the capital markets caused by climate change, biodiversity loss, and inequality cannot be fully mitigated through exclusions or factor integration alone. We note that these strategies still play a role, by conveying investor expectations to companies, incentivizing systemic risk management, and shielding portfolios from the idiosyncratic risks of companies with poor sustainability performance. Stewardship activities – including public policy advocacy – can complement and amplify portfolio risk management by directly targeting contributions to systemic risks.

## Collaborative Engagements to Address Systemic Risk

For decades, it has been common practice for asset managers and owners to collaborate to engage companies on sustainability and corporate governance issues, to develop common approaches to common threats.[66] There is a simple reason why: Systemic risks are too large and complex for any single company or investor to tackle independently.

Our Stewardship Policy states that:

> "Collaboration with other long-term investors and key stakeholders can help us achieve our common aims, particularly with respect to mitigating systemic risks. We have a long-standing commitment to work with other like-minded investors and to participate in investor networks to learn from our peers and to raise standards. When such collaboration is likely to enhance our ability to engage with a company, and it is permitted by law and regulation, we will work with other asset managers and asset owners, depending on the issue of concern and the alignment of views among the investor group. We make our own individual investment and voting decisions regarding focus companies that we engage with collaboratively."[67]

We believe that this collaborative approach is particularly well suited to mitigating systemic risks. One reason is that it is simply more efficient:

- Investors can make more effective use of limited resources by sharing the workload with other investors. They also gain the advantage of different perspectives and areas of expertise.

---

[66] The oldest coordinator of these coalitions is the Interfaith Center on Corporate Responsibility (ICCR), founded in 1970, https://www.iccr.org/

[67] BNP Paribas Asset management (2025). 2025 Stewardship policy, https://docfinder.bnpparibas-am.com/api/files/c0ba61da-9b99-4567-84af-8b6ac312fa67 . Collaborative engagement allows us to share resources and ideas on a pre-competitive basis. We do not share commercially sensitive information such as investment decisions or proxy voting intentions.

- Companies can have greater certainty that their actions will be accepted by the market when responding to a coalition with a common set of requests. Collaborative engagements also reduce the number of touchpoints and engagements companies need to manage.

Collaborative engagement can also help minority shareholders, small and large, to gain access to corporate management teams and boards that normally focus their attention on their largest investors.[68]

We participate in formal and informal collaborative engagements. Formal collaborations include Climate Action 100+ and Nature Action 100. (We helped to design and launch NA100.) These public initiatives are coordinated by third-party organizations and governed by memoranda of understanding and terms of reference. We also frequently engage with companies in informal, self-organized collaborations with other investors.

## Strategies for Escalation in Stewardship

Investor-issuer dialogue is the foundation of good stewardship – it enables trusting relationships to be built, which permit candid solution-oriented discussions on issues that might otherwise remain unaddressed. Dialogue is a two-way street, and we listen at least as much as we talk. However, there are times when stronger measures are necessary.

Our stewardship approach includes a range of escalation strategies to be used, if necessary, when concerns are not adequately addressed after dialogue, or when companies refuse to talk. These include:

- Voting against board discharge, elections, or financial accounts
- Submitting private or public questions to management and at general meetings

---

[68] Across many issues, from corporate governance to climate, critical long-term risks were raised first and promoted successfully by small investors working collaboratively. This has been particularly true in the United States where large investors have been traditionally reticent to challenge management.

- Filling or co-filing shareholder proposals
- Making public statements

The purpose of these tools is, in almost all cases – but particularly for complex issues like systemic risk – to encourage the company to engage in constructive dialogue to find effective solutions. Escalation decisions are made on a case-by-case basis.

## Examples of Engagements Focused on Systemic Risk69

The following table highlights specific examples of our stewardship efforts addressing key systemic risks through collaborative engagement and escalation strategies.

| Example | Systemic Issue Targeted | Investor Influence Mechanism | Evidence of Collective or Market-Wide Effect | Differences from Conventional ESG practices |
|---|---|---|---|---|
| Climate Risk Engagements | Misalignment of corporate activities with global climate goals risks systemic financial instability and environmental harm. | Collaborative investor dialogues, escalation strategies, and support for science-based targets across multiple firms and sectors. | Adoption of net-zero commitments and climate disclosures by numerous companies, influencing market norms and regulatory expectations. | Company-focus list and investors' expectations focused on reducing risk to the system, in addition to risks to individual companies. |

---

[69] Most examples in this section are as at end of December 2024, with a few details in the horseshoe crab engagements from 2025.

| | | | | |
|---|---|---|---|---|
| **LABOR RIGHTS AND SUPPLY CHAIN RESILIENCE** | Weak labor protections and human rights abuses undermining social stability, opportunity, and mobility. | Collaboration with other investors and local stakeholders, coordinated engagement with key purchasers and industry associations | Too early to provide evidence of impact. | Addresses root-cause drivers (e.g. supply chain structures), to achieve structural improvement in the sugar supply chains in India, ultimately unlocking social mobility and economic opportunity, rather than focusing exclusively on reputational risk to brands. |
| **BIODIVERSITY AND HUMAN HEALTH: PHARMACEUTICAL DEPENDENCY ON HORSESHOE CRABS** | Over-reliance on a keystone species for medical testing threatens global health, ecosystems, and pharmaceutical industry resilience. | Multi-year sector engagement, shareholder resolution, industry collaboration, and event facilitation to spur adoption of synthetic alternatives. | Support of industry working group (PSCI) to facilitate an industry-wide approach to addressing this challenge, publication of good practices, and sector-wide commitments to reduce horseshoe crab use. | Prioritizes ecosystem health, focusing on an overlooked industry-wide practice that is globally accepted by regulators, but is also an extinction driver. |

| | | | | |
|---|---|---|---|---|
| **PUBLIC POLICY ADVOCACY: CATALYZING SUSTAINABLE CHANGE** | Policy misalignment or gaps at the national or regional level impede progress on sustainability, climate action, and equality. | Collective investor advocacy and direct engagement with policymakers, regulatory consultations, and coalition-building to shape sustainable public policy frameworks. | Examples include investor-supported climate policy reforms, enhanced disclosure requirements, and the integration of sustainability criteria into financial regulations. | Extends beyond influencing individual companies to shaping the enabling environment and structural incentives affecting entire sectors and markets. |
| **PRI's COLLABORATIVE SOVEREIGN ENGAGEMENT** | Systemic environmental risk within sovereign debt markets, such as climate change threatens financial and societal stability. | Coordinated engagement by institutional investors with sovereign issuers, multilateral organizations, to reduce risk linked to the transition to a net-zero global economy. | Market-wide improvements such as reinforcing the positive Australian climate policy, informed its green bond framework development, and built investor confidence in sovereign engagement. | Addresses country-level systemic risks beyond company actions, leveraging investor influence for positive change in national climate policy and frameworks. |

*The securities mentioned hereafter are for illustrative purposes only; they are not intended as solicitation of the purchase of such securities, and do not constitute any investment advice or recommendation. While we set out changes to company practice and disclosure that were in line with our expectations and/or recommendations, we acknowledge that these changes in many cases may not have resulted from our engagement alone, as companies take input from many other investors and stakeholders.*

## Engaging to Address Climate Risk

Climate Action 100+ is an excellent example of the reorientation of attention needed to address systemic risk. By focusing on the world's largest corporate greenhouse gas emitters, the initiative prioritizes the driver of the systemic risk. BNPP AM is an active member of CA100+, and our engagement focuses on encouraging these companies to meet the CA100+ Net Zero Company Benchmark (NZCB) expectations, thereby reducing long-term systemic climate risk to our investment portfolios. The NZCB measures company progress across 11 metrics, including climate accounting, auditing, and lobbying alignment.

The corporate adoption of "net-zero" commitments has become so commonplace it is easy to forget what it really means – a commitment to align corporate behavior (in this case, GHG emissions) with system thresholds, to restore stability and reduce risk. Our approach to engagement is dynamic, adjusting involvement with company groups based on our holdings and other strategic considerations. In 2024, we co-led engagements with Danone, China Petroleum & Chemical Corp (Sinopec), Iberdrola, Nestlé, Power Assets Holdings, PTT, Saint-Gobain, and Stellantis. We also contributed as investors in other company engagements and continued to co-chair the European Climate Lobbying Working Group of CA100+ and representing Asia-Pacific on the CA100+ Steering Committee.

We, along with the Church of England Pensions Board and AP7 were instrumental in bringing the issue of corporate climate lobbying to CA100+ and helped to launch the Global Standard on Responsible Climate Lobbying, seeking to align corporate lobbying efforts with the goals of the Paris Agreement.[70] The notion that companies should prioritize the goals of the Paris Agreement in their lobbying work, in addition to their own business interests, is another example of how systemic risks force us to reorient our actions to focus on mitigating common threats. A shareholder

---

[70] Home - Responsible climate lobbying: The global standard, https://climate-lobbying.com/

proposal we drafted on the topic – explicitly seeking this strategic reorientation – gained six majority votes in 2020 and 2021, a clear signal that institutional investors were ready for a different approach.[71] In 2024, we conducted an exercise to identify the finance industry and trade associations we belong to around the world, and to contact those we believed might lobby on climate issues. We sent them a series of questions about whether and how they engage on sustainable finance policy development and/or climate-focused policy, and how that work is governed. [72]

Corporate responsiveness to our engagement on climate related topics has varied, as did their willingness to implement the requested improvements in climate performance and transparency. Notable progress was achieved with Iberdrola, Nestlé, Power Assets Holdings, and Unilever, and our previous co-lead engagement with Repsol yielded results as well.

- Iberdrola: disclosed more detailed information on decarbonization strategies and capital allocation, aligning with four NZCB metrics. Improved performance on two indicators and participated in the IIGCC Steel Purchasing Roundtable.

- Nestlé: advanced practices and disclosure in its 2023 Creating Shared Value report, including GHG emission reductions against a 2018 baseline and the inclusion of decarbonization metrics in executive incentives. Its Climate Lobbying Review score improved from 36 to 64 percent on InfluenceMap, and Nestlé is now aligned to four NZCB metrics.

- Power Assets Holdings (PAH): initiated frameworks linking climate performance to executive pay, disclosed coal asset phase-out schedules, and committed to decarbonization aligned with Just Transition principles. PAH now aligns with four NZCB metrics.

---

[71] Shareholders approve a climate lobbying proposal at Delta, continuing a winning streak that shows the importance of Paris-aligned climate policy (2021), https://www.ceres.org/resources/news/shareholders-approve-a-climate-lobbying-proposal-at-delta-continuing-a-winning-streak-that-shows-the-importance-of-paris-aligned-climate-policy
[72] BNPP AM, 2024 Sustainability Report, https://docfinder.bnpparibas-am.com/api/files/a270ea84-c2e7-4a3b-8b6d-2094d980763c (see page 69)

- Repsol SA: after persistent engagement, Repsol changed its decarbonization metrics methodology, setting a net-zero target for 2050 that includes Scope 1, 2, and 3 emissions. However, it remains aligned to only one NZCB expectation.

- Unilever: published its first Climate Policy Engagement Review, scoring 100 percent from InfluenceMap - the first company to do so. Unilever now fully meets NZCB disclosure expectations for Indicator 7 and nearly all in the alignment assessment.[73]

Despite all the good work conducted by CA100+ investor participants, global GHG emissions have continued to rise, and the world is likely to cross the critical 1.5-degree threshold. Rather than reject the progress we have made, we must find ways to be more effective with the limited resources that we have and acknowledge that investor engagement can be highly effective, but it cannot, on its own, solve the problem.

## Labor Rights and Supply Chain Resilience: Forced and Child Labor in the Indian Sugar Industry

Weak labor protections and human rights abuses undermine social stability, opportunity, and mobility. In 2024, *The New York Times* exposed widespread human rights abuses – including forced and child labor – in Maharashtra's sugarcane fields, a key supplier to global brands.[74] Abuses cited included lack of basic needs, coercion of women into hysterectomies, and exploitation of migrant workers with limited legal protection.

Our objective on this topic was to engage with investee companies in our portfolios that purchase sugar from India to encourage them to work to put an end to these abuses. We are working in collaboration with other

---

[73] BNPP AM, 2024 Sustainability Report, https://docfinder.bnpparibas-am.com/api/files/a270ea84-c2e7-4a3b-8b6d-2094d980763c

[74] See, e.g. Coke, Pepsi and Other U.S. Companies Face Wall Street Pressure Over Labor Abuses in India - The New York Times, https://www.nytimes.com/2024/12/20/world/asia/wall-street-us-companies-india-sugar-labor-abuse.html

investors, coordinated by the Interfaith Center on Corporate Responsibility (ICCR). To do that, we undertook the following:

- Discussions with a representative of the Working Peoples Charter India, a local labor rights group, to discuss the situation and possible solutions.
- Participation in an informal steering committee to coordinate ICCR's work.
- Initial engagement with several U.S. and European companies that source sugar from Maharashtra, India.
- Sent joint investor letters to Boards of Directors, providing extensive detail on the issue and asking for dialogue.
- After not seeing enough progress via engagement, we submitted two shareholder proposals, jointly with other investors. The companies were asked to report on the effectiveness of their efforts to uphold human rights standards throughout their sugar supply chains in India.

By the end of 2024, we had successfully encouraged Coca-Cola to update its website with a description of some of its efforts and opened dialogue with others. Going forward, we hope to secure better information and, where needed, tangible changes to the various companies' oversight of their sugar suppliers, as well as commitments from them to work collaboratively and with local stakeholders to drive the systemic changes needed to alleviate these abusive conditions.

## Biodiversity and Human Health: Addressing the Pharmaceutical Industry's Dependence on Horseshoe Crabs

Every vaccine, injectable drug, and medical device implanted in the body must be tested for endotoxin contamination. This testing typically uses a component from horseshoe crab blood (LAL, from the North American horseshoe crab, and TAL, from the Asian species). However, the four extant horseshoe crab species (three in Asia, one in the US) are declining due to over-harvesting by the biomedical and fishing industries, threatening both human health and pharmaceutical profitability, as well as dependent species, including a range of migratory shorebirds. Horseshoe crabs are considered a "keystone" species because entire ecosystems depend upon them.

Affordable and effective synthetic alternatives exist but uptake has been slow. We have engaged with the pharmaceutical sector for several years to encourage the industry to make the switch, placing their businesses and human health on a more resilient platform while reducing impacts to fragile ecosystems. The global demand for endotoxin testing will only go up – it makes little sense to continue to depend upon a threatened species, located in a concentrated area (primarily the Delaware Bay), when viable alternatives are available.

A key to successful engagements is to have a clear objective. In this case we have two: reduce industry dependency and impact on horseshoe crabs for endotoxin testing by replacing LAL/TAL with synthetic alternatives, and improve companies' reporting on this issue in nature-related disclosures, both to improve our ability to hold individual companies accountable and to help establish new industry norms.

We began our engagement with the pharmaceutical sector towards the end of 2021. Since then, we have had more than 100 interactions with nearly 30 companies, filed one shareholder resolution, participated in industry initiatives to amplify impact and regularly engaged with local conservationists and scientists.[75] We also co-hosted two events on Cape May, NJ, where we invited pharmaceutical companies to observe the annual horseshoe crab spawn and shorebird migration, hear from local scientists, and discuss solutions with peers, in a confidential setting. Eli Lilly and AstraZeneca served on the steering committee to organize our latest event.

---

[75] Horseshoe Crab Recovery Coalition – Saving the American Horseshoe Crab, https://hscrabrecovery.org/

When we first approached selected pharmaceutical companies on this topic towards the end of 2021, we received little response. We therefore changed our strategy and approached the Pharmaceutical Supply Chain Initiative (PSCI) in 2022, to ask whether it would be willing to facilitate an industry-wide approach to addressing this challenge.

In response to our outreach, PSCI, which works with 80 companies, established a working group and in May 2023 published a set of good practices[76] for the use of horseshoe crab-derived reagents:

- Immediate end to the use of the blood of two species of the Asian horseshoe crab considered endangered.
- Minimize the use of horseshoe crab blood in endotoxin testing techniques worldwide, including by using synthetic alternatives.
- Share data on the health of the horseshoe crab populations, to better understand population health and the impact of industry use.

PSCI has subsequently surveyed its members and published a first-of-its-kind report on the industry's efforts to phase out horseshoe crab blood.[77] The goal of our engagement is for all companies to adopt these practices and disclose their progress in doing so. Ultimately, we'd like to see the industry replace horseshoe crab blood with synthetic reagents, reducing their impact on fragile ecosystems.

Examples of particularly good progress in phasing out LAL include:

- When we began our engagement, Eli Lilly had already reportedly reduced its use of LAL by 80 percent, replacing horseshoe crab-derived reagents with synthetics for all lab water testing and for all new products. All water used in these labs must be pure and free from endotoxins. Lab water testing consumes the largest volumes

---

[76] The use of Horseshoe Crabs in the Pharmaceutical Sector – PSCI (2023), https://pscinitiative.org/bulletin?bulletin=629

[77] The use of horseshoe crab blood for endotoxin testing in the pharmaceutical industry - PSCI (April 2025), https://pscinitiative.org/resource?resource=2806

of LAL, by far. The company is now working to re-register its legacy products with synthetics and has been a leading voice for change within its industry and with regulatory bodies.

- Novo Nordisk disclosed a comprehensive plan to phase out LAL.

- Orion Oyj engaged with the contract research agencies it uses, integrated alternative testing methods, and plans to report related actions in its 2025 CSRD statement.

- AstraZeneca set internal targets for responsible sourcing, reduced horseshoe crab use by 90 percent via microfluidic technology and aims to transition to recombinant alternatives for all water testing and regulatory submissions post-2025. In addition, AstraZeneca partially funded a beach reclamation project that restored critical habitat just in time for the 2025 horseshoe crab spawning season.

- Amgen published a plan to phase out horseshoe crab-derived reagents in favor of synthetic alternatives.

- Bristol Myers Squibb developed methods to transition water testing to synthetic reagents and disclosed commitments to use such alternatives for new medicines.

## Public Policy Advocacy: Catalyzing Sustainable Change

As asset managers grow in scale, influence and market impact, our stewardship practices should reasonably be expected to contribute to the understanding and mitigation of systemic risks. Increasingly, asset owners articulate these expectations when selecting partners, prioritizing those who demonstrate proactive engagement on systemic issues. We anticipate this trend will continue, making stewardship on systemic risk a baseline requirement for credible, long-term investment relationships.

We have consistently advocated for public policy reforms to mitigate systemic risks like climate change, nature loss, and inequality. Shaping legal frameworks, regulations, standards, and guidance relating to sustainable finance is integral to fulfilling our fiduciary duties to clients. This approach aligns with the Principles for Responsible Investment (PRI) recommendation to participate in policy development, regulation, and standard setting.

Over the years, we have partnered with policymakers on corporate disclosure, climate policy, and governance. Our policy priorities include the energy transition, healthy ecosystems and equality. Consistent with the expectations we set for issuers, we seek to pursue our public policy objectives in a transparent manner, with a sufficient degree of specificity disclosed to inform our clients and relevant stakeholders of the positions we take.[78]

Beyond support for the Paris Agreement's goals and a range of nature-related policies, such as support for a Global Plastics Treaty, we also outline policy measures focused on addressing inequality, including mandatory CEO-employee pay ratio and gender pay gap disclosures and country-by-country corporate tax reporting. We also support the concept of 'double materiality' in corporate disclosures to ensure that corporate reporting addresses the environmental and social risks they face as well as the risks they create. Comprehensive information on both dimensions is vital for investors to measure and manage both systemic and idiosyncratic risks that may arise from issuer actions.

## PRI's Collaborative Sovereign Engagement

In 2022, BNPP AM joined the pilot PRI-coordinated Collaborative Sovereign Engagement on Climate Change as an Advisory Committee member, co-leading the Federal Working Group. This initiative brought together

---

[78] Our 2025 Stewardship Policy contains a section outlining our approach to public policy advocacy and our priorities: BNP Paribas Asset Management (2025), Stewardship Policy 2025, https://docfinder.bnpparibas-am.com/api/files/c0ba61da-9b99-4567-84af-8b6ac312fa67

27 global investors to engage with sovereigns on reducing risks linked to the transition to a net-zero global economy. Key objectives included safeguarding the value of sovereign debt investments, maintaining national competitiveness, and mitigating systemic risks through global economic exposure.

Australia was selected as the first country for engagement. Throughout 2024, we participated in numerous meetings in Canberra, Sydney, and Brisbane, engaging with government officials – including the Treasurer, climate change spokespeople, and staff from the Prime Minister's Office, various ministries, and treasury departments. Discussions centered on the reporting needs of investors regarding sovereign green bonds (SGBs), expectations for the next Nationally Determined Contribution (NDC) plan, the importance of policy certainty, and the anticipated passage of mandatory disclosure regulations.

By collaborating in this initiative, BNPP AM and other investors supported government efforts to meet climate policy commitments, contributed to the development of the Australian Government Green Bond Framework, reinforced economic transition arguments, and raised stakeholder awareness about the integration of policy and investment decisions.

## Takeaways

Addressing systemic challenges such as climate change, biodiversity loss, and social inequality is not only a matter of regulatory compliance and fiduciary responsibility, but also essential to protecting long-term value for our clients. If left unchecked, these challenges threaten to undermine our ability to deliver sustainable returns in the future. Additionally, we should recognize that progress in one area can sometimes create new challenges in others. As a result, it is important to stay aware of these potential conflicts and make sure our decisions always serve the best interests of our clients.

A holistic perspective – one that considers the broader interplay between markets and the societies they serve – is required to manage these risks effectively. Stewardship, particularly through thoughtful engagement with issuers and policymakers, is a powerful means of addressing such complex issues. Nevertheless, it is important to recognize the limitations of investors' direct influence; while we can act as catalysts for positive change, implementation often depends on the companies in which we invest (or even their suppliers), policy makers and regulators. Expecting investors to achieve – and document – unrealistic levels of "additional" impact overlooks the realities of the systems in which we operate and may discourage constructive action.

Systemic issues are, by nature, collective action problems, and there is always a danger that responsibility is deferred or diluted. Investors, despite their sometimes-indirect connection to the root causes of these risks, must remain engaged and avoid complacency.

Now is the time for investors to embrace system-level investing: Working collaboratively and taking a proactive, solutions-oriented approach, we can help shape the sustainable and equitable markets upon which our clients and wider society depend.

## Chapter 7:

# How To Organize an Investment Department as a System-level Investor

By Barbara Zvan, Aaron Bennett and Brian Minns[79]

Imagine being entrusted with the opportunity to build a modern, 21st-century pension plan from the ground up – a blank canvas on which to design the policies, structures, technology, and culture needed to safeguard pensions for generations. Where would you start?

This was the challenge facing University Pension Plan Ontario (UPP) at its launch in 2021. UPP is a jointly sponsored, defined benefit pension plan designed by and for Ontario's university sector. After more than a decade of collaboration between university unions, faculty associations, administrators, and other staff groups, UPP launched with three founding universities: University of Toronto, Queen's University, and University of Guelph. The Plan continues to grow each year and now serves more than

---

[79] Barbara Zvan is President and CEO, University Pension Plan Ontario. Aaron Bennett is Chief Investment Officer, University Pension Plan Ontario. Brian Minns is Sr. Managing Director, Responsible Investing, University Pension Plan Ontario.

41,000 members across 5 universities and 14 sector organizations, with CAD $12.8 billion in pension assets under management.[80]

From the outset, we recognized that addressing financially material environmental, social and governance ("ESG") factors, such as climate risk, is fully aligned with both our fiduciary duty and our members' best interests. Two influential books published as UPP was taking shape in early 2021 – *Moving Beyond Modern Portfolio Theory: Investing That Matters*, by Jon Lukomnik and James P. Hawley, and *21st Century Investing: Redirecting Financial Strategies to Drive Systems Change* by William Burckart and Steve Lydenberg – helped frame the concepts and language for the investment approach we needed to build: an in-house investment department that integrates material ESG considerations while embedding many of the principles and practices core to system-level investing.

Much of our approach to system-level investing has been shaped by our size, resources and externally managed investment structure. We had a relatively clear vision of what we were seeking to achieve, which we codified in our investment beliefs. We also looked to what other similarly sized investors accomplished, and the partnerships and initiatives we could lean on to amplify our approach. Ultimately, UPP focuses on the aspects most strategically relevant to our investment approach – stewardship, policy engagement, and long-term portfolio design – anchored by a shared commitment to the principles that define system-level investing.

## The Challenge: Bridging the Gap Between Beliefs and Structure

While system-level investing can serve as a guiding compass, it's up to the organization to build its own path forward. For UPP, that meant acting quickly – but carefully and thoughtfully – to shape an investment team capable of managing the assets we took over from the founding universities while preparing to take on additional pension assets in the future.

---

[80] As of January 1, 2025.

The assets UPP assumed at inception were spread across more than 100 investment mandates and investment managers. We evaluated each mandate we took over against a comprehensive rubric encompassing investment performance, operations and governance, and responsible investing. Next, we developed an action plan to build the portfolio for the new pension plan.

A further challenge was needing to execute this complex dance of building the team, remotely hiring and onboarding, establishing systems and processes, strengthening governance, and hiring talent – all at the same time as the COVID-19 pandemic.

The team we built would need to embrace, or at least support, the core principles of system-level investing at a time when most asset owners and investment managers did not recognize this approach or were not yet aligned with it. Traditional investment practices often assume that the broader systems supporting returns will remain stable and healthy. System-level investing is a newer approach not typically part of traditional finance curriculums. While successful long-term investors may have intuitively adopted frameworks that incorporate the importance of beta and the influence of systemic risks on long-term compounding of returns, they have not been well-articulated or systematically applied. The early insistence by a core group of UPP leaders that these principles were embedded – not simply appended later – within our investment program, together with our strong networks, allowed us to attract investment professionals with the right mix of beliefs and experience.

We next needed to ensure foundational policies and frameworks, like our Statement of Investment Policies and Procedures, and Responsible Investing Policy, translated beliefs into practice. Without policies aligned to our principles, appropriately adjusted and balanced across different asset classes and strategies, we could not fully realize our commitment to addressing system-level implications.

An additional challenge involved setting appropriate measurements and time horizons. In theory, we agree that healthy systems play an important role in generating the absolute investment performance for our members. In practice, we understand the difficulty in correlating that health with long-term performance improvements. As we sought to develop our approach, we knew we'd have to be comfortable with the notion that it might take significant time to develop the empirical evidence to support our theoretical foundation, just as with many other beliefs in the investment industry.

Meanwhile, many of the improvements we hoped to see unfold over timescales that do not neatly align with traditional compensation or performance management cycles. For that reason, it was essential to create conditions where employees felt empowered to act with an emphasis on continuous, incremental improvement.

## The Solution: Embedding System-Level Investing into Governance, Culture and Compensation

To fully integrate system-level investing across UPP, we focused on three reinforcing pillars: governance, culture, and compensation. Together, these elements provide the structure and incentives necessary to embed system-level investing throughout the investment team and across the broader organization.

### Governance

Governance has been central to shaping and sustaining UPP's approach, from the articulation of investment beliefs to oversight and reporting.

**Investment beliefs**: The development of UPP's investment beliefs statement was the most critical step in formalizing our commitment to the principles and practices common to system-level investing. The process began with one-on-one interviews with every UPP Trustee and each member of the management team responsible for overseeing and investing the Plan's assets. These conversations explored perspectives on capital markets, investment costs, internal versus external management, active versus passive, risk, diversification, investment horizon, alpha versus beta, investing versus trading, and system-level thinking.

During this process, we were fortunate to collaborate with Jon Lukomnik, William Burckart[81] and William's colleague at The Investment Integration Project (TIIP). As authors of books that influenced our system-level investing -aligned thinking, the opportunity to work with them brought great perspective and expanded the conversations beyond what might ordinarily be discussed when developing investment beliefs.

These interviews and discussions formed a shared set of beliefs, founded in a purpose to deliver on the pension promise to members now and in the future. We then consolidated and shared the insights from these interviews during an educational session on system-level investing for Trustees and Management, after which we worked together to draft an investment beliefs statement. Following several rounds of Trustee review and refinement, we approved the statement in February 2022.

Today, this statement provides a consistent framework for decision-making across UPP's investment strategies. We expect that healthy capital markets and systems will lead to the positive market investment returns (beta) we require, with acceptable levels of volatility. Adding to this, our ability to discern trends and functions within the different subsystems enable us to better manage risk and capture opportunities as they arise. Several of the beliefs in our statement explicitly reflect system-level investing principles, including:

- As a long-term investor, UPP has a responsibility to promote the health of capital markets and the financial, social, and environmental systems on which capital markets rely.

---

[81] Jon Lukomnik and William Burckart are the editors of this *Handbook*.

- Creating value and managing risk involve exercising UPP's voice to influence outcomes related to material issues through active ownership, policy advocacy, and collaboration with other investors and stakeholders – all of which must be approached with the same intention and rigour as selecting investments.
- UPP embraces partnership as a foundation for enhanced performance and impact.

**Climate risk as the entry point**: Concepts related to system-level investing can feel abstract. At this stage, investment professionals are rarely trained within a framework that embraces system-level investing, and the industry has yet to fully adopt it. Climate-related risks, however, provide a concrete entry point.

Ample, widely understood, generally accepted evidence indicates that there are substantial material macro and micro risks related to climate for long-term investors and the financial system.[82] At the same time, investors have a clear and growing set of actionable responses[83], both traditional and non-traditional, to help mitigate those risks. This made climate risk an accessible on-ramp for embedding system-level investing into practice at UPP.

---

[82] See for example, the work of the Network for Greening the Financial System (150+ central banks or prudential supervisory authorities) and its finding that, "Climate change affects all agents in the economy (households, businesses, governments), across all sectors and geographies. The risks will likely be correlated with and potentially aggravated by tipping points, in a non-linear fashion. This means the impacts could be much larger, and more widespread and diverse than those of other structural changes." Source: Network for Greening the Financial System. (n.d.). *Origin and Purpose*. Retrieved September 7, 2025, from https://www.ngfs.net/en/about-us/origin-and-purpose

[83] See for example, the work of the CFA Institute and its recent publication which says, "This guide reflects the financial industry's critical role in addressing climate change, presenting actionable insights and pioneering approaches for a net-zero future." Source: CFA Institute. (2025, January 23). *Investment Innovations Toward Achieving Net Zero - Full Book*. https://rpc.cfainstitute.org/research/reports/2025/investment-innovations-toward-achieving-net-zero-book

**Education**: Ongoing education and open dialogue were critical to securing UPP Trustee and management buy-in. This approach was equally central in the development and launch of UPP's Climate Action Plan ("CAP") in July 2022, which became the organization's first initiative to operationalize system-level thinking.

The CAP drew on a solid knowledge base about climate-related risks and opportunities, and the tools available to pension plans to address them. Prior to approving the CAP, UPP's Board of Trustees engaged in multiple discussions, beginning with a dedicated session on climate science and potential investor responses. The Board's Investment Committee and Audit and Finance Committee received briefings on actions and metrics across seven meetings, and staff attended two climate-focused education sessions.

Importantly, this comprehensive education and engagement process – much like the development of UPP's investment beliefs statement – occurred within the first year after UPP assumed the assets and liabilities of our founding universities.

None of this work was superfluous: it reflected UPP's commitment to ensuring that those responsible for portfolio alignment and leading and approving investment initiatives have the knowledge required for informed action and oversight.

**Commitments and minimum standards**: Translating strategy into action requires more than vision; it demands clear commitments and minimum standards to guide decision-making and set expectations. As UPP rolled out our CAP, these commitments equipped UPP's investment professionals with the structure and confidence needed to act. This framework allowed teams to work both autonomously and collaboratively in support of the organization's risk and return objectives while safeguarding the broader financial, social and environmental systems that underpin long-term investment performance.

In one example, we committed to engaging at least 20 portfolio companies in dialogue to support their rapid and orderly transition to a resilient, low carbon, net-zero world, with a focus on those contributing most significantly to our carbon footprint. To guide this work, we established an overarching Stewardship Framework that makes clear our stewardship actions are intended to align the interests of issuers and the financial system with long-term value creation for Plan members. That framework then formed the basis of a Climate Stewardship Plan launched in 2023, which sets out specific actions to address climate risks while encouraging the transition to a more resilient economy with net-zero GHG emissions.

Governance features prominently in advancing this commitment. UPP's Management Investment Committee and Investment Committee receive updates annually on our progress. In addition, UPP also provides members and the public with an annual overview of our climate stewardship priorities, along with a summary of notable activity and outcomes in climate-related engagement, proxy voting, and policy advocacy.

We also committed to invest only in new mandates and assets that align with the transition to a net-zero world and with our climate solutions investment target. In 2023, we established a Climate Transition Investment Framework to support this goal. The framework set minimum standards for new fund investments and co-investments and establishes a target to commit at least $1.2 billion to climate solutions by 2030. Oversight of this framework also rests with both the Management Investment Committee and the Board Investment Committee.

This work led us to examine and address other systemic issues. In particular, we explored social factors that affect portfolio performance, long-term investment outcomes, and the stability of the economy and capital markets. Through this process, inequality was identified as a systemic social risk threatening long-term returns and economic stability across asset classes. Consequently, we prepared and launched UPP's Inequality Stewardship Plan in 2024.

**Reporting and oversight**: Oversight is shared across multiple levels of governance, including the Board of Trustees, Investment Committee, Management Investment Committee, executive leadership, and the Responsible Investing team. The authority, delegation, and reporting cadence are clearly defined in our policies and frameworks, consistent with other key investment activities.

This rigor ensures system-level investing is embedded into the core of our investment processes and decision-making, rather than being treated as a side initiative.

*Culture*

One of UPP's core investment beliefs states: "Culture is an essential investment input. How we invest should reflect UPP's culture of collaboration and forward vision." By embedding system-level investing into our organizational culture, we ensure it remains central to how we operate and make decisions.

**Hiring**: Successfully building UPP's investment team in short order required a focused and consistent talent strategy. Our early embrace of system-level investing at the leadership level enabled us to attract strong leaders who were open to and aligned with this approach despite system-level investing's relative newness. We also prioritized candidates who demonstrated curiosity, a commitment to continuous improvement, and a collaborative approach – qualities critical to advancing both performance and impact.

**Continuous improvement mindset**: Because system-level investing is an emerging and rapidly evolving practice within the investment industry, a continuous improvement mindset is essential. Early efforts will inevitably be imperfect. What matters is a willingness to acknowledge challenges, remain flexible, and adapt through iterative learning and innovation. This mindset ensures that system-level investing evolves in ways that consistently serve the best long-term interests of our Plan members.

The importance of culture to everyone at UPP is evident in the tremendous response rates and high engagement scores in our engagement and culture surveys, demonstrating that our collaborative approach and commitment to continual growth truly resonate across the organization. The surveys confirm that employees believe UPP is dedicated to fostering an intentional culture and addressing sustainability in our operations and investments.

**Collaboration**: Another UPP investment belief states: "UPP embraces partnership as a foundation for enhanced performance and impact." In practice, this means actively fostering cross-collaboration rather than siloed expertise and seeking opportunities to learn from investment partners pursuing innovative approaches. Our Responsible Investing team regularly exchanges insights with peers at the forefront of system-level investing, creating a steady flow of insights that inform and strengthen UPP's investment practices.

Importantly, this collaborative mindset recognizes that we cannot take the health of the underlying systems for granted, nor can we address the related challenges by ourselves. Every participant in the investment ecosystem, whether asset owners, investment managers, or other stakeholders, has unique perspectives and faces unique challenges. It is our responsibility to both learn from others and share our own insights and experiences. Furthermore, we don't assume that others intuitively understand the realities or pressures faced by UPP; many spend their days focused on different priorities or operating in distinct contexts. Openly communicating our perspectives and lessons learned enables more holistic, effective collaboration, ultimately supporting healthier systems and stronger long-term outcomes both for our members and the broader investment community.

**Shared language**: Understanding and progress can be accelerated with shared language. At UPP, we have developed a clear and consistent way of communicating about responsible investing and the impactful component pieces common to system-level investing, which has been essential to building organizational buy-in and scaling our approach. To reinforce this, our Responsible Investing team introduces every new hire to UPP's approach within their first weeks. This ensures employees across functions understand how we define responsible investing terms and how their individual contributions connect to our collective goals.

**Modelling behavior**: Organizational priorities are shaped by what leaders say and do. At UPP, leadership demonstrates its commitment by not only modelling engagement and advocacy outside the organization, but also by striving to "walk the talk" and actively applying the system-level lens to internal operations. This means we hold ourselves accountable to the same principles we advocate for externally, ensuring that our practices, policies, and culture align with our goals. A few examples:

- Barbara Zvan, our President & CEO, has exemplified this through her role on Canada's Expert Panel on Sustainable Finance, Climate Engagement Canada, and the Sustainable Finance Action Council, helping to build industry-wide capacity to address systemic issues like climate change in ways that benefit pension plan members.

- Aaron Bennett, Chief Investment Officer, has long championed responsible investing and is an outspoken advocate for embedding system-level investing into institutional investor practices. He advances this agenda through speaking engagements, peer collaboration, and his role with the Principles for Responsible Investment (PRI) Asset Owner Technical Advisory Committee and as a director of the Canadian Coalition for Good Governance.

- Brian Minns, Senior Managing Director, Responsible Investing, promotes system-level investing both within UPP and across the industry. He has worked with UPP's investment department to repatriate a significant portion of UPP's proxy votes to align voting with system-level investing principles, and champions public policy advocacy as a legitimate and necessary tool for pension funds to secure better long-term outcomes for members.

By modelling these behaviors, UPP's leadership reinforces the message that system-level investing is a core component of how we invest and how we serve our members.

**Aligned compensation:** Compensation is a critical lever for aligning organizational, divisional, and individual incentives. Without this alignment, we risk disconnecting our day-to-day activities from the long-term outcomes that matter most to our members.

Our approach to compensation has been very methodical, beginning with the introduction of an organizational scorecard, which we then expanded to divisional scorecards.

Since inception, UPP's organizational scorecard, which measures progress against goals and determine variable incentives, has included responsible investing and ESG considerations. It incorporates a measurable climate component (portfolio GHG emissions intensity) and broader sustainability commitments, directly supporting responsible investing objectives and organizational goals.

As UPP's organizational scorecard matured, divisional scorecards were introduced to strengthen alignment. At the divisional level, additional components are tailored to the unique objectives of each team. The Investment division began incorporating system-level investing, enabling projects such as expanding proxy voting capacity and UPP's investment exclusion criteria to a greater share of assets. The Responsible Investing division integrated system-level, investing-aligned priorities including policy advocacy, promotion of responsible investing and system-level investing practices within the investment industry, and monitoring and engaging investment partners on their responsible investing performance.

At the individual level, employee scorecards include role-specific objectives that connect to system-level investing principles. While individual goals are not "system-level investing" in isolation, together they help embed practices across the organization and activate the levers that bring UPP's investment approach to life.

These scorecards track progress against responsible investing and system-level investing goals, risk management practices, and member service quality. ensuring that both collective and individual performance are measured against UPP's strategic priorities.

Our variable incentive structure is designed to reinforce long-term alignment. For many employees, especially those in senior roles, a larger portion of incentive payments is deferred over multiple years. The deferred amount is first adjusted based on the plan's total rate of return, which we emphasize more heavily than value add – an approach that differs from what is typical in the industry. After this adjustment, the deferred payment is further modified using discretionary parameters reflecting the Board's assessment of our performance in key areas, such as risk and responsible investing.

This layered approach ensures that compensation remains closely tied to the results that matter most for our members, and that prudent risk-taking and responsible investing are embedded across all levels of the organization.

## Lessons Learned: What Worked and What was Challenging

In weaving system-level investing into the DNA of a new pension fund, we quickly discovered where progress was smooth and where we encountered headwinds. Several successes stand out, as do challenges that tested our resolve. We've learned and grown from each in equal measure.

*What Worked*

**Leadership's advocacy for the principles of system-level investing**: UPP's early decision to enshrine the principles and practices common to system-level investing into our investment beliefs and core investing approach was strongly supported by both the Board and management. This helped ensure a central, not siloed, approach. For example, UPP does not maintain a standalone Responsible Investing Committee; instead, the Management Investment Committee oversees responsible investing considerations and system-focused activities alongside all other investment activities. This integration has reinforced that system-focused activities are core to our investment discipline rather than an add-on, with oversight bodies directly monitoring our progress.

**Starting with one systemic risk**: Focusing first on climate risk as a "test case" allowed UPP to apply systems thinking in a targeted and practical way. Climate is widely recognized as a material investment risk, supported by ample evidence and requiring investor action. Starting here provided a strong foundation and led us to understand that not every systemic issue should be incorporated into our strategy. Instead, we prioritized issues that are high-impact, measurable, and aligned with our fiduciary responsibilities.

**Building a culture of continuous learning and humility**: From the outset, we acknowledged that our journey would not be perfect. What mattered was making a start and being prepared to evolve. Our inaugural Climate Action Plan reflected this balance: it included overarching commitments including transitioning to a net-zero investment portfolio by 2040, alongside specific near-term commitments, such as a 2025 target to reduce the GHG intensity of our portfolio by 16.5 percent from a 2021 baseline, and ongoing longer-term commitments such as a target for climate solution investments. This approach enabled us to move forward while leaving space for learning and adaptation.

*What was Challenging*

**Translating high-level concepts into day-to-day actions**: Turning system-level investing ambitions into concrete actions can feel daunting. Investment professionals focused on identifying opportunities in specific asset classes may not immediately see the connection to system-level thinking, and indeed the opportunities to incorporate system-level investing practices may vary greatly between asset classes and investment strategies. Yet, system-level change often comes from "everyday" activities, such as asking targeted due diligence questions, incorporating ESG considerations into manager selection, or sharing insights at industry conferences. Helping staff see these linkages remains an ongoing priority.

It's also important not to get hung up on labels. While terminology like system-level investing, ESG, or responsible investing can help frame objectives, the real value lies in the actions taken and the outcomes derived. By staying focused on practical steps and tangible outcomes, organizations can make meaningful progress, even if the precise label isn't always clear. This mindset encourages employees to engage with the underlying principles, rather than getting caught up in definitions, and supports a culture of proactive, action-oriented change.

**Hiring systems-savvy investment professionals**: Given that system-level investing remains at a relatively early stage of understanding and practice, there is a limited pool of professionals with both deep investment expertise and experience in system-level approaches. Industry training programs, such as the Chartered Financial Analyst and Chartered Alternative Investment Analyst programs, have not yet fully incorporated system-level concepts. Building this expertise internally and contributing to the industry's broader capacity remain ongoing challenges.

**Understanding timeframes and perceptions:** A further challenge lies in reconciling short- and long-term perspectives. Systemic disruptions often unfold in a nonlinear manner: Short-term risk-return impacts can appear modest, even when the long-term consequences may be material. Systemic risks tend to accumulate gradually, often without immediately affecting financial fundamentals. However, when these risks do manifest, their impact is typically rapid, non-linear, and highly material. This dynamic can create a perception of lower returns or higher risk until the disruptive event materializes.

Navigating this dynamic demands careful communication and thoughtful strategy from any pension plan, as the need to balance immediate performance with preparedness for future disruptions remains a persistent challenge.

## High-Level Takeaways: Practical Insights for Institutional Investors

Implementing system-level investing focuses on long-term transformation, not short-term fixes. At UPP, embedding system-level investing into our governance and culture has shown us what success looks like, while ongoing challenges – such as developing strong system-level investing-oriented talent and translating principles into daily practice – remind us that progress is rarely easy or linear. As we continue on our own journey, we share the following recommendations for peers embarking on or advancing their system-level work:

- **Treat system-level investing as integral, not additive**. Done right, system-level investing is not an overlay, but part of the wiring of organizational purpose, process, and decision-making.

- **Operationalize system-level investing through beliefs, policies, and frameworks.** These are foundational, providing practical mechanisms to guide decision-makers and support consistent, day-to-day action.

- **Design culture intentionally**. Leadership buy-in, and hiring for curiosity, openness and alignment – not just credentials – are essential.

- **Use climate risk as a starting point.** You won't be able to do everything you think should be done at once. Focus on the highest-impact systemic concerns first. Climate risk is widely recognized, clearly linked to investment risks and returns, offers multiple pathways for investor response and reasonable standards and metrics for measurement.

- **Learn from and collaborate with others.** System-level change requires collective learning and effort.

Finally, we invite peers beginning their system-level investing journey to connect and share experiences. Collaboration strengthens us all.

## Conclusion: Making System-Level Investing Stick

At UPP, we had the unique opportunity to build a pension plan from the ground up – without legacy systems, processes, or beliefs to untangle. Our experience demonstrates that system-level investing is achievable with the right foundations and a leadership team committed to the journey.

Most organizations will not have the same "blank slate" we started with, but many of our steps can be adopted over time with deliberate planning and intentional execution. Aligning governance, culture and compensation with system-level investing is not a one-time exercise but an ongoing discipline that requires continuous reflection and recalibration as an organization.

We call on other institutional investors, and particularly other pension funds, to embrace system-level investing with courage and clarity of purpose – embedding the ideas at every level of the organization. In doing so, together we can strengthen the systems on which long-term investment performance, economic stability, and the prosperity of our beneficiaries.

Chapter 8:

# Where to Focus: Identifying Systemic Risks and Setting Goals

By Steve Lydenberg and Carole Laible[84]

We share here a key challenge Domini Impact Investments encountered in its implementation of system-level investment: setting goals for the management of systemic risks. We committed to incorporating a system-level approach in 2016. By 2018, we had focused on a single systemic challenge: forests. When we began implementation, we thought that setting goals for forests would be straightforward. Resolving it turned out to have complications. This is the story of that challenge, detours encountered on the road to its resolution, and lessons learned along the way.

Investors articulate their financial goals. These goals typically include such things as absolute and relative return targets, risk tolerance, time horizon, and the like. In traditional investment theory, market risks are referred to

---

[84] Steve Lydenberg is Partner, Strategic Vision. Carole Laible is CEO at Domini Impact Investments LLC.

as exogenous or systematic. They are viewed as forces beyond investors' control. According to this conventional wisdom, investors cannot influence them and are not responsible for them. As a result, conventional investors don't set goals at system levels.

By contrast, system-level investors do because they recognize the importance of their influence on those critical environmental and social systems on which they depend for financial opportunities and market stability. As a result, these investors recognize their responsibility to steward the incalculable worth of these foundational systems and integrate their well-being into risk management practices.

Bell and Morse and Donella Meadows, experts in system dynamics, make it clear that the initial step in systems analysis is to "define the system."[85] Establishing definitions was our first task on the way to setting goals.

To define something is to draw a line around it. When it comes to physical systems – say, a river watershed – it's crucial to clarify where that system starts and ends. This is true in system-level analysis because one system inevitably connects to another. Limits and boundaries need to be drawn for the sake of clarity and practicality.

## Defining Our Focus

At Domini Impact Investments, our interest in systems and their impact on our portfolios surfaced in the wake of the Global Financial Crisis of 2008. The meltdown of the U.S. residential real estate market created impacts so large it caused a global systemic failure. Assets across virtually every asset class lost value. Diversification did not offer the protection most investors had expected it would.

---

[85] Bell, Simon and Stephen Morse. *Sustainability Indicators: Measuring the Immeasurable?* (Abingdon-on-Thames, England) 2008. Donnella H. Meadows. *Thinking in Systems: A Primer* (Chelsea Green Publishing: White River Junction, Vermont) 2008.

Over the next decade, our journey to a system-level approach progressed by fits and starts, but by 2018 it became clear that we could not ignore the various ways in which our portfolios rely on environmental, societal, and financial systems for their success. We also learned that systemic challenges by their nature are vast and complex. For us to have influence, it was important to focus on a particular system. We considered many different systems and landed on forests because they are a key but often underappreciated part of our global climate system.

As we began our work, public attention was focused primarily on the tropical forests of Brazil and Indonesia. But we soon realized the fates of other major tropical forests around the world were crucial as well. In addition, we considered the vast boreal forests of the Northern Hemisphere equally important. All of which led us to the question: What did we mean by "forests" and how should we define them?

Initially, we thought of forests along the lines of wild, undeveloped forestlands. Our concept was that of intact forest landscapes (IFLs), which are defined as a class of forest that is large, contiguous, self-regenerating, and undisturbed by commercial activities, but with the door open to habitation by indigenous peoples.[86] These constitute a substantial portion of today's forestland and occupy about nine percent of the habitable land of the Earth, although that percentage has been declining in recent years.[87]

We also realized that at the other end of the spectrum of types of forests were planted, commercial forests. These commercial forests are grown for timber and pulp and paper.

---

[86] Intact Forest Landscape. Website. Home Page. Available at https://intactforests.org/index.html on September 25, 2025. The definition of an IFL is "a seamless mosaic of forest and naturally treeless ecosystems within the zone of current forest extent, which exhibit no remotely detected signs of human activity or habitat fragmentation . . ." This definition allows for the presence of low-impact habitation by Indigenous Peoples." Home Page. Available at https://intactforests.org/index.html on September 25, 2025.
[87] Op.cit.

Single species tree plantations are the ultimate efficient forests, typically harvested by clearcutting and then replanted every 20 to 100 years, depending on the tree species and climate. Another type of commercial forests are mixed-species forestlands. They are less intensively managed than plantations and with somewhat greater opportunities for sustainability that helps preserve biodiversity and sequester carbon. By the time we arrived at forests as plantations, we were a long way from our initial thoughts of wilderness. Together, these two types of "production" forests occupy an estimated 7 percent of the Earth's habitable lands.[88]

In between these extremes of Intact Forest Landscapes and commercial forests lie forestlands consisting of naturally regenerating trees, shrub lands, savannahs, and pasturelands. National governments or large private landholders own much of this land. Some are formally designated as national parks or conservation areas; others are simply in government hands. Parts of these lands are left in their natural state, other parts are made available or leased out for pasturing, mining, drilling, timbering, hunting, fishing, tourism, and other public and private purposes. They are primarily undeveloped but often put to multiple uses. We define these as Primary Green Spaces. They are dominated by trees that occupy about 22 percent of the Earth's habitable lands and include lands dominated by low-lying shrubs and bushes that take up an additional 13 percent. Grouped together as Primary Green Spaces, they occupy a combined 35 percent of habitable land.

We also confronted the question of whether to include Agricultural Lands in our definitions of types of forests. Were large-scale fruit and nut plantations the equivalent of tree plantations? Were they a form of forests? Or put conversely, weren't tree plantations another form of crop grown like any agricultural product? In the end we decided to include Agricultural Lands among our six types of forests. The same types of environmental

---

[88] World Resources Institute website, *Global Forest Review:* "Production Forests" Available at https://gfr.wri.org/forest-designation-indicators/production-forests as of September 22, 2025.

risk characterize both: soil conservation and degradation, biodiversity loss, and carbon sequestration. Fruit and nut tree plantations look like tree plantations but are just not grown for their wood. Moreover, in terms of land use, agricultural lands occupy an impressively large portion of the Earth's habitable land: 45 percent by some estimates.[89] From a land-use perspective, it was hard to ignore them.

We also wondered if we should include "urban forests." Should we consider urban trees, municipal parks, arboretums and botanical gardens a type of forest? They don't look like forests, but they provide many of the same ecoservices as other types of forestlands and highlight the importance of nature to those living in cities. Compared to the other types of forests, the land they occupy is *de minimis*, but when it came to people's relationship to nature, we felt they played an important role. We decided to include them in our definitions, describing them as Secondary Green Spaces.

Our definitions of six types of forests for our system-level efforts were therefore as follows:

- Agricultural Lands (45 percent of the Earth's habitable land)
- Primary Green Spaces (35 percent)
- Intact Forests (9 percent)
- Planted Forests – Mixed Species (3.5 percent)
- Planted Forests – Monoculture Plantations (3.5 percent)
- Secondary Green Spaces – Secondary (de minimis)

## Implications of Definitions

This simple act of distinguishing different types of forests led us to four insights that we leveraged for goal setting.

---

[89] Hannah Ritchie and Max Roser. "Half the World's Habitable Land Is Used for Agriculture" Our World in Data website (2019). Retrieved at https://ourworldindata. org/global-land-for-agriculture on October 8, 2025.

- Defining forests by types helped clarify goals.
- Common themes that unified the different forest types emerged.
- Our interactions as investors were either direct or indirect depending on the forest type.
- The balance of companies' ability to create value or extract value from these forests differed from type to type.

From an investor perspective, clarifying types of forest helped set goals. We could now see that each type had a distinct purpose or function. For Plantations and Mixed-Species Forests, commercial purposes dominate. For Agricultural Lands, commercially oriented as they are, their basic function of feeding the world is of existential importance and hence demands acknowledgment of their public purpose. The very definition of Intact Forest Landscapes eliminates the commercial from their purpose. For Primary Green Spaces, which reside largely in governments' hands, the line between their uses as public goods and for commercial interests is flexible and often fuzzy. Secondary Green Spaces are lands used to signal the intrinsic value of nature and consequently generate little commercial value.

Struggling through the definition process helped us see these differences clearly. Consequently, we realized that the goals for each would also differ. More than that, the goals often could, and would, conflict – for example, Intact Forest Landscapes can be in direct competition with Agricultural Lands for how land is used, and that conflict is likely to intensify as the world's population expands from eight to ten billion.

In addition, it became clear that our goal for "forests" as an overarching system that encompasses all six types was not straightforward but consisted of a judgment of how well this overarching system allows each of its six types of forests to simultaneously satisfy their purposes, functions, and goals. Understanding each type of forest's potential role was a logical and critical step toward setting our goals.

The second realization was that, despite the differences among the six types of forestlands, four unifying themes ran through them that help confront the great challenges of this century such as climate change, biodiversity loss, income inequality, and economic justice. They were:

- **Sequestering of carbon.** Forests sequester carbon. Knowing which types of forests (tropical forests versus boreal, intact versus plantations, agricultural lands of different sorts) sequester how much and under what circumstances could then become part of our goal setting.

- **Preservation of biodiversity.** Forests are the primary means for biodiversity preservation on land. Again, some forestlands are better than others at preserving biodiversity. That knowledge would also be useful in goal setting.

- **Acknowledgement of intrinsic worth**. Forests are the lungs of the world and provide a wide range of ecosystem services. We came to stress the recognition of the intangible and difficult-to-value aspects of forests. They are "priceless." The market price of forestlands and their ecosystem services is important, but their intrinsic worth is invaluable.

- **Recognition of Indigenous Peoples.** Indigenous Peoples around the world have a historical record of preservation of forests and other green lands. Their traditional environmental knowledge has proven worthwhile, most recently in wildfire prevention. In addition, they play a valuable role in "systemic stewardship," particularly when they retain control of its design. That concept could also now be integrated into specific goals in different ways for different types of forests.

Third was the straightforward observation that as investors, the six types of lands fell neatly into two categories: those with which we interacted directly and those for which our interactions were indirect. These two categories are:

- **Direct interest**
  - Agricultural Lands
  - Planted Forests - Mixed Species
  - Planted Forest – Monoculture Plantations
- **Indirect interest**
  - Intact Forest Landscapes
  - Primary Green Spaces
  - Secondary Green Spaces

As an investment manager, we interact through our security selection of publicly traded companies with business models that play a direct role in the first three types of forests. We consequently have a direct interest in the attainment of goals we set for these lands and their impact on our specific holdings and portfolios. However, opportunities for investments in Intact Forest Landscapes are, by definition nonexistent. Similarly for Primary Green Spaces, opportunities for direct investments arise on occasion but are not a primary consideration. Secondary Green Spaces are also seldom of interest to investors.

Consequently, the more direct an investor's interest is in a type of forest, the more likely their goals are to focus on those assets and use diversification and other traditional tools for the management of risks and opportunities. Conversely, the more indirect that interest is, the more likely their goals are to focus on these forestlands' indirect but systemic impacts on the economy and hence on their assets across all classes, and the more likely investors are to use tools and techniques specifically designed for influence at a system level to mitigate those risks and enhance those opportunities.

Finally, we realized that the definitions and their implications intersected with a parallel track of work we were pursuing: sharpening our ability to distinguish corporations that were creating system-level value by addressing climate-related risks and opportunities from those that were extracting value at a system level in ways that exacerbated those risks without creating opportunities. This insight became useful as we realized the crucial role that balancing the impacts of value creation with those of value extraction was to play in goal setting at portfolio and system levels.

## Setting Goals

We now arrived at a point where we could set goals. Still, before putting all the pieces together, we reminded ourselves that our system-level approach should complement, not replace, our core business of managing portfolios. Specifically, we want to minimize our portfolios' risks and create additional investment opportunities in the short and long term. In doing so at the portfolio level, we seek to benefit ourselves and, at the system level, build a stable and resilient foundation on which to invest for the long term. The two serve different purposes that together make for a resilient and sustainable foundation for investing. We consequently set goals and devised metrics to measure success at both the portfolio and the system level.

We could now fully comprehend what setting goals entailed – how the pieces of the puzzle fit together to generate desired outcomes. We understood that our goals required an effective balance between extraction of value in the short term and the preservation and creation of value in the long term. For each type of forest that balance would be different and would manifest itself at both the portfolio and the system level.

Determining these goals for each forest type and the metrics through which their achievement could be measured was an intense and time-consuming process. It involved consideration of the beneficial roles that each type of forest could ideally play in an overall system of forest and green lands. It meant defining metrics that could measure their progress toward socially and environmentally desirable outcomes. It also implied identifying one set of actions to facilitate that achievement at a system level and another set of actions to do so at a portfolio level. Like the goals, the metrics and actions would be different for the portfolios and for the systems.

The details of the goal setting for each type of forest may have differed, but several basic steps were involved in each process:

- Determine the overarching goal for each of the six forest types.
  - Value creation or value extraction.
    - Understand if value creation or value extraction dominates or are they in equal balance.
    - Determine the specific actions that promote the appropriate balance, given the characteristics of forest type.
      - Identify those actions at both the portfolio and system levels.
      - Select metrics that determine whether those actions are achieving our desired goals at both levels.

This process resulted in a mosaic of interrelated goals indicative of improved systems health, along with actions necessary to achieve these goals and metrics to measure progress toward them. The table below summarizes the results of this goal-setting process.

## Goals and Metrics for Six Types of Forests and Green Lands

| Forest Type | Overarching Goal | System-Level Goal |
|---|---|---|
| Intact Forests | Stop and reverse loss of intact forests | • Increase in intact forests<br>• No roads in intact forests |
| Mixed Species Planted Forests | Rigorous sustainability management certification | • Global management of these forests conducted in accordance with the most rigorous sustainability practices |
| Monoculture Plantation Forests | Business model transition to one that promotes carbon sequestration and enhances biodiversity | • Transition of at least 50% of monoculture plantations to mixed species, selectively harvested lands, agroforestry, or related approaches |

| System Goal Metrics of Success | Portfolio-level Goal | Portfolio Goal Metrics of Success |
|---|---|---|
| • Data availability on increase in intact forest lands<br>• Data availability on road construction in intact forests | • Forest products, construction and related industries implement rigorous no deforestation policies | • 100% of our holdings in these industries have adopted rigorous no deforestation policies |
| • 100% of these lands certified to at least one sustainability standard, with at least 50% certified to FSC standards by 2030 | • Forest products, food products, and retailing and related industries with direct and supplier exposure to mixed species forests are certified to FSC standards | • 100% of our holdings in these industries have certified 100% of their land to these standards by 2030<br>• In addition, 50% of these lands are FSC-certified for sustainable management practices |
| Data availability for:<br>• Number of companies with policies in place to transition at least 50% of monoculture plantation lands by 2028<br>• Percentage of commercial forest land in agroforestry<br>• Percentage of plantation lands managed with high-conservation value principles<br>• Conservation principles that include contiguous or intact forest landscapes<br>• Number or percentage of monoculture plantations that have undergone business model transition | • Forest products, food products and retailing and related industries undergo business model transitions away from monoculture plantations to mixed-species, mixed-age forests, agroforestry and similar approaches | • 100% of our holdings in these industries have committed to business model transitions for 50% of their plantation lands by 2028 and have begun the transitions by 2030 |

149

| Forest Type | Overarching Goal | System-Level Goal |
|---|---|---|
| **Agricultural Lands** | Transition to regenerative agriculture to enhance soil health, biodiversity, and carbon sequestration | • Food producers and retailers and their direct food suppliers worldwide commit to transition 50% of their lands to at least a minimally credible standard of regenerative agriculture principles |
| **Primary Green Spaces** | Investors use at least the following system-level investing techniques to enhance these lands' sustainable management:<br><br>• Engagement<br>• Evaluation<br>• Polity | • Communication of best practice in these system-level initiatives for these Green Spaces by the investment community<br><br>• Broad uptake of three system-level investing techniques by peers in the investment community |
| **Secondary Green Spaces** | Use of urban and rural forests to communicate the value of nature | • Promotion of the usefulness of Miyawaki forests and similar initiatives as a signaling device on the importance and value of nature and its role in addressing climate change and biodiversity loss risks |

| System Goal Metrics of Success | Portfolio-level Goal | Portfolio Goal Metrics of Success |
|---|---|---|
| • Management of 50% of agricultural land worldwide committed to regenerative agricultural by 2028; underway by 2030 | • Food product and food retailers adopt credible regenerative agriculture policies and practices for 50% of their agricultural lands and the lands in their supply chains | • 100% of our holdings in these industries have adopted a transition policy by 2026 and have begun transition for at least 50% of land by 2028 |
| • Number of communications about best practice implementation of these tools and techniques by investors by year-end 2026 | • Companies in our portfolios explore the intersection of finance, philanthropy, and lessons from Indigenous Peoples to enhance primary green spaces | • Communicate at least five examples from our holdings of best practices in these techniques by year-end 2026 |
| • Development of examples of support for Miyawaki forests and similar initiatives by 2026 | • Communication to our holdings of the importance of urban forests as a tool in climate-change risk mitigation | • Complete a Miyawaki urban forest event for shareholders and their guests by end of 2026<br>• Provide one web-based educational communication on Miyawaki forest technique by end of 2026 |

# Next Steps

When we began our Forest Project, we had no roadmap to guide us toward goal setting and lacked a clear picture of our destination. Identifying systemic risks and defining goals was a journey of research, definition, leverage points, suitable actions based on our size and resources, and what we hoped to achieve. Having reached this milestone, we can now assess implications for the next steps in this process.

The first relates to data, its nature and availability. Given the goals and metrics specified in the accompanying table, two challenges need to be addressed. It is unclear how much of the data required is readily available. In addition, to the extent that it is not in quantifiable form, it will require analytical judgment to assess the progress that is made. These challenges can be overcome but will require work. Portfolio-level metrics will be easier to gather and analyze than those at system levels. Better data sets for the system-level metrics will need to be developed. Proxies for that data may also be necessary.

A second important consideration stems from the nature of the systemic risks of the 21ˢᵗ century: they are likely to have characteristics that we as investors are not accustomed to contending with. Among other things, these risks involve:

- **Irreducible uncertainties**. We are accustomed to calculable probabilities on which to base investment decisions. We have, however, limited past data to clarify the uncertainties of today's risks to Forests and Green Lands and how they will impact the complex evolution of tomorrow's uncertain paths for climate change, biodiversity loss, food insecurity, and income inequality, among other things.

- **Balanced business models for investors and corporations**. Currently, the focus is on the near-term maximization of returns and profits. Companies and investors need to move to a model of balancing tangible and intangible values, value extraction with value creation, and the needs of the future with those of the present to promote resilience while maintaining profitable businesses.

- **Conflicting goals.** Misaligned interests among the six forest-related subsystems as they relate to the larger system can undercut the effective implementation of the change necessary to reach desirable goals. As the world's population approaches 10 billion, for example, competition for land use between forests and agriculture will likely increase.

These challenges have implications for the paradigms upon which investors' current practices and models are based. Because we live in a world that has changed radically over the last century, fundamental aspects of how we as investors relate to that world will need to change as well.

How that change will manifest itself is in large part *terra incognita* for investors, but it is likely that a system-level approach incorporating goal setting that includes balanced business models and actions taken at both portfolio-level and system-levels will play an important role.

## Lessons Learned

In retrospect, had we known where we would end up when we set out, we could have saved much time and effort. In addition, we have learned much along the way about goal setting when confronted with the management of the risks of systemic social and environmental challenges.

The following are a few of those lessons:

- **Focus on a single systemic risk and its environmental and societal challenges**, one that impacts assets across all classes and poses acute risks. The number of these that investors face today is limited. As the 21st century progresses with its complexities and global interconnectedness, that number will likely grow.

- **Recognize that systems are made up of subsystems** with specific risks and opportunities of their own.

- **Understand the nature and purpose of each of these subsystems.** Each has a "job" – a purpose and a function – that plays a role in the outcomes of the overall system.

- **Accept that it is not necessary to understand the complexities of how or why each subsystem does its job.** It is sufficient to understand what that job is and how that subsystem interacts with the others.[90]

- **Recognize that each subsystem creates a mix of both public and private goods** and that the balance between the two differs, often dramatically, from one subsystem to another.

- **For each subsystem, set an overarching goal that accounts for the balance between public and private purpose.** Then set specific goals and actions for each subsystem as it relates to portfolios and to the overall system of which it is part.

- **Accept that these subsystems with their different outputs and goals can conflict with one another.** Their interests can be misaligned and that misalignment is a risk that will need to be managed.

- **Select metrics that help measure each subsystem's progress toward its system-level and portfolio level goals.** The combination of those two will be the measure of the subsystem's progress toward its overarching goal.

- **The degree to which all the subsystems' goals can be met will be the degree to which progress is being made for the overall system** itself with its own overarching goals.

- **Comprehend the fundamental paradigm shift that is implicit in goal setting when it comes to systemic social and environmental risks and opportunities.** Ultimately, a willingness to manage systemic social and environmental risks and opportunities at the highest level involves change in underlying investment paradigms.

---

[90] For a discussion of this concept in cybernetics, see Davies, Dan. *The Unaccountability Machine.* (Chicago: University of Chicago Press) 2024:40-82.

# Conclusion

Goal setting plays an important role in investors' management of environmental and social systemic risks and opportunities. It opens the door to deep considerations of how these systems affect investors and how investors influence them in return. It allows investors to identify how key subsystems can help overall systems generate desirable outcomes or avoid ones that undermine long-term investment opportunities. It suggests that systemic-risk management in the investment and corporate communities needs business models that strike a balance between value creation and value extraction.

Ultimately, goal setting provides a roadmap that can guide investors toward investing at the portfolio and system level in ways that promote resilience and sustainability. The details of this roadmap remain to be filled in, but it points investors in a clear direction. As the 21$^{st}$ century progresses, the importance of investors' role in the management of systemic risks and opportunities will only grow more crucial in this world of ever-increasing complexity and interconnectedness.

## Chapter 9:

# Measuring Success: Evaluation and Measurement

### By Emilie Goodall[91]

When seeking to measure and evaluate progress, investors typically focus on and report against sustainability measures at the asset or fund level, if outcomes are considered at all.[92] At this early maturation stage of system-level investing, it is rare to see robust measures for evaluating investor practices that seek to influence the environmental and social systems on which capital markets rely.

Moving environmental and social systems from their current state to a truly sustainable state involves multiple, competing influences and influencers, which makes isolating the effect of any one investor's actions difficult.

---

[91] Emilie Goodall was Head of Stewardship, Europe, for Fidelity International until March 2025.

[92] The World Benchmarking Alliance's 2025 assessment found that while 60% of financial institutions assign formal responsibility for sustainability, only 1% have evidence-based strategies linking financing activities to material impact. World Benchmarking Alliance, 2025. Financial System Benchmark. [online] Available at https://www.worldbenchmarkingalliance.org/publication/financial-system/.[Accessed 29 July 2025.

As articulated in the blog series "does sustainable investing work?" by Walkate and Gosling, there is "hardly any evidence to support the notion that [sustainable investing] practices are resulting in meaningful systemic effects, such as overall emissions decreasing in an industry or companies contributing additionally to SDGs. This does not mean that they are never having such effects – systemic effects are inherently hard to measure. But rockets clearly reaching orbit are rarely seen."[93]

This is also true of measuring the financial outcomes of such activities. As articulated in "*Moving Beyond Modern Portfolio Theory*, to calculate "the quantitative impact of [such] activities is difficult, as there is no 'control' group, precisely because the attempted mitigation of systematic risk is designed to affect the entire market, not just a subset of it."[94]

This chapter makes the case that despite these challenges, striving to measure and evaluate system-level investing is still worthwhile. It explores how one investor – Fidelity International – sought to balance a more traditional linear input-output-outcome approach to measuring its stewardship efforts with wider considerations of system health and resilience.

## Why Measure?

There are three main reasons why investors may set out to measure and evaluate their system-level investing efforts:

- **Learn**: to support organizational reflection and build shared understanding of what works (or doesn't) in contributing to mitigating systems risk. A learning approach can help evolve the culture, capabilities, and partnerships required to act at a system level.

---

[93] Gosling, T. and Walkate, H. (2024) Does Sustainable Investing work? Part 1, available at https://www.ecgi.global/publications/blog/does-sustainable-investing-work-part-1-the-three-stage-rocket-analogy-0 Accessed 30 July 2025.
[94] Lukomnik, J., Hawley, J.P. (2021) *Moving Beyond Modern Portfolio Theory: Investing That Matters*.

- **Improve**: to generate feedback that can strengthen investment decision-making, refine engagement approaches, and better target resources. This is especially important for investors, but also challenging in systems work, where learning loops are often long and impact is diffuse.

- **Prove**: to build credibility, both internally and externally, by showing that strategies and actions are meaningfully aligned with long-term systemic outcomes.

Learning, improving and proving can coexist as aims, but there is a tension between the three. A prove emphasis risks chasing easier, more observable outcomes and cherry-picking positive evidence. Given the nascency of system-level investing, it may make sense to first learn to track legitimate, meaningful signals and test what they reveal about effort and wider change. But pursuing a wholly open-ended learning approach risks weak discipline and wasted effort if credible indicators are not defined and reviewed.

There are few established standards and no mandatory reporting requirements specific to system-level practices. Even so, the need to justify resources adds pressure to prove results. In an industry that is highly quantified and highly competitive – with increasing pressure on costs and margins – whether the allocation of resources creates value is a valid question for the board, clients and other stakeholders to ask.

There is also a tension between a more quantified, linear approach to measuring and evaluating activities – an input-output-outcomes approach – and a systems approach that recognizes a more complex, interdependent set of influences, pushing and pulling through complex feedback loops. A curiosity mindset can reconcile these by leaning into the learn to improve approach, although this may be at odds with the dominant models of quantitative measurement, further influenced in recent years by anti-greenwashing regulation. As one observer noted, "in recent years, Chief Financial Officers have become responsible for sustainability functions as regulatory requirements to disclose material risks related to climate change increased (not specifically the finance sector). This shift may better integrate sustainability and financial decision-making, but it can also subject sustainability considerations to traditional financial thinking, priorities and metrics."[95]

## What Can Investors Influence?

A key consideration is what changes investors can meaningfully influence. For large, diversified investors, direct effects on real-world outcomes are typically limited. The notion of contribution – additional influence, relative to what others do[96] – remains a useful concept from impact investing, even if not yet adapted for systemic change.

This chapter focuses on evaluation and measurement for active engagement, one of four investor contribution strategies as defined by Impact Frontiers.[97] Engaging actively includes filing shareholder resolutions, helping investee companies engage with affected communities, and contributing to broader industry or policy efforts. Investor engagement with listed companies is widespread and longstanding. There is statistically significant data available for its effectiveness in terms of investor influence. "A

---

[95] Loveridge, D. (2025). Background Paper 1 – Viewing stewardship through a systems lens, University of Melbourne. Loveridge, D. (2025). Systems-Informed Stewardship, Background Paper 2.

[96] Impact Frontiers website. Available at https://impactfrontiers.org/norms/investor-contribution/ Accessed 31 July 2025.

[97] The other three strategies outlined by Impact Frontiers are: signaling that impact matters to investors; growing new or undersupplied capital markets; and providing flexibility on risk-adjusted return. The latter two are more commonly found among concessional investors or investors working with others in the form of blended finance, typically but not exclusively in private markets. These are promising avenues for system-level investing, but far less common amongst institutional investors, with fewer examples and much rarer evidence therefore of their 'success' in terms of systems influence. Available at https://impactfrontiers.org/norms/investor-contribution/ Accessed 31 July 2025.

number of studies document correlations, and plausible causality, linking engagement on environmental and social issues with changes in company actions and, in some cases, outcomes, such as environmental incidents."[98]

Evidence is stronger for company-level influence than for persistent real-economy effects. As Walkate and Gosling argue, it is a leap from proving that an investor triggered a company change, to proving real-economy impact of that change, to proving that impact "persists even after second order impacts and must not be (entirely) unwound by the response of competitors and consumers to the company's actions."[99] Evidence for lasting systemic change is weaker still.

But this framing is rooted in a linear cause-effect attribution approach to measurement, which is at odds with the inherent complexity of how change occurs in systems.[100] For example, in systems change, identifying and shifting key feedback loops is crucial to understanding how change happens, as these loops often sustain existing patterns – or, when disrupted, can unlock transformation. Each is influenced by public, private and civil society actors, who have competing aims.

A pragmatic approach could be to combine traditional, linear engagement tracking of observable company changes, aiming to understand potential investor influence rather than prove contribution, with tracking indicators of systems health and resilience. Adapted from Donella Meadows, the four core characteristics of which are:[101]

---

[98] Gosling, T. and Walkate, H. (2024) Does Sustainable Investing work? Part 2 – Launch and reaching the earth's lower atmosphere. Available at www.ecgi.global/publications/ blog/does-sustainable-investing-work-part-2-launch-and-reaching-the-earths-lower Accessed 30 July 2025.

[99] Gosling, T. and Walkate, H. (2024) Does Sustainable Investing work? Blog series https://www.ecgi.global/projects/responsible-capitalism/does-sustainable-investing-work Accessed 30 July 2025.

[100] Meadows, D. (1999) Leverage Points: Places to Intervene in a System. Available at https://donellameadows.org/archives/leverage-points-places-to-intervene-in-a-system/ Accessed 3 September 2025.

[101] The Investment Integration Project (TIIP), 2023. (Re)Calibrating Feedback Loops.

**Adaptability** – The capacity to self-organize, learn, and evolve in response to changing conditions, a pivotal leverage point for resilience and transformation.

**Clarity** – Transparent, timely information flows that enable informed decisions.

**Connectivity** – Strength of relationships and feedback channels linking system parts, supporting coordination and dynamic response.

**Directionality** – Coherence of feedback loops that reinforce desired dynamics or balance deviations, signaling purposive movement over time.

Tracking investor activities and company behavior changes alongside these more macro indicators can help investors interpret whether system health is strengthening or weakening, and guides adjustments – even if causality cannot be proven. This was the approach of Fidelity International:

> "[Measurement in systemic investing] requires grappling with different ways of seeing the world – the alternative mental models – that come with systems and complexity thinking. By engaging at this deeper level, it becomes clear that we need to ask different questions about what should be measured, why, and by whom. For example, the question 'what is the impact of my investment?' may become less important than the question 'what does my investment allow me to learn about the system I want to change'?"[102]

---

[102] Daggers, J. (2025). What could and should impact measurement look like in systemic investing? Available at: https://medium.com/transformation-capital/what-could-and-should-impact-measurement-look-like-in-systemic-investing-858281efb77b] Accessed 31 July 2025.

## An Attempt at Measuring and Evaluating
## System-Level Stewardship

Fidelity International is a global asset manager investing actively across multiple asset classes, including equities, fixed income, multi-asset and real estate. It serves millions of clients in Europe and Asia with deep bottom-up research. As a long-term, diversified investor, Fidelity and its clients are exposed to systematic risks such as climate change, nature loss, social inequalities and fracturing global governance.

These risks were identified via internal research that used "uncertainty" as one of several criteria, defined as the ambiguity around how system-level disruptions or investor actions might unfold, given unclear causal pathways or outcomes.[103] This helped frame Fidelity's approach to measurement, recognizing that indirect causal chains with many actors lead to unexpected outcomes. Although uncomfortable, it felt a more honest reflection of the reality of systematic risks than linear cause-effect logic.

Together, the criteria supported a "learn-to-improve" rather than "prove" stance, cautioning against claims of results of activities where causality could not be established, a common challenge in public markets. This helped set boundaries for what Fidelity could reasonably measure and claim.

Fidelity's approach built on its existing sustainability targets, including halving the portfolio carbon footprint by 2030 and a net-zero aim by 2050.[104] These focus on Fidelity's own portfolio (and operations) rather than a system-level goal, acknowledging the limits of its influence and the myriad drivers of climate outcomes.[105]

---

[103] The Investment Integration Project (TIIP), 2023. (Re)Calibrating Feedback Loops.
[104] Fidelity International, 2024. Climate Investing Framework. Available at https://www.fidelity.com.tw/s3files/documents/reports-and-policies/Fidelity-Climate-Investing-Framework-2024.pdf Accessed 30 July 2025.
[105] *Getting to net zero requires collaboration, and the success of our climate plan is dependent on broader system level change. That means we need a broad range of stakeholders to collaborate towards solutions if we are going to achieve our shared ambition of getting to net zero.'* Fidelity International, 2024. Climate Investing Framework. Available at https://www.fidelity.com.

Fidelity categorized activities that could both meet its carbon targets and influence others beyond the companies whose securities were held in its portfolios using an "influence framework." This internal, simple tool identified four main levels of influence, which map closely to The Investment Integration Project's levels of investor action: system-wide, industry, sector and/or portfolio level firm/entity (i.e. the individual assets in which Fidelity invested), with the additional layer of individuals.[106] The latter was added to highlight the importance of education and engagement, both internally with colleagues and externally with clients. Although there may be a degree of consensus as to the systematic risk, industry actors do not always agree on the most appropriate or effective influencing activities, which can hinder progress at other levels of influence. Aligning understanding amongst colleagues, clients and others with influence continues to be where a large amount of effort is needed, to identify optimal strategies that may reinforce or weaken feedback loops. In terms of the characteristics of system health and resilience, this means intentionally strengthening the system's adaptability, clarity and connectivity, to improve directionality. Otherwise, efforts across the influence framework may be confused at best, and at worst, conflicting.

Figure 1 provides a generic example, used periodically by Fidelity as an internal diagnostic and communication tool to ensure coverage across each of the four levels (the scale of the risk requires multiple strategies) and alignment (in any large organization, there is a risk of overlapping and conflicting activities). It was used to inform start/stop/scale decisions and, along with additional assessment tools, assess probability of success.

---

tw/s3files/documents/reports-and-policies/Fidelity-Climate-Investing-Framework-2024.pdf Accessed 30 July 2025.

[106] Adapted from a more detailed version available in Fidelity International, 2024. Sustainable Investing Principles. Available at https://professionals.fidelity.co.uk/static/master/media/pdf/esg/sustainable-investing-principles.pdf Accessed 30 July 2025.

# Figure 1: Influence Framework

| Level of influence | Examples of Fidelity's actions |
|---|---|
| **System**<br>Our economic, social and ecological systems are interconnected, and affected by the loss of natural capital in ways that are not yet fully understood but that have wide-ranging implications for capital markets. | • Active engagement in development of market standards, regulatory consultations and industry groups<br>• Firmwide sustainability commitments and targets (market signalling) |
| **Industry, sector, and/or portfolio**<br>Systemic risks arising from unsustainable economic practices are already informing change across industries. This change requires collaborative efforts to accelerate the necessary transitions. | • Thematic engagements, undertaken individually and in collaboration<br>• Engagement with data providers, proxy voters, index providers<br>• Finance-sector specific engagements |
| **Firm, entity**<br>Capital allocation, engagement, and voting inform company behaviour change. | • Outcomes-driven company engagements |
| **Individuals**<br>Individuals' knowledge, skills, and experience are key to effecting and informing change. | • Training<br>• Client engagement |

Fidelity chose to focus its system-level investing efforts on engagement, reflecting Fidelity's asset mix and longstanding legacy of active management. Fidelity traditionally engaged individual companies on idiosyncratic issues relevant to shareholder value (i.e. engaging at the 'firm/entity' level of the influence framework). System-level investing requires engaging at the 'system' but also 'industry, sector and/or portfolio' level, too. As one of Fidelity's sustainable investing beliefs states, "Effective stewardship combines bottom-up, thematic, and system-wide approaches."[107]

In practice, this meant looking beyond idiosyncratic factors and engaging via thematic engagements with 'bellwether' companies that can "start a ripple through the sector and incite changes in behavior across other market participants."[108] Thematic engagements matched Fidelity's priority systematic risks, and were highly focused, anticipating a minimum of 3-5 years' engagement, targeting companies where Fidelity felt it could engage directly and meaningfully (either individually or in collaboration) in "sector-level engagement that can help inform progress at the system-level."[109]

---

[107] Fidelity International, 2024. Sustainable Investing Principles. Available at https://professionals.fidelity.co.uk/static/master/media/pdf/esg/sustainable-investing-principles.pdf Accessed 30 July 2025.
[108] The Investment Integration Project (TIIP), 2023. (Re)Calibrating Feedback Loops.
[109] The Investment Integration Project (TIIP), 2023. (Re)Calibrating Feedback Loops.

Measurement was used to inform learning and resource allocation, rather than prove causality, with transparent reporting against portfolio targets.[110] Setting out to learn helped establish the right incentives for the stewardship team, with broad activity targets set against overarching systematic risk, avoiding perverse incentives to choose easy, near-term outputs.[111]

Observable company changes were calibrated against wider system signals (regulatory, sectoral, scientific or social). Each thematic engagement used milestones - credible and measurable signals of progress from the company - aligned wherever possible with industry goals and standards, as proxies for connectivity and directionality, characteristics of system health.

For example, Fidelity's climate transition engagement prioritized companies contributing most to Fidelity's calculated financed emissions, and where Fidelity's influence was judged to be greatest. It focused on issuers in material sectors representing the top 70 percent of Fidelity's Scope 1 and 2 financed carbon emissions (aligned with the IIGCC's Net Zero Investment Framework) that were not transitioning to a net-zero pathway, plus issuers representing the top 25 emitters across Scopes 1-3. Target companies were assessed using Fidelity's proprietary Climate Rating, combining service provider data and in-house research to assess an issuer's alignment to 2050 "net zero."[112] Given the time lag and occasional errors with ESG data, Fidelity would engage data providers to correct errors, where possible, as an industry- or sector-level intervention, seeking to improve clarity, another characteristic of system health.

---

[110] Having established a set of climate targets, Fidelity is committed to publishing progress against these in the form of regular climate reports. See, for example, Fidelity's latest Climate and Nature Report 2024, available at https://www.fidelity.co.uk/media/PI%20UK/pdf/corporate-governance/tcfd-report.pdf Accessed 29 July 2025.

[111] Such asks may still be valid to pursue to enhance **directionality** (one of the characteristics of system health), contrary to the thinking that these wouldn't be valid efforts as they weren't 'additive' (in traditional investor contribution thinking) but are unlikely to be sufficient in the pursuit of change.

[112] For more detail, see https://professionals.fidelity.co.uk/sustainable-investing/integration Accessed 16 October 2025.

Milestones were contextualized by the company's starting point (often relative to sector and region) and assessed using the Climate Rating. Milestones were based on industry best practice and sectoral pathways, centering around carbon emissions disclosure; presence of emissions reduction targets; and evidence of integration into corporate governance. Where progress stalled or conflicting corporate actions emerged, escalation options included votes against directors, shareholder resolutions and, potentially, divestment.[113]

A tracking system that included all the above was incorporated into Fidelity's cross-asset class research platform in 2025, after thorough testing. The platform gave all investment professionals real-time engagement data, helping tighten feedback loops and investment decisions. Quarterly meetings of analysts reviewed company- and sector-level progress and learning for each thematic engagement, sharing knowledge across regions and sectors. This brought together different perspectives, informing analysis of patterns and changing regional contexts. An annual review of portfolio holdings and target companies resulted in adding or discarding milestones as needed. Progress (or lack thereof) at this company level was thus cross-checked against observations of wider market activities (the sum of others' influencing activities) at the industry- and system-level, such as shifts within industry initiatives or changing policy.

It is tempting to concentrate activities where direct influence feels more observable and therefore actions accountable, such as with company engagement (even though, as noted earlier, there is weak evidence for lasting real-world outcomes from such practices). But to strengthen alignment and the potential for influence and lasting outcomes, Fidelity also worked at the industry- and sector level with civil society and with industry standard setters and initiatives. Analysts' engagements with industry networks and civil society also helped sense feedback loops and redirect effort when

---

[113] Fidelity International, 2024. Climate Investing Framework. Available at https://www.fidelity.com.tw/s3files/documents/reports-and-policies/Fidelity-Climate-Investing-Framework-2024.pdf Accessed 30 July 2025.

bilateral company engagement asks were likely to prove unrealistic. This was intended to increase the connectivity and understand directionality of efforts around the systematic risk, for example, helping make the internal case to shift focus to policy change efforts when bilateral company engagement was improbable or insufficient.

Industry networks were monitored for weak governance or poor responsiveness to external feedback, red flags for adaptability and directionality in terms of system-level health. Influencing options include bilateral or collaborative engagement with the initiative itself or, as a last resort, leaving.

Figure 2 indicates an iterative learning approach to systems stewardship, reflected in Fidelity's learn-to-improve approach.[114]

## Figure 2: Integrated Shifts to Move Towards Systems-Informed Stewardship[115]

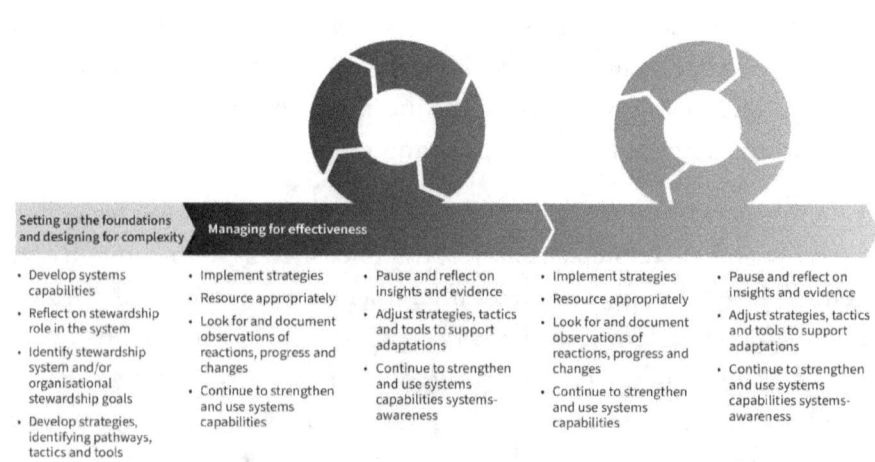

---

[114] Loveridge, D. (2025). Systems informed stewardship: reimagining investment stewardship for a sustainable future, University of Melbourne.
[115] Loveridge, D. (2025). Systems informed stewardship: reimagining investment stewardship for a sustainable future, University of Melbourne.

To improve alignment, quarterly and annual meetings included policy specialists in parallel tracking and engaging relevant legislative and regulatory developments, which could hinder or help company behavior change. These insights formed the basis for Fidelity's regulatory engagement, often in collaboration with others, and were tracked similarly to company engagements – with even greater caution in drawing direct causal links.[116]

The higher the levels of influence (from individual up to system), the more challenging it is to make the connection from actions to results, even when influencing actions concentrate on one systemic risk, in one sector and in one market (see the Rio Tinto example). Fidelity is in the relatively early stages of deploying the influence framework (having formalized it in 2023) and making connections between the levels of influence; further work is needed on analytical frameworks that can move beyond data collection and pattern spotting, and that can better account for the interconnecting nature of systemic risks.[117]

---

[116] Further detail of thematic and policy engagements are detailed in Fidelity's annual reports, see for example Fidelity International (2025) Sustainability Report https://www.fidelity.com.au/sites/fidelity/assets/Sustainability-Report-2024_final.pdf and Fidelity International (2025) 2024 UK Stewardship Code Report, available at https://professionals.fidelity.co.uk/static/uk-professional/media/pdf/sustainable-investing/Fidelity-UK-Stewardship-Code.pdf Accessed 3 September 2025.

[117] For example, the Accelerator for Systemic Risk Assessment (ASRA) has devised transdisciplinary assessment and response tools for systemic risk, on which it seeks feedback: https://steer.asranetwork.org/ Accessed 16 October 2025.

## Capturing the "Whys" of Progress

As part of Fidelity's tracking system, analysts recorded why an engagement ask was – or was not – met. For example, when an engagement ask was paused (or pulled altogether), reasons could relate to Fidelity (e.g. shares sold) or the company (e.g. management constraints). Across hundreds of engagements, this data revealed selection criteria strengths/weaknesses as well as sector/region dynamics. Meeting an ask was not necessarily "Fidelity's success"; analysts would record perceived drivers of change, whether external (e.g. regulatory change) or internal (e.g. management commitment). This was subjective and open to challenge. Companies occasionally credited investors explicitly, though Fidelity did not solicit attribution, in part due to the power dynamics and the risk of companies saying what they thought an investor might want to hear.

An example where the company cited Fidelity as a contributing factor is Rio Tinto, a long-term holding and the subject of years of engagement. Rio Tinto is a "bellwether" company, one of nine Australian companies targeted through Fidelity's climate thematic engagements. Fidelity, alongside the Australian Council of Superannuation Investors (ACSI) and representing Climate Action 100 investors, had been pressing Rio Tinto since 2021 for transparency on green steel investments and scope 3 emission reduction efforts, particularly related to iron ore processed in China. In March 2024, following sustained collaborative investor engagement and a tabled AGM proposal from ACCR, Rio Tinto committed to report spending on steel decarbonization projects, provide three-year spending forecasts and progress milestones, and enhance Scope 3 disclosures for its 578 million tons of 2023 emissions (70 percent from iron ore).[118] Tracking the system-level outcomes of this example requires ongoing engagement and monitoring for another few years, including its partnership progress with BHP and BlueScope on near carbon-free steel production.

Alongside company engagement, Fidelity engaged the Australian government on climate, including as co-lead for the PRI's Collaborative Sovereign Engagement on Climate Change.[119] The aim was to align strategies and strengthen **connectivity** and **directionality** between regulatory and investor signals and company action. One of the key influences bringing together mining rivals Rio Tinto and BHP to work on reducing emissions in steel production was the threat to company profits triggered by the clean energy transition.[120] An independent review commissioned by PRI found that the collaborative sovereign engagement reinforced the positive direction of travel on Australian climate policy across 2024, supporting a more effective and orderly market transition.[121]

This highlights that not all measurement should sit with individual investors; third parties are often better placed to track collaborative progress and system health indicators.

---

[118] Rio Tinto, 19 March 2024. Continuous improvement in climate disclosures for steel decarbonization. Available at https://www.riotinto.com/en/news/trending-topics/accr-commitment .Accessed 31 July 2025.

[119] Fidelity International, (2023). Influence and Stewardship Report, Australia. Available at https://www.fidelity.com.au/sites/fidelity/assets/FD24710_Influence+Stewardship_Report_2023_D3.pdf Accessed 31 July 2025.

[120] Australian Financial Review (February 9, 2024). Push to save iron ore golden goose. Available at: https://www.afr.com/companies/mining/green-steel-push-unifies-rivals-rio-bhp-and-bluescope-20240208-p5f3k8 Accessed 31 July 2025.

[121] PRI (2025) Collaborative Sovereign Engagement on Climate Change: Progress Report 2025. Available at https://www.unpri.org/download?ac=23909 Accessed 3 September 2025.

## Lessons Learned and Future Developments

Other investment managers use similar milestone-based engagement tracking. This chapter shows how a systems lens – specifically, considering characteristics of system health and resilience – can evolve, not replace, such practices.

- **Clarify upfront why you measure or evaluate your activities.** Is it to learn, improve or prove? This can help highlight potential tensions. Prioritizing any one purpose can influence your activities and measurement approach.

- **Challenge the impulse to prove and attribute**. This can feel counter-cultural in what is a highly competitive and quantified field, but increasingly investors recognize that to mitigate systematic risk, actors need to align around goals of the system, improving directionality and increasing the chances of collective success. Establishing a learning culture around systems thinking and system-level investing can help balance the desire to prove and attribute success.

- **Anchor engagement asks in industry standards wherever possible**, preferably industry standards that are rooted in planetary boundaries and that reflect the latest science and social change movements, even if they are emergent and imperfect. This can be challenging, as the nature of feedback loops means that standards can find themselves quickly out of step with reality. In which case, they can be challenging to unwind. Industry standards are critical indicators of connectivity and directionality within a healthy system. This includes investors being prepared to act to inform those standards where connectivity is weak, or directionality is misaligned.

- **Deploying additional and complementary influencing strategies**, ideally collaboratively, such as engagement with data providers and regulators, to strengthen system health characteristics of clarity and connectivity.

As the field matures, tracking individual investors' efforts could be supplemented with occasional independent evaluations of these strategies and their connection to characteristics of system health and resilience. This could include other system-level contribution strategies, such as blended finance. Given potential conflicts of interest (the pressure to prove), such work may best be led in collaboration with independent evaluators, potentially instigated by third-party investor networks given the wider market value of such research.

# Tools and Techniques for System-level Investing

Chapter 10:

# Investment Beliefs as a
# Strategic Compass

By Saksham Malhotra[122]

HESTA is an Australian profit-to-member industry superannuation (pension) fund. We invest more than A$100 billion on behalf of more than one million members who work predominantly in the health and community services sector. HESTA's purpose is to invest in and for people who make the world better. This purpose drives HESTA to invest in sectors aligned with the fund's members, who play a vital role in supporting the well-being of others.

As an investor, HESTA's approach to incorporating system-level investment thinking is underpinned by the fund's investment beliefs. Investment beliefs are a strategic compass providing a coherent framework that guides all aspects of the investment process and decision-making. Investment beliefs are particularly important in system-level investing, as they help investors clarify and articulate their fundamental views on the nature and purpose of financial markets, how investors intend to create value, the

---

[122] Saksham Malhotra is Manager Responsible Investments at HESTA

roles markets play in society, and how investors should act within them. In this way, HESTA's investment beliefs articulate how the fund connects its fiduciary duty to the long-term health of the systems on which members' retirement outcomes depend.

## The Role of Investment Beliefs in the Investment Management Process

There has been evolving research on the topic of investment beliefs, from the theoretical foundations of Markowitz[123] in the 1950s to Ambachtsheer and Ezra in the 1990s.[124] The research on investment beliefs has evolved from the understanding that portfolio construction depends on beliefs about risk and return, to the importance of explicitly stating these beliefs and their connection to high-performing funds.

As the Initiative for Responsible Investment's paper on Investment Beliefs Statements[125] states, investment beliefs have both conceptual and functional importance.

Investment belief statements are conceptually important because as they articulate the perceptions that trustees hold about the financial markets in which they operate and their role within them. They also act as a bridge between institutional goals and practical day-to-day decision-making and help institutions clarify and communicate the underlying rationale for investment decision making. Lastly, they increase transparency by making explicit what would otherwise be implicit, hence making it easier to distinguish one investor from another. This transparency results in asset owners attracting aligned partners and assessing beliefs of asset managers to gauge alignment.

---

[123] Markowitz, H. (1952). Portfolio selection. The Journal of Finance, 7(1), 77–91

[124] Ambachtsheer, K., & Ezra, D. (1998). Pension Fund Excellence: Creating Value for Stakeholders

[125] Lydenberg, S. (2011). Investment Beliefs Statements. Initiative for Responsible Investment at Harvard University, IRI Working Paper.

Investment belief statements are of functional importance as they serve as the guidepost for capital allocation, stewardship, and risk management. Investment beliefs guide practical decisions across asset allocation, manager selection, security selection and stewardship. They align investment practices with the institution's beliefs, reducing the risk of inconsistency or drift. This also helps maintain strategic direction and effective governance over time. Beliefs are a benchmark against which investors can evaluate decisions and outcomes. Lastly, the process of developing investment beliefs is itself invaluable. It fosters debates, builds dialogue, and brings in views from across teams irrespective of asset classes and titles, thereby helping the institution clarify its own identity and focus, and drives alignment throughout the organization.

## HESTA's Belief System in Context

HESTA has five investment beliefs.

- As long-term investors, our members' best financial interests are served by a deep commitment to responsible investment.
- A forward-focused total portfolio approach strengthens alignment with investment objectives.
- Targeted active management, working alongside leading global partners, delivers outperformance.
- Proactive and strategic risk awareness creates portfolio resilience.
- Value can be enhanced by effective governance, harnessing technology and data, and disciplined implementation

HESTA has given each investment belief additional context to bring the statements to life.

We added context to the first investment belief to provide an insight into how the investment belief includes managing system-level risks to deliver on long-term returns:

"HESTA recognizes the importance of pursuing a growing, sustainable and inclusive economy. By managing systemic risks (such as climate change), integrating responsible investment factors, catalyzing innovative investments, and being a 'gutsy advocate' for a fair and healthy community, we can deliver strong, long-term returns for our members and help accelerate our contribution to a more sustainable world."

Context around the second investment belief describes how to foster an environment that leverages a total portfolio approach mindset in the investment process, rather than an individual asset class perspective. It puts investment team collaboration and constructive debate at the heart of decision-making:

"Market returns vary over time but are somewhat predictable over the medium- to-long term. A total portfolio approach actively balances forward returns and risks with an unwavering focus on investment and impact objectives. A total portfolio approach facilitates the sharing of diverse ideas and market insights, encourages cross-team challenge and collaboration, and builds conviction to drive performance."

Framing accompanying the third investment belief goes to the practical signposts that investment beliefs provide, in this case, active management and partnerships to deliver on outperformance. The key here is that the belief outlines the basis for, and the environment within which active management and broad market exposure can add value:

"Cost-effective strategies that provide broad market exposure, combined with targeted and dynamic active management where inefficiencies are identified that can be exploited efficiently, have the potential to enhance returns, protect capital, whilst providing unique market insights and opportunities. Our hybrid model, which combines internal capability working together with a global network of trusted expert partners, is expected to improve net returns to members."

The fourth investment belief's context frames proactive risk management as essential for long-term investment success and portfolio stability, incorporating the use of active ownership as one of the levers to deliver on this:

"We must take investment risks to generate returns. Risk awareness requires us to understand the world around us and how it is evolving, including the impact of valuations, business cycles, thematics, economic environments and responsible investment factors to build more resilient portfolios. Success requires proactive risk analytics, stress testing and scenario analysis, as well as disciplined mitigation activities and active ownership."

Context for the last investment belief focuses on their earlier highlighted strength in emphasizing good governance and disciplined execution as crucial for realizing their benefits:

"Good governance promotes effective decision-making and accountability. Harnessing 'fit-for-purpose' technology and data can improve investment insights, and also supports disciplined implementation which reduces costs, improves net returns and minimises execution risks ."

The most recent update to HESTA's beliefs was made in 2023. The process took around six months. We conducted it with an eye towards the fund's competitive advantages. These include both structural advantages, such as the fund's scale, investment horizon and growing membership base drawn from beneficiaries working in health and community services, as well as cultural advantages, such as the fund's strong purpose, total portfolio approach, partnerships and knowledge management. We involved a broad range of stakeholders in developing the investment belief statements including, but not limited to, HESTA's Investment Management Leadership Team, Executive, Investment Committee and

Board. Reviewing and updating the fund's investment beliefs followed a period of significant growth of the investment team and at a time when the fund had commenced a process of partially internalizing investment management. This meant that beyond the value of the beliefs in supporting decision-making, the process of development was also very valuable in facilitating the forming, storming, norming and performing of a newly changed team.

This development process demonstrates the adaptive nature of institutional belief making that takes in both organizational learning and stakeholder feedback. Kim Farrant, The General Manager of Responsible Investment noted that "HESTA's approach to responsible investment is necessarily different than that of its peers." The why, what and how of responsible investment at HESTA reflect the way the fund thinks about itself – as a diversified super fund with global investments, needing to respond to risks related to some of the world's biggest (systemic) issues, and reflecting the fund's willingness to be a 'gutsy advocate' for a fair and healthy community based on its health and community services membership. HESTA's processes make sure the investment beliefs are a living document, actively informing processes and decision-making. By way of example, each paper to the fund's Investment Committee identifies how the discussions and recommendations in the paper link to the investment beliefs. Similarly, investment memos documenting decisions include reference to the relevant investment beliefs relied upon in reaching the decision, helping to support consistent decision-making.

In addition to establishing the framework for investment decision-making, HESTA's investment beliefs are also designed to connect with the organization's "Super with impact™" strategy. "Super with impact™" is described as the positive outcome HESTA creates by supporting the fund's members to face the future with confidence, being a gutsy advocate for a fair and healthy community and delivering investment excellence with impact. The investment beliefs are linked to HESTA's "Super with impact™" purpose through the third pillar of the purpose, which seeks to deliver investment excellence with impact.

Investment excellence with impact is about HESTA using its expertise and influence to deliver strong long-term returns while accelerating HESTA's contribution to a more sustainable world and is core to HESTA's organizational strategy. Superannuation is a long-term investment, and HESTA has a history of delivering strong long-term returns for members. Four investment options – Balanced Growth, Conservative, Sustainable Growth and High Growth – have all been ranked in the top 10 for investment performance against their respective peers over the 10 years ended 30 June 2025.[126]

## Designing Beliefs for System-Level Influence

HESTA's investment beliefs, in particular the first – *"as long-term investors, our members' best financial interests are served by a deep commitment to responsible investment"* – are primarily put into practice through HESTA's Responsible Investment Policy.[127] For HESTA, responsible investment is an approach to investing that incorporates the consideration of environmental, social and governance risks and opportunities into investment decision-making and active ownership, to deliver strong long-term returns.

HESTA recognizes how important a growing, sustainable and inclusive economy is to delivering strong long-term returns for members. As a super fund with diversified global investments, we are structurally exposed to risks related to some of the world's biggest issues and therefore manage these risks on an ongoing basis. This framing is important to recognize the "why" behind incorporation of system-level thinking into how a large asset

---

[126] Balanced Growth, Conservative and High Growth option rankings in the respective SuperRatings Accumulation Fund Crediting Rate Surveys June 2025. Sustainable Growth ranking in the SuperRatings Sustainable Fund Crediting Rate Survey June 2025. Product ratings are only one factor to be considered when making a decision. Visit SuperRatings for important information about this rating. Investments may go up or down. Past performance is not a reliable indicator of future performance.
[127] https://www.hesta.com.au/content/dam/hesta/Documents/Responsible_Investment_Policy.pdf

owner manages risks. This framing often also forms the basis of HESTA's public submissions to policy makers, engagement with companies that can materially influence achievement of the active ownership objectives (also known as "keystone actors" within the portfolio) and integration of responsible investments across asset classes.

HESTA's approach to identifying material system-level risks and opportunities is underpinned by the framing of a portfolio supported by a growing economy, delivering strong positive market beta influenced by systemic risks. We identify material responsible investment risks and opportunities through a materiality assessment of the system-level costs and opportunities of various factors with an ability to influence the growth and stability of markets. The identified risks and opportunities then guide HESTA's responsible investment approach. Factors such as gender equality, decent work, and good health and well-being support strong market fundamentals, including economic growth, that drive member investment returns. Systemic risks such as climate change and biodiversity loss have the potential to undermine these.

Systemic risks are those that threaten the functioning of the economic, financial and wider systems on which investment performance relies. They create systematic risk in the capital markets, which cannot be mitigated through diversification or divestment. HESTA contextualizes systemic risks by using the UN Sustainable Development Goals ('SDGs'), endorsing the ambitions of the SDGs as a framework to address systemic risks and identifying areas of opportunity. We prioritize several SDGs through the responsible investment program. We believe this is aligned with members' best financial interests given that SDGs are a focus of global policy and initiatives and therefore associated with material financial opportunities and risks.

Let's look at a few practical examples of how the statement of investment beliefs can facilitate a system-level investing approach. We do this by connecting research at economy level to risks and/or opportunities within the investment portfolio.

- For gender equity, economy level research has shown that addressing Australia's gender norms would boost GDP by A$128 billion annually.[128] We then approach this system-level opportunity from a portfolio perspective where research has demonstrated the benefits of gender diversity on company performance (return on assets, return on equity and profit margins)[129] and investment returns.[130]
- For climate change, at an economy level, the Network for Greening the Financial Sector conservatively estimates that global GDP may be 7 percent lower annually by 2050 unless the world can shift toward a net-zero pathway.[131] Conversely, the Australian economy stands to add up to A$65 billion in GDP by 2050 through investment in renewables, critical minerals, green iron ore and steel, and other technologies.[132] Translating this to a portfolio level, companies that are taking action to mitigate climate-related transition and physical risks and strategically considering opportunities within a low carbon economy are more likely to maintain and enhance long-term shareholder value.

The translation of each system-level factor to portfolio-level context is important for not just understanding how the risks and opportunities can manifest in the portfolio, but also to determine the actions HESTA can take to put into practice its investment beliefs. The examples highlight how introducing an investment belief statement can encourage institutions to seek system-level influence and drive system-level change.

---

[128] https://www.deloitte.com/au/en/services/economics/blogs/remaking-norm.html

[129] 2022 Beyond Lip Service by RQI Investors showed gender diverse companies are typically 'higher quality firms' and gender diversity in leadership is positively correlated to return on assets, return on equity and profit margins

[130] Gender Equity Insights 2025: The Power of Balance by Workplace Gender Equality Agency (WGEA) and Bankwest Curtin Economics Centre showed that gender balanced leadership can boost company value by close to A$93 million for a A$1 billion ASX-listed business.

[131] https://www.ngfs.net/sites/default/files/medias/documents/ngfs_climate_scenarios_for central_banks_and_supervisors_phase_iv.pdf

[132] https://www.ey.com/en_au/sustainability/the-energy-superpower-opportunity

Investment beliefs set the direction to manage system-level risks and capture opportunities, acknowledging the role that system-level challenges have on long-term returns. What follows is how the HESTA Responsible Investment Policy puts the beliefs into practice by finding the materiality of system-level risks and opportunities and breaking those into sub-systems for objective setting, action identification and progress measurement.

## Embedding Beliefs Though Governance and Culture

We review the investment beliefs on a triennial basis; the Investment Committee reviews the investment beliefs and recommends them for the Board's approval. Separately, HESTA management reviews the Responsible Investment Policy every year and tables it for reapproval by the Investment Committee at least every three years.

Another way investment beliefs come to life is through the translation of HESTA's organizational values into the Skills and Capability Framework of the Investment Management Team. Within this framework, key proficiencies are identified which support the organizational values – Lead with Purpose, Build Trust, Embrace Change, Foster Inclusion and Optimize Outcomes. These proficiencies strongly reflect implementation of HESTA's investment beliefs, including a focus on system-level interconnected thinking.

## How Beliefs Shape Day-to-Day Activities

The investment belief statement serves as a foundational framework that directly influences the day-to-day activities of investors. Active owner-ship (or stewardship) is an important part of how HESTA manages and addresses risks arising from systemic issues. HESTA considers whether companies suitably manage risk and create or enhance value, and whether they do so in a way that promotes broader economic resilience for the benefit of HESTA members. Active ownership can include engagement with investment managers, with companies, using shareholder rights to file/co-file shareholder resolutions, and voting across the thousands of companies HESTA invests in.

HESTA's Active Ownership Priorities demonstrate how the system-level component of investment beliefs comes through in HESTA's day-to-day active ownership activities. The Active Ownership Priorities explicitly state that:

> "Identification and management of material issues and sys-temic risks and opportunities – we expect companies to act in a responsible way considering how their business contributes to systemic issues. This includes identifying and managing material risks and opportunities both in the present and over the long-term. Assessment of risks and opportunities should consider financial, regulatory, operational, reputational and legal impacts."

The priority themes in HESTA's responsible investment program all con-nect to one or more economy-level changes that can support the manage-ment of system-level risks faced by the investment portfolio. For example:

- For active ownership within good health and well-being, one of the economy-level changes sought is to reduce the use of antibiotics in food supply chains. Antimicrobial resistance occurs when bacteria change over time and no longer respond to medicines that were designed to treat them. WHO provides guidelines on the use of medically important antimicrobials in food-producing animals. HESTA actions this system-level objective through its membership of FAIRR[133], where through collaborative engagement with companies, investors seek restrictions on the marketing of antibiotics for growth promotion, responsible manufacturing that avoids antimicrobials

---

[133] https://www.fairr.org/

entering the environment, and comprehensive company policies on the use of medically important antimicrobials.

- For active ownership within natural capital and biodiversity, the economy-level change sought to manage risk is to increase corporate ambition to halt and reverse nature loss in line with the Global Biodiversity Framework. This system-level objective is actioned through HESTA's direct and collaborative engagement through Nature Action 100 with keystone actors in material sectors to encourage these companies to assess and disclose nature-related impacts and dependencies across their material value chain.

Public policy advocacy is another lever for influence connected to HESTA's investment beliefs. HESTA may use its voice, both independently and collectively, to address systemic issues that are at odds with maintaining and building a growing, sustainable and inclusive economy. This is important in delivering strong long-term performance. HESTA's Active Ownership Priorities and priority SDGs guide our public policy advocacy. Like with active ownership, HESTA's system-level objectives underpin this public policy advocacy work. For example:

- The fund engaged in public policy advocacy on natural capital and biodiversity, where the economy-level change sought to manage risk was the establishment of mechanisms in Australia that align with the objectives of the Global Biodiversity Framework. To address this system-level challenge, HESTA advocated for the establishment of robust Australian laws to deliver environmental protection with a focus on halting nature loss.

- The fund contributed to Climate Change advocacy in Australia, where the economy-level change sought to manage risk was that policy settings in Australia support orderly reduction in greenhouse gas emissions across the economy toward consistency with Australia's commitment to the Paris agreement. To address this system-level challenge, through HESTA's collaborative relationship with the

Investor Group on Climate Change (IGCC), the fund has shared investor perspectives on the importance of Australia's 2035 Nationally Determined Contribution. Furthermore, HESTA has been an investor lead in the Principles for Responsible Investment (PRI) Sub-Sovereign Engagement Pilot, which seeks to support Australia's state governments in climate policy development.

Capital allocation is the final lever influenced by our investment beliefs. HESTA seeks to manage risks and capture opportunities through responsible investment integration, exclusions and thematic investments. For instance, the fund connected its capital allocation to a system-level objective in HESTA's work on housing affordability. Research shows that the provision of 250,000 social dwellings can deliver A$5 to A$11 billion in savings to the government through reduced costs to the social security system in just over ten years. This is in addition to the creation of 46,000 jobs per annum, and a A$40 billion contribution in GDP to the Australian economy.[134] Therefore, the economy-level change sought to manage risk in housing affordability is for institutional capital, where prudent, to deliver on housing supply at scale in a system that is driven by clear and consistent policy. HESTA seeks to address this system-level challenge by capital allocation through investment in apartments and build-to-rent projects in Australia which is set to deliver on mixed-tenure dwellings blending social, affordable, market-rate and specialist disability housing.

We also use the levers in combination. In addition to capital allocation for housing, HESTA made public submissions and participated in Australian state and federal housing working groups to provide feedback on models to scale investment in housing supply, utilizing the levers of capital allocation and advocacy to support system-level outcomes.

---

[134] https://believehousing.org.au/news/how-housing-benefits-peopleeconomies/

## Takeaways

Investment beliefs are crucial for achieving coherence across the investment process. They articulate the core principles that guide all investment decision-making, support alignment across the organization, provide transparency and accountability to beneficiaries, and offer a consistent framework for action and evaluation. However, equally important is the framework that exists around the investment beliefs to bring the beliefs to life. This framework consists of additional context for each investment belief, a purpose and strategy that underpins and aligns with the beliefs, policies that implement the beliefs, and a governance structure that provides oversight and includes accountability. For HESTA, system-level thinking is manifest across the framework, from the investment beliefs down to the identification of a keystone actor within the portfolio identified as a priority company in the active ownership program.

In setting investment beliefs, organizations should consider a focus on long-termism accounting for system-level risks and opportunities that impact the strength and stability of the market, and acknowledgement of system-level externalities that impact portfolio investments. Investors should also leverage the interconnections among asset classes. When designing the beliefs, discussion should include implications of each belief for the investment process, evidence of each belief's value-add, and a counterview to each investment belief to ensure a reasoned debate and consideration of alternative perspectives. Throughout the life of the investment beliefs, investors should continue to question whether the enabling environment for the beliefs is sufficiently supportive.

In conclusion, investment beliefs are not only essential tools for clarifying the internal goals and practices of investors but also play a critical role in shaping how investors engage with the broader financial system. By explicitly articulating their perspectives on the functioning of markets and the system-level risks and opportunities that exist within markets, investors can better identify and seek to address systemic-level challenges. Investment beliefs are most effective when they are not only clearly articulated but also embedded within an enabling framework that supports their realization. This means that investment beliefs should be supported by a broader context, an aligned strategy, and robust policies that translate principles into practice. When organizations integrate investment beliefs across the investment function, they become a powerful tool for guiding decision-making, fostering alignment among stakeholders (both internal and external), and enhancing the institution's ability to achieve its long-term objectives while navigating the complexities of financial markets.

Chapter 11:

# Engagement and System-Level Stewardship: Lessons Learned from the Net Zero Asset Owner Alliance

By Jake Barnett and Patrick Peura[135]

Institutional asset owners (such as pension funds, insurance companies, sovereign wealth funds, endowments, and foundations) independently manage trillions of dollars worldwide. Representing the long-term interests of their businesses and beneficiaries, these institutions are highly diversified, with investments spanning virtually all investable asset classes in the global financial market.

Historically, asset owners' broad diversification has led to more predictable and stable returns as idiosyncratic events to the upside or downside averaged out over time. This diversification also makes overall returns

---

[135] Jake Barnett is Managing Director Sustainable Investment Strategies, Wespath Benefits and Investments. Patrick Peura is Head of Investment Stewardship and Engagement, Allianz Investment Management.

contingent not just on a few companies succeeding but on broad economic health and prosperity. Thus, asset owners are increasingly aware that they are exposed to system-level risks and opportunities that impact the broad economy – factors that cannot be enhanced or mitigated solely through investment selection or diversification. This exposure means two things for asset owners. First, they rely on the growth of the global economy to achieve the investment results that they depend on, and second, that system-level risks are material to asset owner's portfolios and businesses.

The co-authors of this chapter believe that one of the best ways to address such system-level risk is through system-level stewardship and have collaborated for several years on advancing system-level stewardship through work in the Net-Zero Asset Owner Alliance (NZAOA). We define system-level stewardship as investors seeking to address financially material system-level risks and opportunities in methodical, logically-ordered ways that advance the long-term interests of the institution undertaking the action. While this chapter is about lessons and best-practices from this work, it is important to start by appropriately scaling expectations for a methodical, logical approach to stewardship that addresses system-level risks and opportunities.

Institutional asset owners' size, global reach, and importance to the underlying economy have, at times, resulted in a tendency among some stakeholders to overestimate the power and influence of asset owners. When asset owners are represented by others as powerful directors of companies or even the global economy, it is natural for other stakeholders within civil society to try to push asset owners to take more aggressive stewardship action, allocate more capital, or divest from certain investments – all in the hopes of addressing the concerns of said stakeholders.

The truth of what asset owners can accomplish is not so straightforward or so strident. This is especially true because asset owners act individually and independently. Addressing societal-level problems requires wide societal buy-in, and asset owners do not have a "silver bullet" to circumvent the important multi-stakeholder and often democratic process for generating this societal acceptance.

With that said, there are impactful actions an asset owner can take to advance their individual and independent long-term interests via system-level stewardship. In this chapter, we share the story of action taken on system-level stewardship by asset owners who participate in the Net-Zero Asset Owner Alliance to address system-level risks and opportunities associated with climate change. The bulk of the chapter details the origins for this work and how a system-level lens naturally evolved to become central to the engagement approach of the NZAOA, sharing practical learnings along the way. We end with lessons learned for stewardship professionals seeking to lead their firm in developing a system-level stewardship approach.

## Context of Author's Perspective

The work of the NZAOA is organized through different work "tracks" whereby asset owners work on advancing understanding and best-practices of how to fulfill their institution's independent net-zero commitments. The co-authors of this chapter served as the Engagement Track (E-track) co-leads for the NZAOA from 2021-2024. In practice, this meant we were responsible for furthering the NZAOA's interest in each member effectively representing their long-term interests to their respective stakeholders, with a particular focus on their investee companies and their asset managers (or prospective asset managers).

While we write about our experience as co-leads, many others contributed to this work. Our interpretations and thoughts are our own and do not represent those of any organization or specific participant in the alliance. We also do not intend to edit or change the meaning or intent of the outputs of the E-Track, and our recount of how they came to being are individually our own.

Lastly, when we use the term "asset owners," we speak specifically to those asset owners who have recognized their long-term interest in addressing system-level issues like climate change. We also believe this categorization covers most asset owners, as argued in the NZAOA's paper *Addressing Climate Impacts: An overview of NZAOA asset owners' long-term interests and responsibilities* (2025).

## The Origins of the NZAOA Engagement Track: Wrestling with Limits of Corporate Engagement

The NZAOA launched in 2019. This was a time of grand investor ambition, new initiatives, and excitement about how corporate engagement could address climate change. As a tool best suited to address idiosyncratic risks, corporate engagement was already maturing into investor initiatives like Climate Action 100+ – a very positive development overall, but with many misinterpreting what such initiatives could achieve absent a focus on system-level solutions.

This era's dominant paradigm was mirrored in early E-track conversations. Initial strategy discussions focused on exploring if there was value that independent NZAOA members could add through corporate engagement. However, as these strategic deliberations continued, conversations centered on how to overcome recurring themes E-track members experienced in engagements with companies:

1. Companies understood (in most cases very well) the risks of unabated climate change;
2. Most acknowledged science's warnings that society would be severely disrupted by rapidly rising global temperatures;
3. Most had heard from numerous investors with similar climate-related concerns;

4. But very rarely could any of these investors demonstrate credible paths for businesses to reach net zero in line with 1.5-degree Celsius warming scenarios.

Importantly, further climate ambition by companies was not achieved by stronger will or heightened levels of morality. It was blocked largely by a technological and economic inability to respond to investor asks in the existing (or projected) policy and regulatory environment while remaining profitable.

Don't get us wrong: it is the perspective of the authors that investors were and continue to be fully within their rights to communicate their perspectives and long-term interest to companies within relevant jurisdictional and regulatory context. However, it was clear that corporate engagement alone was not going to solve the more fundamental obstacles standing between investors' broad long-term interests and companies' immediate practical realities. Realizing the E-track was butting up against the limits of where engagement dialogue with companies could advance members' long-term interests, the E-track started to discuss what could come next.

## Early Days – Developing our Theory of Change

The E-Track centered discussions on three central, shared goals within the NZAOA:

1. Mitigating portfolio and business risks associated with climate change,

2. Pursuing and preparing for new opportunities that will result from the economy-shaping transformations climate change will inevitably create and,

3. Addressing climate change in the real economy as the primary means to fully execute on our independent long-term interest in addressing

climate risk and capturing opportunities as covered in the earlier referenced *Addressing Climate Impact* paper.

These three goals were grounded in a desire to facilitate efficient operation of capital markets that would support long-term value creation. All these goals were also using a system-level lens, even though we had not yet named it as such.

In exploring how to pursue these goals, the E-Track sought to steer clear of over-promising impact. Discussions instead focused on the unique and differentiated strengths of the NZAOA as a major, global, asset-owner-led climate initiative. These conversations led to three conclusions:

1. Asset Owners Make the NZAOA Unique: The NZAOA's member composition – asset owners representing themselves and their own interests – contrasted with many other investor coalitions of the time, most of which tended towards multi-stakeholder participation that included asset managers and service providers. While these coalitions are valuable and play a productive role in the investor ecosystem, they could not practically and fully cater to asset owner interests, ambitions, and internal expertise in the same way the NZAOA could.

2. Corporate Engagement is Not the Most Impactful Lever for NZAOA: We also identified the low marginal impact of the NZAOA pursuing climate-focused corporate engagement given the existence of effective initiatives like Climate Action 100+. Instead of recreating the wheel, we simply suggested asset owners within the NZAOA learn more about CA100+ and similar initiatives if they were interested.

3. Initiative-Supported Asset Manager Engagement Barely Exists: Despite the crucial need for asset owner-asset manager relationships to include both clear understanding and integration of asset owners' long-term interests, the authors did not see this happening in a well-ordered methodical way, especially when it came to asset manager stewardship activities.

Based on these conclusions, the E-track set forth a strategy that supported independent asset owner-to-asset manager engagement on key climate stewardship topics.

## Moving into the Work: Testing Theories and Forging Best Practices

With vision in hand, the E-Track began testing assumptions on best-practices that could help inform asset owner selection, appointment, and monitoring (SAM) processes of asset managers. For all the best practices we will discuss, this iterative process involved multiple rounds for drafting and refinement of best-practices internal to the NZAOA E-Track, testing those drafts with external stakeholders, and thoughtful integration of feedback. When considering the full scope of work described throughout this chapter, this iterative process involved dozens of dialogues with hundreds of professionals across the investment ecosystem over multiple years. Parties engaged included asset manager partners, academics, scientists, civil society experts, and asset owner peers. These discussions were invaluable to creating relevant and actionable resources.

Proxy voting emerged as an early flashpoint in need of such resourcing. While ecosystem voices clamored for asset owners to demand more "yes" votes on climate resolutions, the E-track respected that there was value in the perspective represented by asset managers in private dialogue: Thoughtful stewardship is nuanced and not always best-captured by a "yes/no" metric such as proxy voting.

On the other hand, we were also dissatisfied with the current status quo for asset manager proxy voting processes. Many asset managers adopted a black-box approach to voting, with answers to our questions on how they evaluated votes frequently boiling down to *"trust us."* Naturally, asset owners could not systematically evaluate the efficacy, or consistency, of such methodologies in advancing their long-term interests. There was also an expression by some asset managers of hesitancy around upsetting company management via support for climate-related votes that did not resonate with many in the E-track. The observable results from many managers on proxy voting was thus a tendency to side with company management.

With the two poles of "overly aggressive" and "unhelpfully opaque" in mind, the NZAOA E-Track set out to find a new way to determine how our interests were being represented in proxy voting. The result was the NZAOA's *Elevating Climate Diligence on Proxy Voting Approaches* (2021).

These best practices set out specific criteria that encourage principles-based, transparency-focused voting processes. Criteria are designed to be customizable to fit into independent asset owner SAM processes. They were also designed to allow managers' flexibility in implementation, while setting out explicit characteristics the NZAOA determined were best-in-class: disclose criteria clearly, vote on merit (not to appease management relationships), and escalate thoughtfully when appropriate. Finally, these practices were outlined in a way that allows asset owners to ratchet up or down the scope of criteria they wanted to engage their managers on, depending on what they saw as aligning with the best financial and strategic interests of their institution.

We've heard from over a dozen asset owners that say they've used this guidance to help further alignment between their managers' approaches and their own long-term interests. We can also speak confidently to Wespath's[136] and Allianz'[137] experience that these tools added value to ongoing independent discussions and SAM engagements with asset managers.

---

[136] Sustainability Report 2025 Wespath Benefits and Investments, pg. 26-27
[137] Sustainability Report 2023 Allianz Group, pg. 33.

# Setting Out the Big Picture:
# The Future of Investor Engagement

During the development of the proxy voting best practices, the authors also recognized that a theoretical scaffolding on system-level stewardship was emerging through the initial work of the NZAOA E-Track that could benefit from being made explicit. Thus, began the work on *The Future of Investor Engagement* (2022).

Among core arguments in this paper was an early statement that corporate engagement is a necessary but insufficient lever for addressing systemic issues like net zero. The paper goes on to argue that investors should complement corporate engagement with other activities such as sectoral, policy, and asset manager engagement, with asset owners being uniquely situated to use the lever of asset manager engagement.

This paper clearly laid out a vision for the work of the E-track with both internal and external stakeholders in a manner that proved invaluable for productive dialogue. With internal stakeholders, it gave the authors a direct explanation to the routine question of why we were not working on corporate engagement. With external stakeholders, it helped us level-set the perspective of the E-track on which actions are best suited to support decarbonization, while emphasizing the importance of multi-stakeholder solutions.

The paper also productively influenced public understanding of system-level stewardship within our industry – it's been cited in shareholder resolutions, taught in MBA courses, and referenced among media members in editorial discussions.

## Next Lever: Policy Alignment as a Bridge
## to Systemic Ambition

The E-Track next turned our sight to the tricky question of how to assess and engage on asset managers' alignment on policy engagement.

We saw policy alignment as important because of one of the key points made in the *Future of Investor Engagement*: If the policy and regulatory environment ("rules of the game") were not aligned with the long-term interests of asset owners, no amount of corporate engagement would get companies to move beyond what was profitable and feasible in the fore-seeable future. Thus, the future economic playing field needs to enable corporate behavior that supports long-term value creation for asset owners in a decarbonizing world.

Yet, this was another area where the authors knew it was important not to overstate the asset owner role. Asset owners can't dictate corporate lobby-ing or unilaterally decide on policy - strong and effective policymaking is clearly a place where multi-stakeholder engagement will always be present by design. The E-track also recognized early on that many investors do not want to advance specific political agendas. To help right-size the role of investors, the E-Track focused on alignment between climate commit-ments asset managers and companies had already made at a firm level and how those commitments were congruently applied in relation to policy engagement actions and associations.

Initial drafting of these best practices on alignment was significantly im-proved by feedback from the NZAOA Policy Track on how to make the draft more credible in a policy engagement context. One critical point was helping right-size the initial draft's unrealistic initial expectations on how detailed the asks on transparency could be. Subsequent asset manager meetings enlightened the E-track on the limited amount of resourcing – many asset managers had only a few policy-focused staff who largely prioritized financial regulation. This highlighted that one of the most important aspects of an asset managers' policy approach was their stewardship of underlying portfolio companies. Expecting congruency within asset manager stewardship of investee companies on policy engagement thus became a core principle.

The result: *Aligning Climate Policy Engagement with Net-Zero Commitments* (2023). This document outlined four principles for evaluation: governance frameworks, transparency on positions, accountability mechanisms, and escalation protocols. Designed for SAM integration, these best practices connect dots across siloed teams, encouraging strategic alignment within entities and investee companies. They also provide asset owners a distinct set of guidelines for what alignment looks like on a key issue area – ones which many investors acknowledge are important, but still struggle to meet.

While these best practices were welcomed by fellow investors, the authors also acknowledge this topic remains a frontier issue for many. Nevertheless, we know there are asset managers that are grateful for clear guidance on asset owner expectations in this emerging field and have used this set of best practices as a reference for the development of new firm-wide policies.

## The Capstone: Engagement Best Practices for Smarter Stewardship

The E-Track completed its work on best practices with the publication of the *Elevating Asset Manager Net-Zero Engagement Strategies* (2024). Early exchanges with practitioners on how to best conduct engagement with corporates generally revealed the same dynamics that we highlighted in the *Future of Investor Engagement* – that idiosyncratic corporate engagement is important but can only go so far in addressing underlying system-level risks.

With this in mind, the E-Track sought to develop lines of thinking that would elevate the lessons learned from company engagements by asset managers that reached the limits of the current "rules of the game." We began this exploration from an understanding that hitting these limits does not mean a failure of engagement, but instead the starting point for what to do next to identify and address the system-level hurdles to decarbonization. This approach becomes more powerful when considering that asset managers have unparalleled access to corporate players around the globe across sectors, economies, and geographies. The E-track believed keeping this information siloed within individuals or teams embedded in larger asset management organization did a disservice to informing investor and societal discourse on how to shape a more resilient, prosperous and less risky world. The illumination of these system-level barriers could help the investor ecosystem better engage with regulators, policymakers and real economy actors on finding potential solutions that advance shared interests.

A key piece of guidance in this document was an ask that asset managers publish engagement memos deriving lessons learned from engaging multiple companies within a sector on reaching net zero. This parallels well with the function of proxy voting memos where asset managers have used the practice to explain how their voting actions are aligned with their polices, approach, and merit-based criteria.

## Pulling It Together: A 2024 Call to Action Amid Headwinds

As our tenure as E-track co-leads approached a close, we contemplated how to portray our work on system-level stewardship to the broader investment ecosystem. With the publication of the set of engagement best-practices, existing work on proxy voting and policy alignment, and the *Future of Investor Engagement* paper, the E-track had covered important leverage points we believed were under-represented in stewardship discourse. We also believed these resources created a grounded framework for how to practically advance system-level stewardship within asset owner's context.

Additionally, in 2024, it felt important to lift up asset owner interest on system-level stewardship to contrast with public discourse dominated by tales of anti-ESG sentiment, regulation, and resulting loss of mandates. The result was a call to action entitled *Serving Asset Owner Clients Through Climate Stewardship*.

This call to action was made directly from the NZAOA to the asset manager community. It continued to call for thoughtful, practical, and system-level leadership from our asset manager partners on climate. It also laid out the various published resources as valuable reference points for further engagement, dialogue, and action between the asset owner and asset manager community.

We heard appreciation for this publication from both asset owner and asset manager partners. We also heard feedback that this signal was often most effective when those responsible for allocation decisions within asset managers shared it directly with portfolio management and investor relation functions within asset managers, making it clear that asset owner's interest in leadership from asset managers extended beyond sustainable investment teams.

## Results of Efforts: Anecdotal Wins and Enduring Influence

The impact of stewardship efforts is notoriously difficult to attribute. Often stewardship reports track outputs instead of outcomes – number of meetings held, number of proposals voted for, number of regulations commented upon. This difficulty in quantifying the return on effort between output and outcome only increases when you start dealing with the complexity inherent in system-level stewardship.

Yet, this doesn't mean the investor community interested in addressing system-level risks and opportunities should shy away from evaluation. The authors' experience is that continual improvement is less about trying to quantify exact impact and more about building relationships with trusted peers, practitioners and experts who will help challenge and improve efforts.

The ultimate goal of the efforts described above was to help any interested asset owner who wanted to work on system-level risks and opportunities with asset managers to have access to practical tools that they could integrate independently into SAM processes, and have a strong rationale for doing so. The feedback we received from multiple asset owners is that they do indeed weave the published best practices into SAM, activating the invisible hand in their selection of aligned partners by showcasing that system-level considerations and methodical stewardship to address those systemic risk concerns is important to winning mandates.

## Looking Ahead: What Best Practices Would We Recommend for System-Minded Stewardship Professionals?

The co-authors do not claim to be the foremost experts on addressing system-level risks and opportunities or to be definers of what best-in-class looks like. In fact, we bristle somewhat at the idea that a singular best-in-class for stewardship on system-level topics exists. We've described one paradigm above and we readily acknowledge that effective strategy will differ significantly based on constituencies, end-goals, timelines, resources, jurisdictions, etc.

However, we do believe there are commonalities in any effective system-level stewardship program. These commonalities have more to do with operating from grounded and thoughtful plans of action and being open to iteration rather than established and static theoretical framings.

We therefore conclude with three suggestions on strategy that we think are important if you are going to seek to do such work.

*Start with generating institutional buy-in*: Ambition on system-level topics will not be impactful without organizational buy-in to act on that ambition. Organizational buy-in often runs from the Board all the way to the junior analysts. The most important foundation for a sustainability professional interested in system-level investing is figuring out how they can generate strong support for their work within the institution. Without this alignment, you build a house on a foundation of shifting sand. With it, you position yourself as a trusted strategic thinker seeking to advance the long-term interests of the institution. For example, each co-author made sure to generate strong understanding and buy-in with supervisors and other senior staff within their organizations before publication on any resource.

*Ground arguments in shared long-term interests*: System-level conversations can quickly become abstract and theoretical. This is not a strong position for stewardship professionals. Ultimately, practitioners need to ground any system-level approach in a clear expression of how said approach advances the long-term interests of the party they seek to engage. This begins with the organizational change-agent concept described above, and then should extend outwards. For example, the co-authors got buy-in by focusing on the system-level stewardship approaches that advanced our institution's long-term interests and then spent extensive time getting to know and learning from the investor community present in the NZAOA. This included a consistent curiosity on commonalities and differences of approach among our peers. The resulting understanding allowed us to constantly ground our position in solid credible arguments about why proposed actions were in the long-term interests of the NZAOA community.

*Operate from strong understanding of power*: In arguing for change, one also needs to understand what access and influence they have to the levers of power necessary to advance said vision. Who are your allies, and what are the obstacles internally and externally? What are the pain points and limits of action of the counterparty? What can you do when you reach those limits? This type of power analysis is a well-established lens for many stewardship professionals in the context of idiosyncratic engagement, but the landscape will look different when taking it to a system-level. In advocating for asset owners to do more to engage asset managers, an early understanding of the co-authors was that the power to influence asset managers resided most strongly with the asset owner's CIO or asset class lead, not the stewardship professional. Thus, work on engaging asset manager partners often began with discussions with the internal stakeholders at the asset owner organization about how to best represent asset owners' interests. If successful, this engagement resulted in a shared understanding within the asset owner and a stronger bargaining position when engaging the asset manager.

The journey of advancing system-level stewardship has been some of the most gratifying work of both of our careers. It has brought the opportunity to think big, to work strategically, to iterate organically, and to collaborate with colleagues that became close friends. We would recommend it for anyone hungry for a challenge and eager to make an impact, with only one caveat: Be ready to take intellectual risks and do the work.

# Chapter 12:

# How To Work with Your Consultant on System-level Issues

## By Max Messervy[138]

The chapters in this *Handbook* cover a multitude of system-level investment topics: frameworks for developing strategies and action, how to clarify and articulate an institution's perspectives, and how such considerations might express themselves through investment portfolios. This chapter focuses on practical guidance for how asset owners can engage their investment consultants with respect to system-level issues so as to leverage the tools and perspectives that consultants can offer to effectively advance your institution's objectives. I've included selected case study examples drawn from my own experience working with clients across the institutional spectrum, including reinsurance, endowments and foundations, defined benefit and defined contribution retirement plans, sovereign wealth funds, and development finance institutions.

The functions that asset owners play in our economies – providing secure pensions, backstopping insurance coverage, funding robust educational

---

[138] Max Messervy is Founding Principal, Oakledge Advisors LLC. Available at: https://www.oakledgeadvisors.com/.

systems, etc. – are themselves essential social goods that must be supported. Thus, if fiduciaries knowingly sacrifice returns or accept outsized or uncompensated risks in the pursuit of "the greater good" that is a form of funding a solution to one global challenge by cutting the budget allocated for another – an unnecessary zero-sum game. While it is overly simplistic to claim that there may not be *any* tradeoffs involved in system-level investing, the courses of action that will be most readily supported by consultants (and other stakeholders, by extension) are those that maintain strong risk-adjusted returns while also achieving additional objectives. It is with that background in mind that we can now turn to the main question at hand.

## The Investment Consulting Business Model

It is important to begin our discussion with a review of how investment consultants are organized functionally, as well as how they make money. Why? Because it is highly likely that an asset owner seeking to engage in system-level investing will need to progress *alongside* their consultant(s), in a mutually beneficial learning journey. How consultants are organized affects their functionality; knowing the organizational structure will enable you to tap into the skill sets and resource you need, while avoiding some traps for the unwary. Second, as American author Upton Sinclair noted, "it is difficult to get a man to understand something, when his salary depends on his not understanding it."[139] So knowing how investment consultants get paid, and crafting your relationship with them to be consistent with their business model, or at least not in conflict with it, is a key to convincing your consultants to be willing and able to meaningfully support your system-level investing journey.

This point is underscored by Stephen Heinz and Geraldine (Gerry) Watson of the Rockefeller Brothers Fund, who describe their investment consultant, Cerity Partners OCIO, "not as passive implementers, but

---

[139] Upton Sinclair, "I, Candidate for Governor: And How I Got Licked", University of California Press, 1994 (Reprint of 1934 original).

as co-creators of a strategy that evolves with the times and explores new possibilities. Their willingness to listen, adapt, and engage has been as vital to [RBF's] progress as any policy or performance metric."[140]

Institutional investment consulting firms are generally organized into two broad divisions: external, client-facing roles and internal, research, or operations-focused roles. Client-facing teams – often referred to as "field consultants" – serve as the primary relationship managers. A typical client team consists of one senior consultant supported by a mid-level consultant and a junior analyst, although the composition can vary depending on the client's size and complexity. These teams are responsible for maintaining relationships, understanding client needs, and serving as the conduit between the client and the consultancy's internal expertise. In this capacity, field consultants select from a range of internal resources and solutions, drawing on them as needed to address specific client situations or strategic objectives.

Behind the scenes, internal-facing teams provide the research, analysis, and operational support that underpin the firm's advice. While structures vary across firms, most include specialized groups focused on manager research – conducting due diligence and rating external managers and general partners' strategies and capabilities – along with economic research, portfolio construction, and performance monitoring functions. There may be specialists in specific asset classes such as private credit or infrastructure, or in issues like sustainability or crypto, and even in such enabling areas as communications and presentations. Many firms also maintain internal committees that bring together subject-matter experts to develop policy and guidance for specific asset classes, regions, or investment approaches (such as dynamic asset allocation). These committees collectively produce what is often called the firm's "house view" – a synthesis of current thinking disseminated across the organization and ultimately delivered to clients

---

[140] The Investment Integration Project, "Returns, Risk, and Responsibility: How the Rockefeller Brothers Fund Invests for Long-Term Value and the Public Good." TIIP: 2025. Accessed on Oct 12, 2025: https://tiiproject.com/wp-content/uploads/2025/08/RBF-10-Year-Review-8.1.25_FINAL.pdf

through field consultants, typically in quarterly meetings that cover market trends and portfolio implications.

Consultants offering OCIO services have internal structures that more closely resemble those of traditional asset managers. Because OCIO clients delegate partial or full authority over their portfolios, OCIO firms must maintain operational capacity for daily portfolio management. OCIO providers generally construct portfolios using either their own or third-party investment products. The resulting portfolios reflect the OCIO's strategic and dynamic insights. Ideally, they will be tailored to each client's specific objectives and constraints, though the temptation for an OCIO to impose a "house view" irrespective of those objectives and constraints remains ever-present. OCIO providers typically embed advisory elements into their contracts, allowing for a relatively seamless delivery of a complete package of services to clients.

Across the consulting industry, most large global firms – and a growing number of mid-sized and boutique ones – maintain dedicated sustainability or ESG or, occasionally, impact investing teams. Whether or not your consultant will have such capability, and the quality of that capability, will depend on firm culture, history, and the revenue split derived from different types of institutional clients who may or may not demand them. These specialists may engage clients directly and may in fact have their own revenue models/P&Ls separate from the core business, or they could be more internally focused, contributing specialist perspective related to investment manager research, for example.

These teams clarify clients' objectives and advance progress on environmental, social, or mission-related goals. The prominence and structure of these teams often reflect firm culture, client mix, and revenue sources. Larger firms, especially those serving diverse global clients or operating outside North America, tend to employ staff fully dedicated to sustainability and impact work. These specialists may maintain their own client relationships and revenue lines or function internally to enhance investment research and manager evaluation. Field consultants frequently consult these experts to enrich client conversations or propose additional advisory services (sometimes with additional fees attached). Or, to put it bluntly, the field consultants grew up with a much more traditional MPT-based training and do not themselves have the required skill set or experience, so they bring in specialists. And seldom do these consultants have system-level investing specialists anywhere in house.

In firms without the scale or client base to support a fully dedicated sustainability team, responsibility for such work may fall to traditional consultants with relevant expertise or personal interest. These "dual-hatted" professionals provide sustainability-related advice alongside their standard consulting responsibilities.

## Engagement and Contracting Models

Asset owners typically engage consultants through either retainers or project-based agreements. Retainer relationships can span multiple years and position consultants as an extension of staff, though the consultants still owe their ultimate allegiance to the fiduciaries (generally a Board), not the investment staff. Think of it as working daily with the investment staff, but also acting as an independent check on them, akin to the governance structures used by internal auditors. For asset owners, retainers offer the benefit of a consistent partner with whom to develop institutional knowledge over time. For consultants, they provide stable revenue streams and reduce the frequency of time-consuming procurement processes.

Retainer clients occasionally request services that fall outside the formal scope of work. Field consultants often accommodate such requests – particularly for larger clients, when preparing for contract renewals, or when fee structures allow some flexibility. Alternatively, consultants may need to decline or defer these tasks if they prove disproportionately time-consuming, typically managing client expectations through transparent communication. Some asset owners choose to maintain dual retainers – one with their core consulting team and another with a firm's sustainability or impact specialists.

Best practice is for contracts to define specific deliverables and service levels based on the client's priorities and available budget, and for the fiduciaries of the asset manager to annually perform a performance review of the consultant. Such a review serves three purposes. The first, and most obvious, is to communicate what has worked well and what needs improvement. The second is to scope what may be needed in the upcoming year. The third, and less obvious, is to reinforce that the consultant's ultimate accountability is to the Board, not the staff (even though the consultant may work much more closely and routinely with the staff)

My personal experience suggests that there is no one "best" way to engage with a retained consultant around system-level and related issues. For example, one faith-based institution hired my team to conduct a relatively light-touch annual portfolio ESG review of the funds they invested in, while a foundation client had us support its net-zero investment commitment, utilizing our proprietary tools and seeking our specialist insights in their manager selection and engagement. In addition to those specific assignments, we also worked with various public institutions to help build and mature their climate investment and stewardship programs to ensure robust integration into their core processes. These engagements involved in-depth education of their Board members on system-level topics, particularly articulating and publishing the institution's investment beliefs and objectives related to climate topics and divestment, ensuring that strong governance alignment was achieved prior to any significant (and possibly controversial) portfolio moves being made.

Project-based engagements, by contrast, are for a defined time frame and typically are structured around specific deliverables. These projects aim to advance a client's decision-making or strategic development, such as conducting a portfolio review, designing a new policy framework, or evaluating emerging investment approaches. When considering a project-based engagement, asset owners should assess how much implementation support they require after the project ends. For instance, if a consultant helps design a system-level investing strategy such as those detailed by PGGM or UPP in their chapters, the client should clarify whether follow-on support for updating internal processes is included or whether it will be handled internally.

Clients who already have retainer relationships often engage their consultant's sustainability or impact team on a project basis to advance discrete objectives. Examples include one-off educational sessions, portfolio screenings, or updates to investment policies to align with evolving system-level goals and strategies.

Ultimately, when asset owners seek consulting support for system-level investing, an important first step is to consider the type of consulting relationship they already maintain – retainer or project-based – and whether that structure is fit for purpose to the new assignment. While contracting a consultant for a specific project may seem straightforward, translating ambitious mandates into tangible outcomes often proves more complex in practice.

## The Economics of Non-Traditional Consulting

All new investment practices – and system-level investing is still relatively new – requires that consultants step out of their legacy business functions of advising on strategic asset allocation, portfolio construction, and manager selection, and into areas and topics they may not be familiar with and that are not necessarily in demand for many of their clients. Therefore, if a client asks their consultant whether they could help develop and implement a system-level investing strategy, it could kick off an internal discussion among the consultant's colleagues and leadership regarding the "scalability" of such work – how much demand exists for the type of advice being offered.

It is important to understand that consultants trade largely in *information* and *insights*; they are tasked with researching topics, evaluating market landscapes for trends, and bringing leading-edge analytics to bear to inform their clients' decision making. Consultants also offer third-party perspectives that can give fiduciary comfort to investment committees, trustees, and other stakeholders.

As with any other product, the *production* of investment advice requires an upfront commitment of resources, whether human, data access, or otherwise, to be successful and decision-useful to clients. Therefore, consulting firms want to ensure that those upfront costs to produce specific outputs can be amortized across the greatest number of clients possible to ensure a profitable venture. This has become a recurring issue for consultants: do they gather the resources necessary for a potentially profitable new consulting area, or stick to the tried and true. In the past, traditional consultants faced this issue when real estate, private equity and hedge funds gained popularity. Some consultants did so, while others chose not to, allowing the growth of specialty consultants for those investments.

This business model has clear implications for how consultants respond to anything innovative, including system-level investing inquiries. The more highly tailored to each client's needs, context, and governance structure the services required, the less profitable. At the same time, every institution has its own objectives, stakeholder expectations, and fiduciary boundaries, which makes it both impractical and inappropriate – for reasons of confidentiality and client trust – to replicate one client's deliverables for another.

To reconcile this tension between bespoke advice and scalable business practice, many consulting firms have developed frameworks to structure conversations around emerging or complex topics. These frameworks serve as modular tools that allow consultants to engage clients in repeatable, theme-based discussions while still leaving room for customization. During my time at Mercer, for example, the firm implemented the *Sustainable Investment Pathway*, a framework designed to help clients define their sustainability beliefs, articulate goals, and craft an implementation strategy that aligned with their mission and investment philosophy. Other major firms have since built comparable structures to guide their clients along similar journeys. Although language and branding differ, the intent is the same – to transform highly individualized advice into a process that can be scaled, without losing its depth or relevance.

When clients bring consultants questions about newer topics such as system-level investing, however, they may venture into territory where the firm lacks an established "house view." Moreover, the firm may not even have the resources and skills necessary to create one. In such cases, even the most experienced consultants might hesitate to offer formal rec-ommendations until they have had time to research, confer internally, or consult with subject-matter experts, whether internal or external. A single inquiry might therefore result in the sharing of background materials or high-level discussions rather than a fully formed advisory approach. But as multiple clients begin to raise similar questions, the internal dynamics shift. Patterns of inquiry become a market signal that reaches firm lead-ership, prompting investment in research and the

development of new frameworks or analytical tools. What begins as an isolated client request can thus become the seed of an entirely new practice area – one that eventually shapes how the firm engages with system-level investing more broadly

At the same time, clients who feel some urgency to address system-level investing and related topics within their own mandates may prefer to seek out specialist firms to support their inquiries, rather than potentially waiting for their traditional consultant to decide whether or not it wishes to develop and offer perspectives and materials on the topic, a process that may take years – and may lead to an answer of "no." Specialist consultants in this area may have a mission and/or thematic orientation at the core of their approach, and the history of why their firms launched in the first place may have much to do with the fact that the traditional firms left a significant "gap" in the market for system-level investment advice.

A useful example of how the economics of non-traditional consulting can evolve in practice comes from Cambridge Associates.[141] Initially responding to client inquiries about sustainability and long-term systemic risks, the firm's leadership recognized that meaningful advice in this area required new frameworks, staff training, and data capabilities – investments that could not be justified on a single-client basis. Over time, Cambridge Associates developed a dedicated sustainability and impact platform, embedding environmental and social factors into manager research and portfolio construction, and enabling consultants across its global offices to draw on shared intellectual capital. In effect, early client demand for sustainable and impact insights catalyzed an internal capability that is now core to the firm's advisory model.

## Strategies for Engaging Your Consultant

Given all this context, what should investors seeking system-level investing support from a trusted advisor do?

**Start by defining the nature of your request.** How do you or your institution seek to engage in system-level investing? It helps to have a clear idea of your objectives, to the extent you can define them. If you can't, perhaps you should first ask for a series of educational sessions. You might also consider what views and interests your institution's stakeholders hold on this topic; if you are part of the staff, have your Board or other fiduciaries inquired about system-level investing topics, or are they aware of it? If you are a member of a Board or a fiduciary, have you asked staff for their perspectives? Clarifying such questions internally first is helpful, but it may also be that a key deliverable of the consulting engagement is to elicit and align those perspectives, as when UPP engaged outside consultants to help devise its Statement of Investment Beliefs.

---

[141] See High Meadows Institute and The Investment Integration Project, *Sustainability in Capital Markets: Investment Consultant Case Study – Cambridge Associates*, 2025. https://tiiproject.com/wp-content/uploads/2025/09/Sustainability-in-Capital-Markets_ Investment-Consultant_Case-Study_Cambridge.pdf

**Ask about your consultant's experience, resources and insights on system-level investing.** Inquiring with your lead/field consulting team as to whether their firm has done any work on system-level investing topics is an essential step. Orient your inquiry around the objective(s) you have outlined at the start. If this is a new topic that you are raising, you might share some relevant articles (including a reference to this *Handbook*) with your consulting team for their background. Like it or not, if your consultant is not conversant with system-level theory and practice, both you and it are likely to embark on an educational trip together. Or, if that is impractical, you could seek a specialty consultant for a project engagement.

**Evaluate your consultant's response to your request.** Depending on how conversant your field consulting team is with leading-edge topics, they may be able to respond to you directly, or they may have to seek internal input prior to responding. This process can sometimes take days or weeks (which can be quite frustrating, admittedly) but generally, the field consultants' interests are in keeping their clients happy; they therefore try to avoid providing you with inaccurate information. Hence the need for clear input from the rest of the consulting firm.

**Define the scope of the engagement.** Presuming your consultant offers adequate capability to support your system-level investing objectives, consider how (and how much) you would like to work with them to achieve your goals. Defining these questions can be a tricky combination of factors: budget availability, the consultant's capabilities and team, and certainly not least, your institution's perspective on how deep into system-level investing you want to go and which tools of system-level investing you want to employ.

If your institution believes that system-level investing should be core to its investing approach going forward, then you will likely want an engagement with your consultant to reflect that deep commitment. As the other chapters in this *Handbook* detail, a deep engagement with system-level investing will likely require a rethinking and revamping of an institution's investment approach and portfolio to align with goals and achieve objectives. This will likely require a long-term partnership with an advisor who can support your journey. Practically, this may mean that you should evaluate whether a retainer contract could meet your needs. Such a contract could be structured as a "dual retainer" with a specialist team within your existing consultant, or you might consider rescoping your existing contract. If you think you need truly specialist expertise, you could hire a specialist consultant to work alongside your current general consultant. Such specialist consultants often have experience working with general consultants, as well as investment staff and fiduciary boards. The key in this structure is ensuring clear boundaries for each consultant's scopes of work. I have been involved in various such engagements; transparency and clear communication between parties are essential.

For institutions at the beginning of their system-level journey and/or with more limited budgets, engaging a consultant for a clearly scoped project could be the preferred option. Such projects could focus on working closely with board members and/or staff to articulate the institutional beliefs around system-level investing and specific issues to address. This engagement could take the form of roundtable discussions facilitated by the consultant to identify a consensus, or one-on-one meetings, or surveys issued to board members and/or staff, or a combination of those methodologies. Such projects provide the starting point for the institution's system-level investing journey. My team and I worked with many institutions who could only engage in limited projects, but these were nonetheless impactful for the client's perspective on the given topics covered and set the stage for how they conducted their investment programs in the future. For example, we worked with one insurance entity with environmental commitments and conducted a project where we engaged with each of their external fixed income managers to assess their climate and stewardship capabilities in a structured way. While the client did not make any immediate portfolio changes, they did gain a new understanding of how their managers approached (or didn't) a topic of critical importance for their company.

## Evaluating a Consultant's System-Level Investing Readiness

What if, after moving through this process, it turns out that your current consultant is not the right fit to advise your institution on system-level investing, or they are not interested in pursuing such work? How can you make such a determination clearly, and how can you best evaluate alternates? Here are a few considerations which, if thought of as a mosaic, can help narrow down a list of candidate firms.

**Mission alignment indicators**: While an obvious step in due diligence, simply evaluating a firm's website and publications can provide some indication of the consultant's approach to system-level investing. Does their site have a separate page for system-level investing, sustainability, impact, or other themes? Do they speak about their approach to supporting clients with such interests? Do their published works highlight innovative thinking and/or approaches that can be discerned? Do the principals of the firm – and particularly the team that would be assigned to you – have experience in system-level investing? Have they published on the subject?

**External memberships**: Sometimes a consultant's capabilities and orientation can be identified by the company they keep and the membership organizations to which they belong. Does the consultant indicate that they are members of any mission-aligned organization, or that they regularly participate in any? Impact investment-oriented events and organizations can generally indicate a relative openness to unconventional thinking and may point towards the consultant at least circulating in the "right" circles to have exposure to system-level investment practices. Is the firm, or its principals, in leadership positions within those organizations?

**Client referrals/endorsements**: Given this is an emerging field of investing still, consultants who can point to clients they have worked with, case studies, or other collateral provide clear comfort that they have created value for such clients. Each asset owner will have to evaluate individually whether the consultant's offerings would meet their respective needs effectively, of course, but having a client track record is an important element of due diligence.

## Conclusion

This chapter may be more than you ever wanted to know about the (sometimes opaque) world of investment consulting. However, mapping out some practical ways to effectively engage a consultant is a pre-requisite to ensure that asset owners receive the advice, tools, and support they need to achieve their system-level investing goals. For investment professionals who have been "in the game" for a while, some of this may have been obvious. For newer professionals, I hope you found some useful insights regarding how to contract consultants and how to use the leverage have.

As I noted at the outset of this chapter, system-level investing is still an emerging field. Asset owners may need to collaborate with and learn alongside their consultants about how to implement system-level investing practices. However, I anticipate that following the publication of this *Handbook*, there will be a much greater interest in system-level investing from all corners of the investment world. So, it seems only a matter of time before virtually all consultants will be more well-versed in the topic, to their clients' great benefit.

## Chapter 13:

# Policy as Table Stakes

### By Corey Klemmer[142]

The legal and regulatory backdrop poses a persistent challenge to sustainable investing. It can create enabling conditions and facilitate innovation or create hurdles and chilling effects. This has been true for a long time in jurisdictions around the world - whether it's guidance that creates real or perceived hurdles to using non-traditional financial data, or the absence of required disclosures that leads to inconsistent data and a highly uneven playing field for companies seeking to be transparent about their risks and opportunities, or the availability of fund structures to implement specific investment theses.

System-level investors are particularly affected by the legal environment as they seek returns by benefitting the market as a whole, a notion squarely outside of the norms of traditional finance which therefore does not fit neatly into existing legal frameworks.

[142] Corey Klemmer is the principal and founder of ACK Consulting. She was formerly the Policy Director at the U.S. Securities and Exchange Commission. Prior to that she worked in asset management and financial policy. She is an attorney and a CFA Charterholder. All opinions herein are Ms. Klemmer's, and do not reflect the position of any employer or the editors or publisher of this Handbook. Nothing here provides legal or investment advice.

These challenges have been compounded in our current environment by the politicization of sustainability. Even though in many iterations, "sustainable investing" simply represents an effort to make our financial theories more robust and our markets more efficient, in the US, the whole field has been dragged onto center stage of our deeply divided political discourse.

That was not the case when I joined the front office of the U.S. Securities and Exchange Commission in 2021. At that time, the wind was at our backs. So called "ESG integration" had experienced significant growth over the previous five years and there was a groundswell of support for a rule on climate-related financial disclosure. Voluntary compliance with the TCFD disclosure regime was broad and growing and the relatively strong consensus across the market said that rulemaking would be beneficial.

It appeared that there was a real problem to solve, real world solutions to draw from, and we at the SEC had the tools and authority to act. Yet at the time of this writing (2025), the SEC's climate disclosure rule is stayed (i.e. not effective) and trapped in limbo as the Eighth Circuit Court of Appeals put the case on hold until the SEC takes action,[143] and the current SEC has declined to defend the rule but has not shown any other indication that it will act.

Given the growing threats to the systems on which we rely, an effective and enabling legal environment is more important than ever. It's critical for system-level investors to have a thesis on what that looks like and a strategy to support it. I hope my experience can offer some perspective on how to do that. Though I focus in this chapter on my time at the SEC, I believe the tools and reflections discussed here can apply to other issues, regulators and jurisdictions around the world.

---

[143] *State of Iowa et al.* v. *United States Securities and Exchange Commission*, No. 24-1522 (consolidated with Nos. 24-1624, 24-1626, 24-1627, 24-1628, 24-1631, 24-1634, 24-1685, 24-2173) (8th Cir., Sept. 12, 2025), PDF, accessed October 9, 2025, https://www.knowntrends.com/wp-content/uploads/sites/969/2025/09/State-of-Iowa-et-al-v.-SEC-24-1522-No.-00805348431-8th-Cir.-Sep.-12-2025.pdf

# The Need for Policy Work

For the system-level investor, engaging with policy is table stakes. This is true for two reasons.

First, in the same way that system-level investing recognizes that long-term performance depends on healthy environmental and social systems, it should also consider the market as a system unto itself. A stable, fair and efficient market is a condition precedent for sustainable investing. Conversely, a market with excessive leverage and rent-seeking, and without strong guardrails or governance is prone to crises.

Consider the goals of system-level investing in the context of a crisis: Yes, opportunities may emerge to pick up distressed assets or see declining emissions due to reduced consumption. But the overwhelming context will be investors scrambling to fill financing/funding gaps and scaling back on anything "non-essential." Beyond that, the human cost becomes significant – in the form of lost jobs, lost homes and increasing austerity measures from governments. Investments in energy transition will likely shift towards economic recovery and stimulus. All of these outcomes presumably stand at odds with the goals of a system-level investor.

Second, policy directly affects the ability of system-level investors to engage with and address the issues they seek to affect. If our capital markets were a network of trains moving assets around our financial system, our legal/regulatory system would be the tracks. It's certainly possible to work in finance without ever thinking much about the tracks, but if those tracks run between Point A and Point B and your investment thesis requires you to get to Point C, there is no choice but to deal with how those tracks get built, through law, policy and regulation.

System-level investing fundamentally challenges us to reach Point C - to engage with financial risk and value creation in a way that is outside the conventions of modern portfolio theory (MPT) and traditional finance.

Where MPT ignores, obscures or accepts systemic risks, system-level investing seeks to measure, manage and mitigate them. Whether your system-level investing strategy involves novel financial products or filing shareholder proposals or even just ingesting corporate disclosures – policy plays a role.

Here's an illustrative list of what legal and regulatory policy may affect:

- Corporate engagement – How and when you can add proposals or director candidates to the proxy materials that are sent to all shareholders, when and how you are able to collaborate with other investors, when you must disclose your stake in a company, the subject matter of your dialogues with companies.

- Permissible investment strategies – The boundaries of fiduciary duties, when non-financial information may be considered, how you determine information to be financial or non-financial, appropriate risk exposures for different types of investors.

- Investment opportunities – Pathways for companies or funds to access capital, who can invest, whether registration is required and what is involved in that registration.

- Information environments – Required disclosures from companies and investors, when disclosures or omissions create liability, to whom and for whom the liability is created.

While I would submit that the current legal and regulatory regimes permit system-level investing, they fall far short of creating an enabling environment.

For these reasons, engaging with law and policy – the proverbial train tracks – becomes a critical tool for any system-level investor; critical for the mutually reinforcing goals of supporting a healthy financial system and enabling the function of system-level investing to strengthen the systems on which the financial system relies. What follows are my reflections from my time in key regulatory functions – first, as Counsel to the Chair of the

Securities and Exchange Commission (SEC) and then as the SEC Policy Director – in the hopes that it will make users of this *Handbook* better informed and more effective when wielding these tools.

## Day 1 Ambitions; Year 2 Realities

Each new administration, hot off an electoral win, takes over the U.S. federal government with a wave of fresh energy and big ambition (God bless the career staff that provide the ballast on this sometimes-careening ship). In the Spring of 2021, following the change in administrations, ESG was top of mind. Then again, so was Payment-For-Order-Flow (the payment system that allowed platforms like Robinhood to offer "free" brokerage services), transparency at private funds and the explosion of unicorns (WeWork was in the midst of flaming out), instability in the treasury markets (the "COVID jitters"), and a SPAC bubble, just to name a few. Oh, and crypto.

The ESG-focused investor community was similarly ambitious. At the time I was at Domini Impact Investments and working deeply on climate- and nature-related risks driven by deforestation. It seemed eminently reasonable that any climate disclosure rule should capture something about land use change as it is the second largest driver of greenhouse gas emissions, behind burning carbon. At the same time, other corners of sustainable finance brought forth issues related to environmental justice, methane emissions, the just transition, carbon offsets and credits, and more.

The pressure for the SEC to act came from investors, companies, Congress, the press and the public as evidenced by a growing comment file in response to a Request for Information issued by Acting Chair Allison Lee. Staff and stakeholders worked tirelessly to explore and vet options for how to proceed. Seemingly endless energy was expended in pursuit of consensus. On March 21, 2022, the proposal rule was voted out of the Commission and available to the public.

Then, on June 30, 2022, the Supreme Court (SCOTUS) decided the case of *West Virginia v. EPA*. It was the opening salvo in a series of SCOTUS opinions that marked a generational shift in administrative law. Those decisions will define the regulatory environment for years if not decades to come. Where courts would once defer to the expertise of specialized agencies when interpreting the words of Congress (a principle known as the Chevron doctrine), now courts will substitute their own interpretation. Combined with other decisions, the Supreme Court dramatically expanded opportunities for private litigants to challenge agency actions across time and subject matter (issues with forum shopping pre-existed this shift but peaked in the Biden administration with 40 percent of challenges to agency action filed in the right-leaning Fifth Circuit[144]). Those decisions put significantly greater scrutiny and constraints on the actions of federal agencies, including the SEC.

As time went on, it became increasingly clear that the Overton window had shifted. The final rule would almost certainly face immediate legal challenge. And the opposition only grew bolder against a changing political, legal, and temporal context. Litigious comment letters led to Freedom of Information Act requests and Congressional subpoenas. My conviction prior to joining the SEC about deforestation making perfect sense as part of a climate disclosure rule fell away, not because my beliefs about the financial risks created by deforestation had changed but because our operating constraints were shifting.

Even without any of these challenges though, as it turns out, writing regulations is hard. When putting pen to paper, the devil is most certainly in the details. Regulating almost always requires line drawing, which depends on judgement calls and often limited data. It requires lots of definitions, some of which draw from widely shared understandings, some of which do not. We could dial things up or down by changing the scope of entities covered, the timeline for compliance, or the consequences for failure, but ultimately there had to be a decision about what information was part of the required disclosure and what was not.

---

[144] https://policyintegrity.org/tracking-major-rules/forum-shopping

The finished product involved a staggering amount of work and dedication from the staff of the SEC, folks I worked with, contributions from the public, and engagement with stakeholders (I commend and appreciate all their efforts). The rule ultimately faced nine petitions, including one filed within minutes of the vote of the final rule (i.e. the text of the rule had been public for only minutes when the first brief was filed). The petitions were consolidated in the Eighth Circuit. And as mentioned above, at the time of writing the rule is stayed by the Commission (i.e. paused pending court action), the Commission has declined to defend the rule, and the Court has indefinitely paused further consideration of the rule until the Commission acts.

In light of the legal limbo the rule now faces, I expect it will be a long time before we truly understand the impact those efforts will have for our markets. But I believe they will serve the markets for the better - whether as a model for future legislation, a guidepost for forward looking companies, or as a public record of why and how investors need these disclosures.

## Another Narrative and Reflections

While the SEC's work on its climate rule may have dominated the head-lines, the regular business of the SEC moved along. The policy function is actually quite narrow, all things considered. And much of the policy work focused on issues with a far smaller audience, like corporate disclosures related to executive compensation, or the smallest tradable increment for an exchange-traded security.

In one such rulemaking effort, we put out a proposal on conflicts in secu-ritization that generated a strong and negative response from the market. Industry leaders and trade associations submitted comment letters, then came in and sat down with us to walk through the issues raised in their letters. They provided highly technical feedback, offering specific changes that would address their concerns. They walked through the mechanics of a transaction and explained how various alternatives would affect their decisions and flow through to their clients and the market.

The engagement was tremendously productive and led to a final product that both better accomplished our goals as regulators and avoided potential disruptions to the markets. This counter-narrative is a bit of a simplification – there weren't deeply divided perspectives in the comment file nor was the industry objecting to being regulated, full stop. Still, I mention the experience for two reasons.

First, law firms and trade associations bring a highly valuable technical proficiency and acumen to the table. Of course that's obvious, and it's why they charge such large fees. But policy advocates, system-level or otherwise, might take note of what makes them so effective. Look at the way their comment letters are framed: They often target specific language in the regulatory text, the legal analysis and/or the cost benefit analysis.

Second, and this point may have been obvious within the first, there is a deep structural asymmetry in the markets that the SEC serves. The costs created by proposals are usually borne by a specific group of market actors, while the benefits are generally more diffused and harder to measure. If a proposal imposes a cost on a large market actor (which is generally hard to avoid), that actor has a financial incentive (and in some versions of the world, perhaps an obligation to its shareholders) to vigorously oppose the rule. By contrast, if the benefit of that same proposal is broadly dispersed across market actors, those actors have a (much) smaller financial incentive to engage, and it would be on behalf of a hypothetical gain rather than a certain loss.

This contrast becomes even more extreme where the Commission seeks to regulate in the "public interest." In that case, the beneficiaries of a rule may well in fact receive a significant quantifiable benefit – as in the case of systemic market failures as discussed above – but they are far more likely to recognize the SEC as the South Eastern Conference (a college football conference) than have a view or appreciation of financial regulation. The same goes for "system-level" issues where critical benefits are, by definition, so broadly dispersed they become hard to measure or meaningfully compare to more concentrated costs.

Thus, the structural incentives to engage regulators, and deploy your resources in that effort, fall heavily in favor of larger incumbents who seek individual benefits, often at a cost to broader system health.

## Advice for the System-Level Investing Policy Actor

With all of this in mind, it's critical to be efficient and effective with your policy engagement. To that end, I offer the following thoughts.

**Understand the operating parameters of your decision maker.**

If your theory of change requires a regulator to reach a certain decision, it's critical to understand how that actor reaches decisions.

- Legal authority: In the US, the SEC and other federal agencies are governed by the Administrative Procedures Act, which determines what agency actions can be challenged in court. The SEC's authority comes from statutes that are cited in every rule proposal; every agency's actions must be supported by one of those authorities. The more specific the better. Consider where and how your ask fits in.

- Judicial review: The landscape for judicial review has fundamentally shifted. As discussed above, the ability of private parties to challenge agency review has expanded dramatically. The high-water mark for advocacy is where the agency's authority is clear and the action you're asking for fits squarely within that authority. Anything more ambiguous should be considered in the context of an appellate court strategy.

231

- Congressional oversight: The SEC's budget is approved by Congress, which has oversight and subpoena powers and can directly overturn agency action under the Congressional Review Act.

- Commission approval: SEC action generally requires the approval of a majority of the Commissioners (unless authority has been delegated to the staff level). Every Commissioner and Chair will have their own idiosyncratic drivers to consider but the structural parameters identified here offer framing to hone your message and strategy across the board.

**Read the regulatory text first and know what you're asking for.**

When it comes to policy making, there's typically a lot of discussion and analysis - perhaps hundreds of pages - but the language that matters most is what goes into the regulation. Start there and develop a clear thesis about how it would or wouldn't work and how you would improve it. Bonus points for line edits and/or if you can justify the change legally or with any (quantifiable) cost benefit analysis.

**Survey the landscape.**

- Identify the key decision makers. At the SEC, the Chair determines the agenda, which means the Chair and their staff have a disproportionate influence on what goes into the first draft. The Chair usually needs the support of both majority Commissioners to vote something out, giving them veto power. Minority Commissioners, especially if they support a rule, may also influence the final policy. And career staff are the front lines, they typically hold the pen, bear responsibility for the legal and economic analysis, and play an important role in the outcome.

- Understand who else is on the map, both for and against you. Reading comment letters of parties you disagree with can often be the most enlightening. When possible, finding some consensus outside of the Agency can deliver huge value. Rallying allies behind a specific solution or approach can begin to counteract the structural asymmetry described above. Engaging un-aligned voices or unlikely allies to stake out some common ground is doubly impactful.

- Finally, consider your key messengers. Beyond investors, companies and other market intermediaries, they may include experts, elected officials, or leaders from the business community.

**Submit your own letter.**

If you're filing a comment letter, submit your own. Sign on letters are often reduced to an "et. al." and don't carry the heft of their signatories or assets represented. Even if you write a brief letter generally endorsing another party's submission, it will likely have a greater impact. Investor coalitions play a critical role in building consensus and sharing resources to support these engagements. They can also provide an efficient mechanism for coordinating meetings with regulatory bodies and their staff or directly representing members.

**Engage directly.**

Once you know what you're asking for, ask for a meeting. At the end of the day, these are still systems run by human beings. Connect with them. Government officials can't share information that's not already public so don't expect to leave with new intel. But they are public servants and, I believe, earnest about serving their mission. Yes, there is plenty of naked politics in D.C. (as well as in Brussels, London and other capitals of financial regulation). And yes, these issues are often determined by hyper-specific issues that may reside well outside your wheelhouse, sphere of influence, or ability to engage. But I believe efforts to share specific market insights, even with decision makers with whom you disagree, are worthwhile.

While the current context may present new and growing challenges, the train tracks will still be there, silently determining where you are able to move. A savvy and targeted strategy to lay the tracks needed for system-level investing to succeed is essential for the field today and builds our opportunities to do the work tomorrow.

Chapter 14:

# Capital Market Assumptions and System-level Investing

## By Scott Kalb and Paul O'Brien[145]

## Introduction

To mobilize capital from asset allocators toward system-level challenges, including climate change, we need to build a top-down, systematic approach explicitly focused on risk and return. Sustainability advocates should support this orientation, recognizing that financial performance – both in terms of return potential and risk mitigation – is essential for allocators to take meaningful action in their portfolios toward solutions.

---

[145] Scott Kalb is the former CIO and Deputy CEO of the Korea Investment Corporation (KIC), Korea's $200 billion sovereign wealth fund. Mr. Kalb currently serves as Director of the Responsible Asset Allocator Initiative at the Fletcher School, sponsor of the Responsible Financial Benchmarking Lab (RFBL), and Chairman of the Sovereign Investor Institute at Institutional Investor. Paul O'Brien is former Deputy CIO of the Abu Dhabi Investment Authority (ADIA), one of the world's largest sovereign wealth funds. Currently Paul serves as Trustee for the Wyoming Retirement System and Senior Consultant for the Responsible Financial Benchmarking Lab (RFBL). He holds a Ph.D. in Economics from the University of Minnesota. This chapter reflects Paul's personal views and not those of the Wyoming Retirement System.

One powerful way to operationalize this approach to face, for example, climate change risks, is by climate-adjusting Capital Market Assumptions (CMAs). CMAs provide long term (usually 10- to 20-year) risk and return expectations across asset classes and regions. They serve as foundational inputs for portfolio construction and strategic asset allocation models. By adjusting CMAs to reflect climate-related risks and opportunities, asset allocators can better align their portfolios with emerging realities.

Adjusting CMAs to reflect climate change can be a model for managing other system-level investing challenges. By connecting systematic concerns with tangible economic and financial outcomes, CMAs can be a powerful tool to highlight the consequences of inaction, the potential for better risk-adjusted returns from adjusting portfolios and ultimately help to mobilize capital for system level solutions.

Our research indicates that most current CMAs have not been fully adjusted to account for future climate change impacts. They remain heavily weighted toward historical trends and prices. Yet as global warming accelerates, those historical anchors may no longer apply. We are entering uncharted territory; current projections show us reaching 2.7 degrees Celsius above pre-industrial temperature levels by the end of the century – conditions never seen before in human history. In such a context, heavily weighting historic assumptions leads to mispricing both risk and opportunity.

Most allocators who embed sustainability into their portfolios emphasize that return and risk benefits are essential to justify such investments. Few believe that meeting sustainability objectives alone is sufficient. Adjusting CMAs to reflect climate impacts can help make the financial risk/return case – clearly, credibly, and in terms that resonate with institutional decision-makers.

Climate-adjusted CMAs offer a way forward. They allow asset allocators to align portfolios with probable future outcomes under various global warming scenarios, helping to minimize risks embedded in legacy exposures while capturing upside from investments in climate solutions. This approach is consistent with fiduciary obligations and the legal requirement to prioritize financial performance.

## Defining Capital Market Assumptions (CMAs)

Asset owners spread their investments across multiple asset classes such as stocks, bonds, real estate and private equity. They aim to take advantage of diversification, as different asset classes are not perfectly correlated and will behave differently in different situations. To help in this exercise of allocating capital across asset classes, investors typically start with Capital Markets Assumptions (CMAs).

CMAs are estimates of future risk and returns of different asset classes, as well as the correlations between them.[146] Expected returns are typically expressed as an annual rate of return. Risk is typically expressed as an expected volatility (standard deviation). Correlations between the asset classes suggest how effective diversifying among them is at reducing volatility. Risk is a much richer concept than just statistical volatility, but CMAs make that simplification easier to use.

Asset class CMAs typically look ahead 10 or more years. Shorter time horizons can become dominated by noise and unpredictable events. Looking further ahead averages out some of that volatility, but not too far. Beyond 10- to 15 years, unforeseen trends can start to dominate outcomes, and the range of possible futures grows too wide to be useful. (This point will be important for the sustainability part of the discussion. Outcomes expected only after a much longer time may not emerge from the large uncertainty at that time horizon.)

Here as an example, are the average 2025 CMAs across a range of providers, as compiled by Horizon Actuarial Services, LLC[147]

---

[146] CMAs can also apply to individual securities or investments. We will confine ourselves here to their use with asset allocation and so focus on asset class CMAs.

[147] Horizon Actuarial 2025 Survey of Capital Market Assumptions, Horizon LLC, https://www.horizonactuarial.com/survey-of-capital-market-assumptions

# Chart 1: Ten Year Returns and Standard Deviations for Select Asset Classes

|  | 10-Year Return | Standard Deviation |
|---|---|---|
| US Equity | 6.4% | 16.5% |
| Non-US Developed Equity | 7.0% | 18.2% |
| EM Equity | 7.4% | 22.4% |
| US TIPS | 4.4% | 6.0% |
| US IG Credit | 5.0% | 6.2% |
| US High Yield | 6.0% | 9.8% |
| EM Debt | 6.0% | 10.6% |
| Private Equity | 9.1% | 22.2% |
| Real Estate | 6.2% | 16.2% |
| Private Debt | 7.9% | 11.8% |

*Table by Paul O'Brien. Data from the Horizon Actuarial 2025 Survey of Capital Markets Assumptions*

# Chart 2: Expected Return vs. Standard Deviation

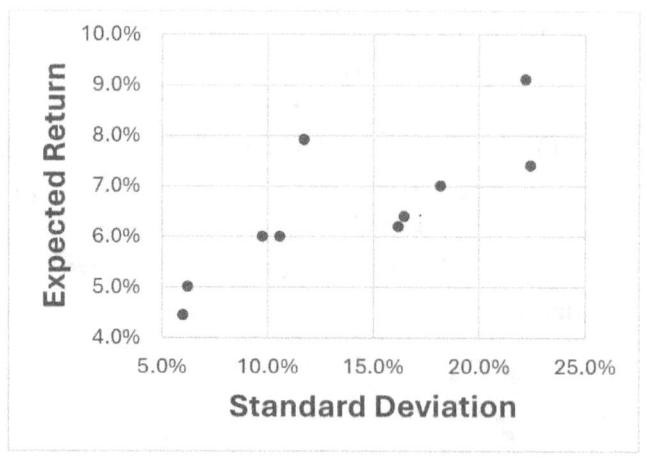

*Table by Paul O'Brien. Data from the Horizon Actuarial 2025 Survey of Capital Markets Assumptions*

These charts reveal two usual characteristics of expected returns:

- Higher returns come with higher risks. This reflects an assumption about how capital markets work: Investors understand risk and demand a higher return for bearing greater risk.

- As projected volatility goes up, so does the range of expected returns across asset classes.

## How are Capital Market Assumptions Used?

CMAs can address the asset allocation problem. For a given allocation of wealth across different asset classes, asset owners can use CMAs to calculate their resulting expected portfolio return and standard deviation. Typically, the asset owner will find their optimal allocation across asset classes, one that gives them the combination of return and risk that best aligns with their goals. For example, the asset owner could fix the highest risk of loss they are willing to accept and seek the highest expected portfolio return within that level of risk.

This balance of risk and return is of critical interest to asset owners. For example, in the defined benefit pension industry, the portfolio expected return is key to determining the actuarial soundness of the pension fund: Will the portfolio be able to support promised benefits? If the expected return is too low, the government or workers may have to increase contributions, or future benefits could be limited. But risk matters too.

Higher risk can be a route to higher returns, but it can also lead to higher possible losses. Investment losses can hurt the fund's ability to pay benefits. Ultimately, it is realized returns that pays benefits, not expected returns.

There is an important technical point here about CMAs that is relevant from the standpoint of sustainability. The attractiveness of an asset class or portfolio is not just a function of its expected return. Risk, especially downside risk, matters too. Potential scenarios of climate change matter for asset classes and portfolios not just through expected return, but also through greater chances of bad outcomes.

## How are Capital Markets Assumptions Determined?

Generally, two sources of information go into creating CMAs. The first is history: Investors assume that the world evolves slowly and that investor and market behavior is reasonably stable. Asset classes are represented by benchmarks, typically comprehensive lists of securities compiled by index providers and weighted by the capitalization of each security. For example, the U.S. equity asset class could be represented by the S&P 500. Future rates of return and volatility of U.S. equities would be assumed to follow the historical averages of the S&P500, which can be measured over the past century or so.

The second source of information is the future, or at least a prediction of the future based on economic models or identifying trends. One common example is demographics. The U.S. population and labor force now grow more slowly than in the past. As labor force growth drives economic growth, this would suggest that future returns on U.S. equities might be lower than past averages.

A second example, relevant for sustainability, would be the potential financial impact of climate. Climate change has had little or no impact on the U.S. economy over the past century and so would not have had much impact on realized equity benchmark returns. If climate impacts become material in the future, CMAs should reflect that.

Different sources of CMAs put different emphases on history versus projections of the future. Most practitioners put some weight on both, but traditionally, CMAs have been as much as 60- to-70 percent weighted in long-term historical returns, volatilities, and correlations. This reflects a foundational belief in mean reversion and trend persistence, especially over multi-decade horizons.

Part of the reason for historical anchoring of CMAs has to do with data availability: Historical returns are abundant and auditable, making them attractive for compliance and documentation. Another has to do with risk modeling: Volatility and covariance matrices are often built from trailing data, and this may reinforce a backward-looking approach.

Overall, allocators tend to favor historical data for asset classes like stocks and bonds that have been around for decades. Future facing models and projections tend to be used for newer asset classes, such as private debt, that have short available histories, or when fundamental forces change, such as when a country successfully implements an inflation target.

While any investor could build their own CMAs, in practice they generally come from a small number of specialist providers, primarily investment banks, asset managers and investment consultants. This partly reflects resource constraints. With dozens of asset classes in capital markets today, doing the work for each requires significant knowledge and resources. In addition, CMAs are not intended to be changed frequently. So, it is more efficient to delegate the derivation of CMAs to specialists serving many investors to take advantage of specialist expertise and smooth the workflow.

## Final Thoughts on CMAs

A number of concerns about CMAs can become important when considering the financial impact of sustainability. A summary might include:

- It's tough to know if they are right. Modern economies and financial markets have been around for less than a century. We don't have enough independent 10-year outcomes to test approaches for creating CMAs.

- The focus on the past surely introduces biases. We know the world is not static. We learn new things over time like, for example, externalities. Activities like burning fossil fuels can have consequences that only become apparent over time.

- Statistical measures like volatility are incomplete measures of risk. For example, volatility is usually modeled to be symmetric (a Gaussian distribution), but many risks can have very skewed distributions of outcomes.

- Providers of CMAs can face commercial conflicts of interest that bias their results. CMAs that are too "pessimistic" can be a tough sell and can turn clients away. And since CMAs cover such long periods, it's not practical to wait long enough to identify biases.

- Another source of bias is the political environment. Some providers and users of CMAs may resist the explicit consideration of climate or other issues related to ESG issues.

Finally, CMAs can be vulnerable to the phenomenon of "herding" that affects many asset owners. While asset owners should prioritize reaching their own goals, they often compare themselves with peers. This discourages using CMAs that differ materially from the consensus. This, in turn, means CMAs don't adequately incorporate information that may imply anything more than incremental change.

## Adjusting CMAs for Climate Change: Methodology and Application

Climate-adjusted Capital Market Assumptions (CMAs) begin with the standard CMA architecture: expected returns, volatilities, and correlations across asset classes over 10- to-20-year horizons. The climate adjustment process builds on this foundation by layering in modifiers that reflect climate-related risks and opportunities, both physical- and transition-related. These adjustments do not seek to replace traditional CMAs, but to refine them with climate-relevant inputs improving realism, strategic clarity, and risk-return fidelity.

Physical risk overlays incorporate hazard-specific data – such as heatwaves, wildfires, and floods – into asset class volatility and downside risk estimates. These overlays rely on geospatial models and catastrophe analytics to assess regional exposure, and they adjust volatility and tail risk assumptions based on modeled hazard frequency and severity.

Sectoral damage multipliers are applied to expected returns based on sector-specific vulnerability to physical risks. For example, infrastructure and agriculture may face higher downside adjustments in high-risk regions. These multipliers derive from historical damage data and forward-looking hazard models, and help differentiate risk exposure across sectors within the same asset class.

Regional vulnerability indices reflect adaptive capacity, governance quality, and infrastructure resilience. These indices are used to adjust both return and volatility assumptions at the regional level, allowing for more granular differentiation across geographies.

Transition risk modifiers adjust assumptions based on policy momentum, carbon pricing trajectories, and technology adoption rates. Sectors exposed to regulatory shifts – such as fossil fuels or autos – may see downward pressure on returns, while climate solution sectors like renewables and green infrastructure may receive upward adjustments.

Adjustments are applied at the asset class level, with sub-regional and sectoral granularity where data allows. All modifications are documented with source transparency and methodological notes to ensure auditability.

## The Challenges of Adjusting CMAs for Climate Change – "Known Unknowns"

While the causes and potential consequences of climate change are well understood, adjusting CMAs to reflect these risks remains a significant challenge. The timing, magnitude, and pathways of global warming remain uncertain, and historical data offers limited guidance, and the uncertainty compounds the inherent difficulty of building effective risk and return models over extended time horizons.

One major challenge is the unknown trajectory of temperature rises. Climate scenarios are not expected to diverge meaningfully until around 2035, with the most dramatic differences emerging after 2050. Recent physical impacts from climate change, for example, the wildfires in LA, heat waves in Europe and floods in Sub-Saharan Africa, have led to disruptions, costly damage and even loss of life, but these events have been manageable and, in a way, may reduce the sense of urgency among investors in the short-term, especially during periods when financial markets are buoyant. Asset allocators manage intergenerational capital, but are not immune to short-term performance pressures – pressures that can inhibit strategies with longer-term climate payoffs.[148]

---

[148] Wong, De Rui, GIC; Kim, Kee Bum, GIC; "Sizing the Inevitable Investment Opportunity: Climate Adaptation" https://www.gic.com.sg/thinkspace/sustainability/sizing-the-climate-adaptation-opportunity/

## Chart 3: Global Warming Pathways in Climate Change Scenarios

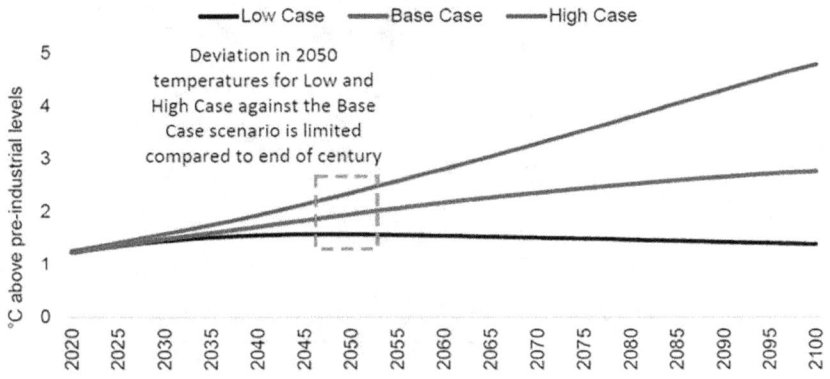

Figure 4: Global warming pathways in climate change scenarios

Source: GIC Sustainability Office analysis, Bain & Company, IPCC

Another challenge lies in the statistical nature of climate models. Temperature projections tend to be positively skewed (skewed to the right) and exhibit fat tails (kurtosis) - meaning they predict a higher likelihood of extreme outcomes than a normal distribution would suggest. Fat-tailed models suggest that the long tail of extreme outcomes will drag mean temperature higher and do a better job of capturing risk than average or median temperatures.

As shown in the chart below, the highest-probability temperature rise is 2.7 degrees above baseline – the current base case. However, there is also a 30 to 40 percent chance of reaching 3.0 degrees, and a 10- to-20 percent chance of hitting 4.8 degrees: both devastating scenarios with non-trivial probabilities.[149]

---

[149] Trust, Sandy; Bettis, Oliver; Saye, Lucy; Bedenham, Georgina; Lenton, Timothy; Abrams, Jesse; Kemps, Luke; "Climate Scorpion– the sting is in the tail;" IFOA, March 2024; https://actuaries.org.uk/media/g1qevrfa/climate-scorpion.pdf

## Chart 4: Fat-Tailed Distribution of Global Warming Outcomes

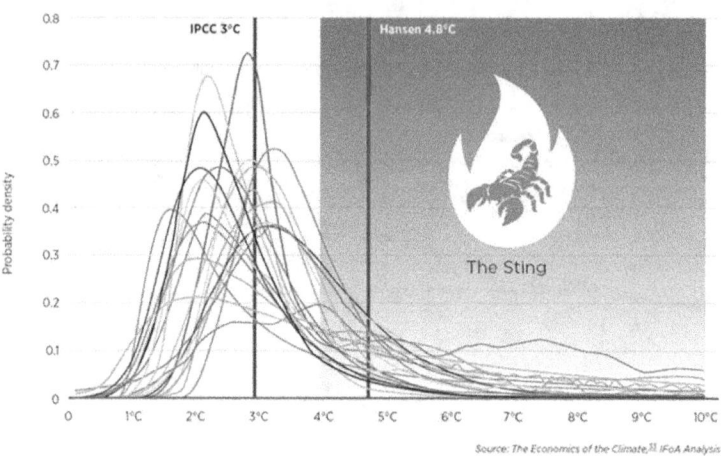

*Source: The Climate Scorpion: The Sting Is in the Tail,*

A third challenge is the phenomenon of "distributional shift" or "mean shift," where the entire probability curve shifts to the right over time. As temperatures rise, events once considered rare – such as heat waves – become part of the normal distribution. These events also tend to accelerate faster than less extreme ones, leading to a nonlinear increase in climate-related damage and cost.[150] In effect, as temperatures rise, the curve of probable climate impacts shifts to the right. While the area in the older curve which included the probability of severe heat waves (shown in orange in the chart below) was very low, the probability of heat waves increases dramatically in the new bell curve due to distributional shift, as does the likelihood of breaching climate thresholds or tipping points.[151]

---

[150] Dr. Kapnick, Sarah; "Introduction to Climate Intuition. Navigating the New Climate Era;" JP Morgan; https://www.jpmorgan.com/content/dam/jpm/cib/documents/Building_intuition_for_strategic_decision_making.pdf

[151] Tandon, Ayesha. *Q&A: The Evolving Science of "Extreme Weather Attribution,"* Nov 18, 2024, Carbon Brief https://www.carbonbrief.org/qa-the-evolving-science-of-extreme-weather-attribution/

## Chart 5: Distributional Shift in Heatwave Probability

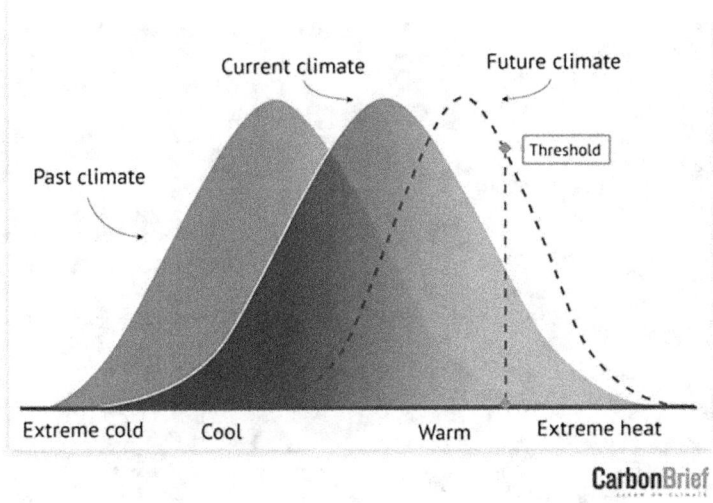

*Source: Carbon Brief. The changing probability of crossing a threshold in the past, present and future climates.*

A fourth challenge involves the reclassification of extreme events. What were once considered "Black Swan" events – unknown unknowns that are rare and unpredictable – are increasingly part of the normal distribution. Today's fat-tail risks would have been seen as Black Swans in earlier models. These events are no longer outside the frame of reference; they are becoming embedded in daily life.[152] This can be seen in the chart below.

---

[152] Ibid

## Chart 6: Tail Risk and Shifting Distributions (flood risk example)

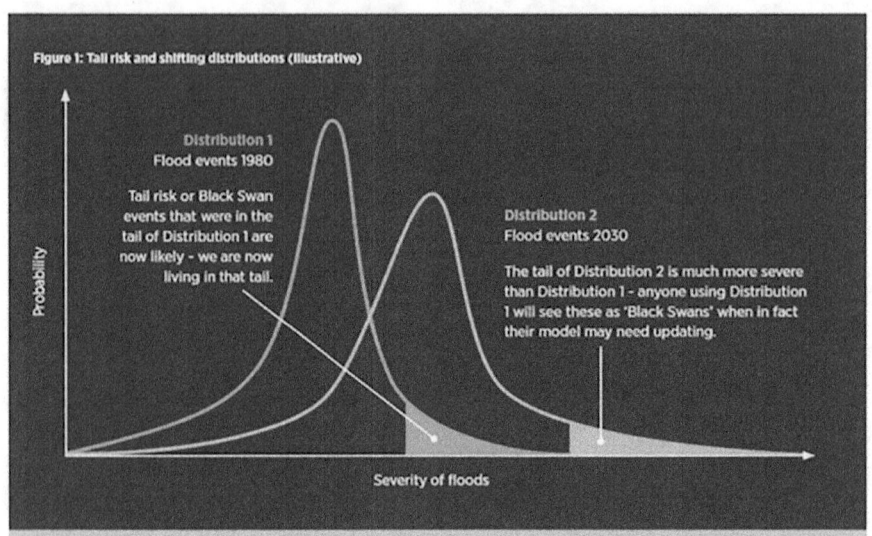

*Source: Climate Scorpion: the Sting is in the Tail, (IFOA)*

Asset allocators can no longer afford to treat climate risks as Black Swans. Instead, they should be viewed as "Black Elephants" – known unknowns that combine the ignored obviousness of the elephant in the room with the unpredictability of Black Swan events. While we may not fully understand the timing or magnitude of future climate risks, we can plan for them, research them, and build contingencies into portfolios.

Perhaps the most daunting challenge in modeling climate change risks is that we are entering uncharted territory. As shown in the chart below, before the end of the century, global temperatures are expected to exceed levels not seen in human history.[153] For over 10,000 years, humanity has lived

---

[153] FIGURE 4 - Humanity's journey on Earth – Human population size and global temperature from 500,000 years before present (BP) until 2100. **Planetary Boundaries Science (PBScience)**. 2025. *Planetary Health Check 2025*. Page 37. Potsdam Institute for

in a stable climatic environment (the green corridor) in which civilization has evolved, adapted, and thrived, but this period appears to have ended. We already find ourselves in new terrain (the yellow and orange corridor) and it remains unclear how a still-growing world population will contend with impacts from a warming planet going forward. Without historical comparisons or case studies to work with, it is difficult to calculate the potential impacts of climate change on society as well as on asset prices, risks and returns, fueling uncertainty and doubt for investors.

### Chart 7: Human History of Temperature Distributions

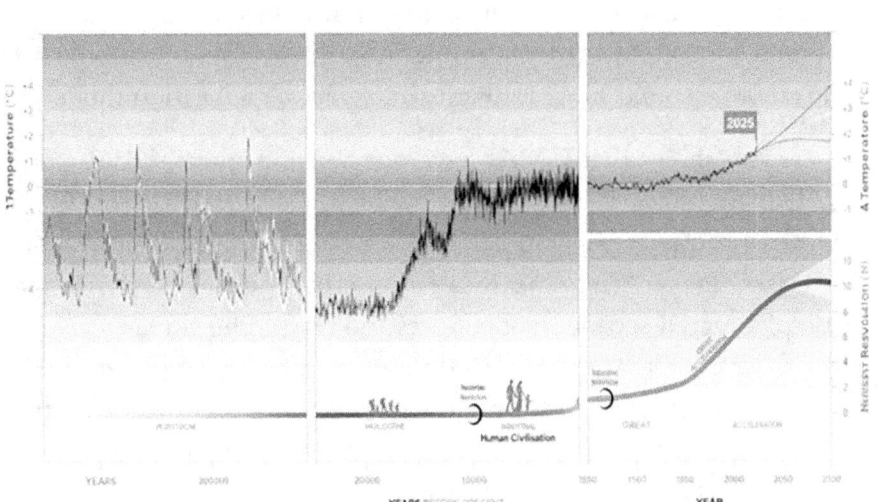

*Source: Planetary Health Check 2025*

---

Climate Impact Research (PIK), Potsdam, Germany. https://publications.pik-potsdam. de/rest/items/item_32589_5/component/file_33151/content

Finally, climate risks are not the only Black Elephants facing asset allocators. Strategic asset allocation models must also contend with technological disruption, artificial intelligence, tariffs, geopolitical instability, inflation, and policy shifts. Uncertainty is an enormous challenge in long-term risk modeling, and climate change is no exception. Adjusting CMAs for climate change must therefore include a focus on expected volatility – not just returns.

## Incorporating Climate-Adjusted Risk and Return Considerations in CMAs

As noted earlier, CMAs are the basic building blocks of portfolio construction, helping asset allocators decide where and how much of their capital to deploy across asset classes to meet long-term objectives. Today, allocators should adjust CMAs to reflect not only climate risks but also broader systems risks, to build more resilient strategic asset allocation models.

Our research shows that CMAs have not been adequately adjusted for future climate impacts. The table below presents average 20-year CMAs for U.S. asset classes. As you can see, long-term forecast returns have been revised upward across nearly all asset classes compared to five years ago, despite record-setting temperatures and worsening climate events.[154] While it's possible that the CMAs do include a climate adjustment that has been overcompensated for by other systemic factors such as technologic advances, our research does not indicate that is the situation. Rather, climate risk has been systematically under-considered.

---

[154] Horizon Actuarial Services LLC; Horizon Actuarial 2025 Survey of Capital Market Assumptions, Exhibit 7m Page 7. https://www.horizonactuarial.com/survey-of-capital-market-assumptions

# Chart 8: Average Expected Returns, U.S. Asset Classes (20-Year Horizon)

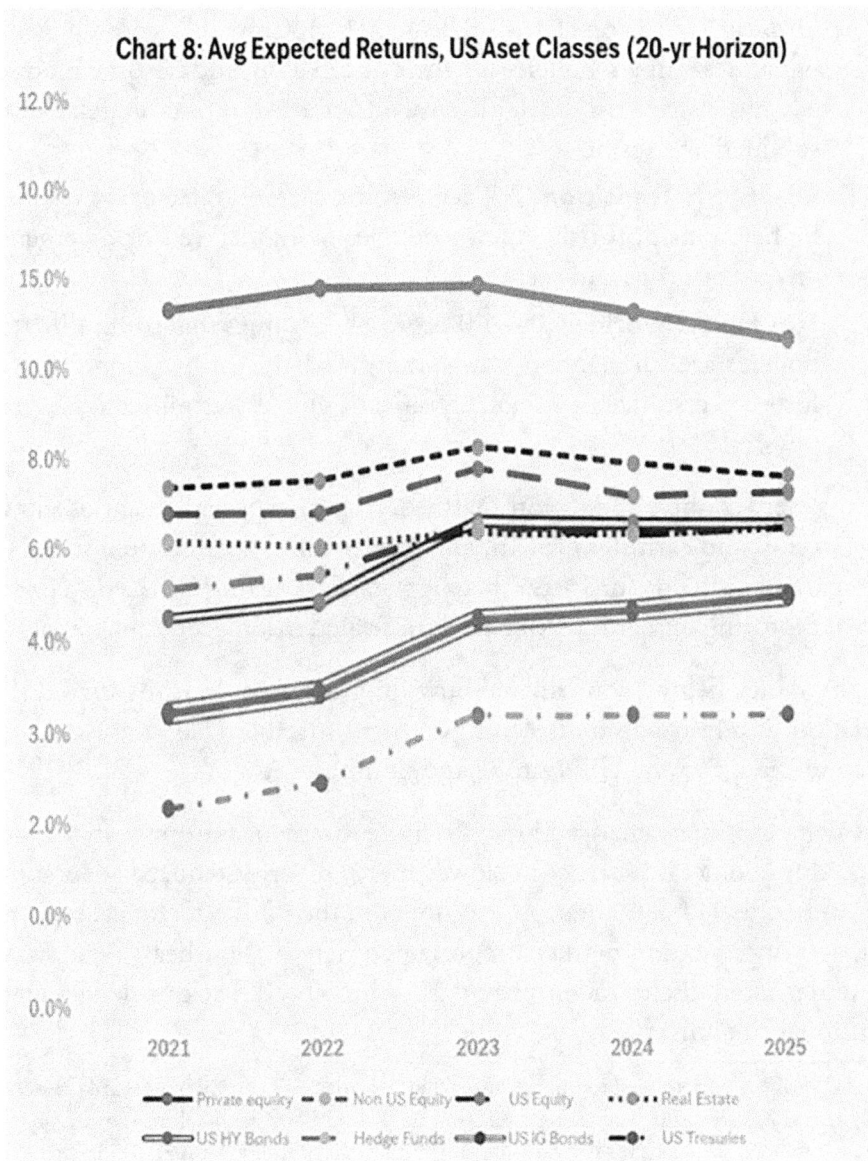

*Source: Horizon Actuarial 2025 Survey of Capital Market Assumptions*

Using tools from the Network for Greening the Financial System (NGFS),[155] we tested these outlooks by climate-adjusting baseline macroeconomic forecasts under three scenarios:

- **Orderly Transition** (1.5 – 2.0 degrees, Paris Climate Accord-aligned) - assumes climate policies are introduced early and become gradually more stringent. Both physical and transition risks are relatively subdued as a result.

- **Disorderly Transition** (2.7 degrees, the current trajectory) explores higher transition risks due to policies being delayed or divergent across countries and sectors.

- **Hot House World** (3.0 – 4.0 degrees) - assumes that some climate policies are implemented in some jurisdictions, but globally, efforts are insufficient to halt significant global warming and severe physical risks.

Across every country and region analyzed, climate-adjusted scenarios show lower GDP and earnings growth, and higher inflation and interest rates, compared to baseline forecasts. This suggests that existing CMAs do a poor job of capturing forward-looking climate-related macroeconomic impacts.

In the tables below, you can see how long-term projections for GDP, inflation, interest rates and earnings growth, decline when adjusted for climate change in the US, Europe and Southeast Asia.

The delta of climate change impacts is more severe for Europe than for the U.S., due to older infrastructure, lower energy security, reduced adaptability, and political fragmentation – as noted in the NGFS technical report. Impacts on emerging markets, represented here by Southeast Asia, may be understated due to incomplete data, which NGFS acknowledges and continues to address.

---

[155] The NGFS is a membership organization that includes 147 central banks and prudential supervisors from 90 countries. It released its fifth vintage of the "long-term climate macro-financial scenarios for forward-looking climate risks" in November 2024. (https://www.ngfs.net/en/publications-and-statistics/publications/ngfs-climate-scenarios-central-banks-and-supervisors-phase-v

## Table 1: U.S. 20 Yr Macroeconomic Projections Adjusted for Climate Scenarios

| United States - 20 year Climate Adjusted Projections | | Orderly 1.5°C | Disorderly 2.7°C | Hothouse 3.0–4.0°C |
|---|---|---|---|---|
| Indicator | Baseline | | | |
| GDP Growth (%) | 2.2 | 2.0 | 1.7 | 1.5 |
| Inflation (%) | 2.3 | 2.6 | 3.2 | 3.5 |
| Interest Rate (%) | 3.2 | 3.5 | 4.1 | 4.4 |
| Earnings Growth (%) | 4.6 | 4.3 | 3.9 | 3.6 |

Notes:

-Sectoral damage multipliers applied to earnings growth reflect exposure in energy, real estate, and manufacturing.

-High ND-GAIN score (~70), shows strong adaptive capacity, but regional disparities (Gulf Coast, Southwest) increase physical risk.

-Aqueduct overlays highlight rising water stress and flood risk in key urban corridors (e.g., Miami, Houston, New York).

-Orderly scenario assumes early carbon pricing and green infrastructure investment; Disorderly reflects abrupt policy shifts and stranded assets; Hothouse models chronic physical disruption, migration, and productivity drag.

## Table 2: Europe 20 Yr Macroeconomic Projections Adjusted for Climate Scenarios

| Europe (EU-27 + UK, Norway, Switzerland) -20 yr Projections | | Orderly 1.5°C | Disorderly 2.7°C | Hothouse 3.0–4.0°C |
|---|---|---|---|---|
| Indicator | Baseline | | | |
| GDP Growth (%) | 1.8 | 1.6 | 1.3 | 1.0 |
| Inflation (%) | 2.0 | 2.4 | 2.9 | 3.3 |
| Interest Rate (%) | 2.8 | 3.1 | 3.6 | 3.9 |
| Earnings Growth (%) | 4.0 | 3.6 | 3.1 | 2.7 |

Notes:

-Sectoral drag from manufacturing, transport, and energy-intensive industries.

-Southern Europe faces rising water stress and heat exposure (Aqueduct Tier 3+).

-ND-GAIN scores reflect moderate vulnerability but strong adaptive capacity (Germany 70+, Spain 65+).

-Disorderly and Hothouse scenarios assume delayed carbon pricing and higher physical damage costs.

## Table 3: Southeast Asia Macroeconomic Projections Adjusted for Climate Scenarios

| Southeast Asia (Indo, Malaysia, Thailand, Vietnam, Philippines, Singapore) | | | | |
|---|---|---|---|---|
| Indicator | Baseline | Orderly 1.5°C | Disorderly 2.7°C | Hothouse 3.0–4.0°C |
| GDP Growth (%) | 5.0 | 4.7 | 4.2 | 3.6 |
| Inflation (%) | 3.2 | 3.5 | 4.0 | 4.5 |
| Interest Rate (%) | 4.2 | 4.5 | 5.0 | 5.4 |
| Earnings Growth (%) | 6.0 | 5.5 | 4.9 | 4.3 |

Notes:

-High exposure to coastal flooding, typhoons, and heat stress (Vietnam, Philippines flagged Tier 4+).

-Sectoral vulnerabilities in agriculture, infrastructure, and informal services.

-ND-GAIN scores indicate low adaptive capacity (Vietnam ~45, Philippines ~50).

-Hothouse scenario assumes chronic disruption to food systems and urban infrastructure.

*Source: These tables were compiled by Scott Kalb, Director, Responsible Asset Allocator Initiative (RAAI) at the Fletcher School, based on data analyzed and sourced from the Horizon Actuarial 2025 Survey of Capital Market Assumptions and the NGFS Phase Five long-term climate macro-financial scenarios for forward-looking climate risks.*

Next, we tested how climate-adjusted CMAs would affect expected returns and volatility across asset classes – equities, fixed income, private equity, and real estate – under the three NGFS scenarios. Consistent with the macroeconomic projections, we found lower expected returns and higher volatility for all asset classes in all regions. Performance deteriorates most sharply under the Hot House World scenario. The tables below make clear that baseline CMA models widely used by the asset allocator community today do not adequately reflect forward looking climate risks.[156]

[156] The NGFS climate adjusted CMA use a building-block approach: Return = income + growth + valuation change. Climate adjustments are applied to earnings growth (equities), yield curves and credit spreads (fixed income), dispersion and scaling risk (private equity),

## Table 4: U.S. 20 Yr Asset Class CMAs Adjusted for Climate Scenarios

### United States - 20 Yr CMA by Asset Class, Baseline vs Climate Adjusted

| Asset Class | Baseline Return (%) | Baseline Volatility (%) | Return @ 1.5°C | Return @ 2.7°C | Return @ 3.0–4.0°C | Volatility Range (%) |
|---|---|---|---|---|---|---|
| Equities | 6.5 | 16 | 6.3 | 5.8 | 5 | 17–21 |
| Fixed Income | 3.9 | 7.5 | 3.8 | 3.5 | 3.2 | 8–10 |
| Private Equity | 8.7 | 20 | 8.4 | 7.5 | 6.3 | 21–25 |
| Real Estate | 5.9 | 12.5 | 5.6 | 4.8 | 3.9 | 13–17 |

Notes:

ND-GAIN score: 61.3 (high readiness, moderate vulnerability).

Aqueduct 4.0 flags increasing drought and flood risk in western and coastal states.

Transition risk is moderate under 1.5°C but accelerates under 2.7°C scenarios.

## Table 5: Europe 20 Yr Asset Class CMAs Adjusted for Climate Scenarios

### Europe - 20 Yr CMA by Asset Class, Baseline vs Climate Adjusted

| Asset Class | Baseline Return (%) | Baseline Volatility (%) | Return @ 1.5°C | Return @ 2.7°C | Return @ 3.0–4.0°C | Volatility Range (%) |
|---|---|---|---|---|---|---|
| Equities | 6.2 | 15.5 | 6 | 5.5 | 4.8 | 16–20 |
| Fixed Income | 3.7 | 7 | 3.6 | 3.3 | 3 | 7–9 |
| Private Equity | 8.4 | 19 | 8.1 | 7.2 | 6 | 20–24 |
| Real Estate | 5.7 | 11.5 | 5.4 | 4.6 | 3.8 | 12–16 |

Notes: Europe includes EU-27 + UK, Norway, Switzerland

ND-GAIN scores: Norway (76.7), Switzerland (72.8), EU average ~65.

Aqueduct 4.0 shows rising flood risk in low-lying and coastal zones.

Sectoral multipliers highlight energy and transport sensitivity.

location-specific damage and insurance costs (real estate). Volatility ranges reflect scenario dispersion and tail risk.

## Table 6: Southeast Asia 20 Yr Asset Class CMAs Adjusted for Climate Scenarios

| Southeast Asia - 20 Yr CMA by Asset Class, Baseline vs Climate Adjusted | | | | | | |
|---|---|---|---|---|---|---|
| Asset Class | Baseline Return (%) | Baseline Volatility (%) | Return @ 1.5°C | Return @ 2.7°C | Return @ 3.0–4.0°C | Volatility Range (%) |
| Equities | 7 | 19 | 6.6 | 5.7 | 4.5 | 20–25 |
| Fixed Income | 4 | 8.5 | 3.9 | 3.6 | 3.2 | 9–11 |
| Private Equity | 9.2 | 21.5 | 8.7 | 7.4 | 6 | 22–27 |
| Real Estate | 6.1 | 13.5 | 5.7 | 4.8 | 3.6 | 14–19 |

Notes: Southeast Asia includes Indonesia, Thailand, Philippines, Malaysia, Vietnam, Singapore

ND-GAIN scores range from 43.5 (Vietnam) to 72.7 (Singapore).

Aqueduct 4.0 flags extreme flood and water stress risk in Vietnam, Philippines, and Indonesia.

Sectoral multipliers show high exposure in agriculture, coastal infrastructure, and energy.

*Source: Compiled by Scott Kalb, Director, Responsible Asset Allocator Initiative (RAAI) at the Fletcher School, based on data analyzed and sourced from the Horizon Actuarial 2025 Survey of Capital Market Assumptions and the NGFS Phase Five long-term climate macro-financial scenarios for forward-looking climate risks.*

Below we show the major sources and tools used for adjusting the baseline macroeconomic and asset class CMAs under the NGFS climate scenarios and a table that summarizes the key differences between climate-adjusted and unadjusted portfolios.

## Table 7: Methodology Summary

| Climate-Adjusted CMAs (2025–2045) Methodology Summary | |
|---|---|
| Component | Description |
| Baseline Source | Horizon Actuarial 2025 Survey, IMF World Economic Outlook |
| Climate Adjustment Source | NGFS Phase V Explorer, IMF Climate Stress Testing Framework |
| Sectoral Damage Multipliers | IMF Working Paper WP/22/145 (firm level productivity studies, agriculture, energy, infra) |
| Physical Risk Indices | ND-GAIN Country Index (vulnerability, readiness), WRI Aqueduct 4.0 (water stress, flooding) |
| Aggregation Logic | Country-level weighted averages by region |

## Table 8: Key Differences, Climate-adjusted vs Unadjusted CMAs

### Key Differences – Unadjusted vs Climate-Adjusted CMAs

| Dimension | Unadjusted Benchmark CMA | 1.5°C (Orderly Transition) | 2.7°C (Disorderly Transition) | 3–4°C (Hot House World) |
|---|---|---|---|---|
| Return Drivers | Historical averages + valuation-based forecasts | Adjusted for green innovation and sector rotation | Adjusted for abrupt policy shocks and stranded assets | Adjusted for severe physical risk and sovereign stress |
| GDP & Inflation Inputs | Consensus macro forecasts | NGFS orderly overlays with stable inflation | NGFS overlays with inflation volatility | NGFS overlays with stagflation and supply chain shocks |
| Sector Weighting | Market-cap weighted | Tilted toward low-carbon sectors | Penalizes carbon-intensive sectors | Penalizes climate-vulnerable sectors (infra, agri) |
| Earnings Growth | Historical trend extrapolation | Boosted by green capex and policy certainty | Lowered due to transition disruption | Lowered due to physical damage and migration pressure |
| Fixed Income Yields | Yield curve extrapolation | Stable rates with moderate credit spreads | Elevated spreads and downgrade risk | Sovereign fragility and inflation-linked repricing |
| Private Equity Dispersion | Historical IRRs and scaling assumptions | Upside from climate tech scaling | Higher dispersion due to policy volatility | Extreme dispersion; stranded innovation risk |
| Real Estate Valuation | Income + appreciation models | Enhanced by adaptation investment | Adjusted for permitting delays, regulatory shifts | Adjusted for location-specific damage and insurance cost |
| Volatility Profile | Based on historical standard deviation | Slightly elevated due to transition uncertainty | Wider bands due to policy fragmentation | Highest dispersion due to systemic physical risk |
| Tail Risk Exposure | Typically under-represented | Mitigated by policy coordination | Elevated due to transition shocks | Elevated due to climate catastrophe scenarios |
| Time Horizon Fit | Long-term strategic (20Y) | Strategic planning and net-zero alignment | Tactical stress testing and risk budgeting | Long-term adaptation and resilience planning |

*Source: Compiled by Scott Kalb, Responsible Asset Allocator Initiative (RAAI) at the Fletcher School, based on the climate-adjusted CMA scenario analysis in tables above.*

If climate change significantly reduces expected portfolio returns, the implications for long-term investors, such as sovereign wealth funds, insurance companies, endowments, foundations and particularly pension funds are serious – especially in the U.S., where funding ratios are already low. Two-thirds of pension payouts come from investment returns rather than contributions. If returns fall short of actuarial assumptions, funding ratios decline, and plan sponsors and pensioners must contribute more to avoid shortfalls. According to NASRA's June 2025 Issue Brief, "in terms of its effect on a pension plan's funding level and cost, the investment return assumption is the most consequential of all public pension plan actuarial assumptions."[157] This is a critical message for policymakers: ignoring climate risks could lead to pension fund failures.

We estimate that contributions would have to increase by 5- to-10 percent above current levels under a 1.5-degree scenario, and by 50 percent under a hothouse world scenario. See below:

## Chart 9: Public Pension Sources of Revenue (1994-2023)

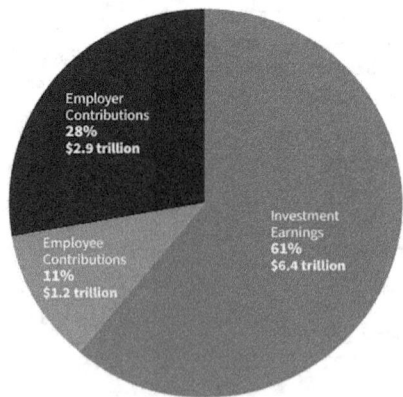

*Source: National Association of State Retirement Agencies*

---

[157] NASRA, "Issue Brief: Public Pension Plan Investment Return Assumptions;" June 2025.

## Table 9: Impact of Climate Change on Pension Returns and Payouts

| Climate Scenario Sensitivity — Pension Payout Impact | | | | |
|---|---|---|---|---|
| Temperature Pathway | Time Horizon | Return Impact | Payout Funding Impact | Key Notes |
| 1.5°C (Net Zero by 2050) | 2025–2030 | −5% to −10% | Mild strain; ~10% contribution rise | Transition risks dominate; long-term stability improves |
| 2.7°C (Current Policy Path) | 2025–2040 | −15% to −25% | Moderate strain; ~25–30% contribution rise | Physical risks rise; equity-heavy portfolios suffer most |
| 3–4°C (Hot House World) | 2030–2040 | −30% to −50% | Severe strain; >50% contribution rise or benefit cuts | Physical risks dominate; infrastructure and real assets hit hardest |

Notes: Based on a portfolio that is 50% equities, 30% fixed income and 20% alternatives, a 6.5% baseline CMA return asumption, weighted average payout mix of 65% investment returns and 35% contributions, a time horizon of 2025-2040, and a discount rate of 6.5%.

*Source: Scott Kalb, Director Responsible Asset Allocator Initiative (RAAI) at the Fletcher School*

## Upside Opportunity: Climate Optimized Portfolios

To make a strong financial case for investing in climate solutions, it is not enough to focus solely on the downside risks of system-level challenges – we must also demonstrate the upside potential of anticipating and managing systemic transitions in the investment environment. Adjusting CMAs to reflect system-level risks is a practical way to accomplish this.

In the below table, we examine the expected returns and volatility of a typical asset allocator portfolio – 50 percent equities, 30 percent fixed income, and 20 percent alternatives – based on widely used benchmarks. When adjusted for the three NGFS climate scenarios, this portfolio shows lower returns and higher risks, consistent with the analysis shown above.

The table also presents a sample "climate optimized portfolio" using the same asset class weightings but based on benchmarks adjusted to reduce risks and capture higher returns from climate-related investments. This

259

optimized portfolio consistently outperforms the legacy portfolio across all climate scenarios, with lower risk.

Under the Hot House World scenario, the optimized climate portfolio outperforms the legacy portfolio by 2.3 percent annually. Compounded over 50 years, this would result in a threefold increase in total value, compared with current portfolios. Notably, even assuming the mildest climate scenario, where global temperatures remain at current levels of 1.5 degrees above baseline, the optimized portfolio still delivers superior performance with lower risk.

## Table 10: Legacy Portfolio vs Climate-Optimized Portfolio Returns and Risks

| Legacy vs Climate Optimized Portfolio, Return & Volatility Forecasts (10–20 Year Horizon) | | | | | | |
|---|---|---|---|---|---|---|
| Portfolio | (Horizon CMA) | | (NGFS Climate Scenarios) | | | |
| | Base Return | Base Vol | 1.5°C CMA | 2.7°C CMA | 3-4°C CMA | Volatility Range |
| Typical Portfolio | 6.50% | 11.50% | 5.10% | 4.20% | 2.80% | 12.2% – 15.0% |
| Optimized Climate Portfolio | 6.20% | 11.00% | 6.00% | 5.60% | 5.10% | 10.5% – 12.2% |

Typical Portfolio Benchmark Weightings: 50% Global Equities (MSCI ACWI), 30% Global Fixed Income (Bloomberg Barclays Global Aggregate), 10% Private Equity & Private Credit (Cambridge Associates Global PE Index and Cliffwater Direct Lending Index (CDLI), 10% Infrastructure & Real Estate (EDHEC infra Broad Market Index and NCREIF Property Index (NPI))

Optimized Climate Resilient Benchmark Weightings: 35% Climate Transition Equity (MSCI ACWI CTB), 15% Adaptation & Resilience Equity (Composite: MSCI Climate Action, S&P Global Water, FTSE Environmental Opportunities (Adaptation subset), 25% SDG-Aligned Fixed Income (Composite: World Bank Green Bond Index, JPMorgan ESG EMBI Index), 15% Clean Tech & Impact PE (Benchmark: Cambridge Associates Clean Tech & Impact PE, 10% ESG Infrastructure & Real Estate (Composite: FTSE Environmental Markets Index, GRESB Infrastructure Benchmark).

The climate optimized portfolio shown above is for illustrative purposes only and does not constitute a recommendation to invest in any specific securities or benchmark indexes. In its current form, it may not be fully investable for most asset allocators due to liquidity constraints and risk budgets. However, this optimization exercise demonstrates that a strong risk-return case can be made for investing in climate solutions. It is not solely about downside protection. Using NGFS models and other tools, asset allocators can adjust CMAs and SAA models to optimize returns – reducing climate risks while benefiting from climate-aligned investments.

## Final Thoughts on CMAs and System-level Investing

Despite uncertainty surrounding the exact outcomes, timing, and trajectory of climate change, there is high confidence that some combination of physical and transition risks will materialize. Asset allocators recognize that they must plan for these contingencies in their portfolios.

Asset allocators need a top-down, systematic approach to investing in climate change and other system level challenges – one explicitly focused on risk and return – to take action in their portfolios. Sustainability advocates should support this orientation, recognizing that financial performance is essential for allocators to mobilize capital.

By adjusting CMAs, we can make a powerful economic case for investing in climate change solutions and other system level challenges. Adjusted CMAs deliver a more accurate picture of the long-term risks of inaction inherent in building portfolios based on legacy benchmarking practices. Unadjusted CMAs that suggest a business-as-usual future – one in which risks are subdued and returns remain stable – can make it very challenging to justify climate-aligned investments.

Climate-adjusted CMAs can help to mobilize capital from asset allocators toward climate-aligned investments by demonstrating better risk-adjusted returns from resilient portfolios. They also can help provide a financially sound basis for a non-political call to action for policymakers.

The Network for Greening the Financial System (NGFS) released the fifth vintage of its long-term climate macro-financial scenarios in November 2024. This technical study provides macroeconomic projections and modeling tools that asset allocators can use to adjust CMAs for climate risks under three core scenarios. In May 2025, the NGFS introduced a complementary model for short-term (3-5 year) macroeconomic projections and CMAs. While not reviewed in this chapter, the short-term model is a valuable addition. It may help allocators develop credible near-term pathways for adjusting asset allocation models and assist policymakers in understanding how today's decisions shape tomorrow's climate costs.

Allocators should critically evaluate the CMAs provided to them by advisors – or build their own – ensuring that climate impacts (and other systemic risks and opportunities) are appropriately incorporated. Climate-adjusted CMAs show unequivocally that long-term returns for legacy portfolios will be lower and risks higher in a warming world. CMAs that suggest otherwise should be carefully scrutinized. Tools such as the NGFS Phase 5 models are available to support this work but further tools are needed.

Asset allocators also should revise their strategic asset allocation (SAA) models to reflect climate-adjusted CMAs. These revised models can serve as a framework for guiding investment decisions around climate strategies and provide a strong financial case to support investing in climate solutions, which would reduce risk and improve long-term performance.

Speaking more generally, this approach of adjusting CMAs to reflect forward looking risks offers a way to bring a broad array of system-level concerns to the attention of asset allocators. We know that systemic risks can translate into impacts on portfolio returns. By adjusting CMAs to reflect those risks, asset allocators can steer the right types of capital into effective solutions and achieve better risk-adjusted returns.

Chapter 15:

# Guardrails and Standard-shaping

By Takeshi Kimura[158]

## Introduction

Currently, the global economy simultaneously confronts several profound structural risks, including climate change, biodiversity loss, and widening inequality. Each of these constitutes a system-level risk that fundamentally undermines the earnings base of capital markets – that is, the stability of market returns.

In addressing such risks, the limits of traditional investment approaches have become increasingly apparent. Conventional impact investing, while valuable in mobilizing capital toward social or environmental objectives, often focuses on single-point solutions – isolated interventions designed to improve outcomes in specific projects or sectors. These efforts, by their nature, generate positive but bounded results rather than transforming the broader systems that give rise to those issues in the first place.

---

[158] Takeshi Kimura is Special Adviser to the Board of Nippon Life Insurance Company, a PRI Board Member, and a Steering Committee Member of the Taskforce on Inequality and Social-related Financial Disclosures (TISFD).

Similarly, the aim of traditional ESG integration is to improve outcomes by integrating environmental, social, and governance factors into company analysis and by encouraging improvements in corporate behavior. Yet risks that affect the market as a whole cannot be resolved through entity-level action alone. Because negative externalities are cumulative and systemic, unless they are addressed collectively, they will remain embedded across markets and continue to erode long-term stability.

System-level investing has emerged as an approach designed to fill this gap. Its purpose is to secure the stability and sustainability of the economy and society as a whole. To achieve this, system-level investing rests on two strategic pillars. The first is *guardrails*: Investor-set criteria that function as internal boundaries to ensure investment activity remains consistent with the long-term health of social and environmental systems. The second is *standard-shaping*: efforts that extend beyond one's own investment actions to influence industry, markets, and policy frameworks, to elevate common rules and expectations.

Importantly, these two pillars are not entirely self-contained. They are connected by an intermediate function – norm-setting. Norm-setting refers to the articulation of investors' fundamental values and outcome orientations, which are then (1), embedded as the design principles of guardrails within investment processes, and (2), externalized as a compass for standard-shaping, offering orientation that can evolve into a common language across peers, markets, and institutions. In other words, it serves as the basis for both internal discipline and external signaling of values.

In this way, guardrails and standard-shaping function as the two wheels of a single vehicle, with norm-setting acting as the axle that links them. Only when combined strategically can they address system-level risks and lay the foundation for a sustainable financial system. This chapter examines the core elements of guardrails and standard-shaping, their complementarities, examples of practices, and the challenges that lie ahead.

# Guardrails: Discipline from Within

Building on the principles of norm-setting, guardrails are operationalized, concrete, mandatory requirements within the investment process. They span asset allocation, mandate and benchmark design, risk controls, proxy voting, and engagement. In the context of system-level investing, guardrails are self-imposed operating boundaries – pre-commitments that keep investment activity aligned with long-term system health.

## *Layers of Guardrails*

Three interrelated layers of guardrails operate at different levels of discipline. First, *stewardship to reduce externality risks* directs company behavior to limit negative impacts. Second, *addressing sustainability arbitrage and trade-offs* ensures that progress on one front does not come at the expense of another. Finally, *universal portfolio consistency* aligns the portfolio as a whole with system-level objectives. Together, these layers form a continuum from company-level action to portfolio-wide discipline.

## *Entity-level Stewardship to Reduce Externality Risks*

Classic guardrails in ESG integration include negative screening and best-in-class selection. Both focus on risks and opportunities at the entity level and aim to improve risk-adjusted returns by selecting or excluding companies. While they function as guardrails to some extent, but are insufficient for system-level investing. Excluding companies with low ESG scores and investing only in those with higher scores does not insulate investors from system-level risks, so long as those and other companies continue to generate harmful externalities.

What is needed as a first step in system-level investing guardrails is *en-tity-level* stewardship that pushes companies to reduce their negative externalities – their adverse impacts on society and the environment. (We emphasize "entity-level" here because later we introduce "system-level" stewardship, and the distinction between the two is important.) For instance, Nippon Life Insurance has about 1,400 domestic equity holdings, and just the top 75 emitters account for roughly 80 percent of the portfolio's total greenhouse gas (GHG) emissions. Supporting the net-zero transition of these high-emitting companies is therefore critical from a system-level perspective. In 2023, Nippon Life developed and published a *Transition Finance Framework* to encourage high-emitting companies to formulate transition plans aligned with the Paris Agreement and the 1.5-degree target. Divestment is considered only as a last resort if engagement yields no improvement. Similar frameworks to press high emitters to develop and execute credible transition plans are now being adopted by many other investors.

### Addressing Sustainability Arbitrage and Trade-Offs

When investors press companies to reduce negative externalities and generate positive outcomes, they must keep in mind two related risks: sustainability arbitrage and trade-offs. While they may appear similar on the surface, their underlying dynamics differ. Arbitrage refers to intentional and avoidable practices where improvements in one metric are achieved by shifting harms elsewhere – for instance, reducing costs through labor exploitation to finance "green" investments. Trade-offs, by contrast, are structural and contain often unavoidable tensions: Advancing one sustainability objective inevitably imposes burdens on another. For instance, accelerating decarbonization may impose short-term shocks on employment and local economies in carbon-intensive regions. The former therefore calls for prevention and deterrence, while the latter requires anticipation and mitigation measures.

For both risks, a common first line of defense is to establish minimum requirements. To operationalize a dual focus on environmental and social dimensions, investors need to apply consistent thresholds simultaneously across both dimensions and institutionalize them as *integrated guardrails* within stewardship policy. In practice, many institutional investors have adopted social enforcement floors alongside climate policies, targeting issues such as human rights abuses, exploitative working conditions, tax avoidance, and public health harms. Building on this, integrated guardrails may include, for example, interim net-zero targets aligned with the Science Based Targets initiative (SBTi) and credible transition plans on the environmental side, as well as minimum safeguards grounded in widely recognized standards – such as the UN Guiding Principles and the OECD Guidelines – on the social side, covering human-rights due diligence and zero tolerance for severe violations. A crosscutting "Do No Significant Harm" (DNSH) constraint should also be imposed to ensure that progress in one dimension is not nullified by regression in another. These minimum requirements should be codified as mandatory elements of corporate transition plans and disclosures, ensuring that compliance is binding at the entity level and not merely aspirational.

## Universal Portfolio Consistency

While stewardship to address environmental and social externalities is vital, entity-level engagement alone is not enough to determine whether an entire portfolio is aligned with the long-term health of systems. Here the next guardrail is Universal Portfolio Consistency (UPC). UPC is a framework for reviewing portfolios across asset classes and testing their alignment with system-level objectives such as climate stability and social resilience.

A typical application is setting net-zero-aligned targets (including interim milestones) by asset class – equities, bonds, and alternatives – and monitoring progress across the portfolio. This practice is already well-established among many institutions. Another is incorporating climate scenarios into long-term capital market assumptions (CMAs), thereby ensuring that return and risk estimates themselves are grounded in system-level realities. For passive investors, adopting Paris-Aligned Benchmarks (PABs) or Climate Transition Benchmarks (CTBs) aligns index construction directly with system-level goals, ensuring that stock selection and weighting support long-term market stability. These methods embed externality reduction into the market's structural design, beyond engagement with individual companies.

Alongside environmental UPC, adoption of a social UPC is growing. Beyond entity-level engagement, it embeds ex-ante social floors – human rights, labor standards, and non-discrimination – into the investment architecture itself, spanning capital allocation, index construction, and manager mandates. In practice, this can include standing watchlists and in some cases exclusion lists based on human-rights criteria; norm-based screening and social KPI tilts codified into index rules for passive strategies; and embedding minimum standards in investment mandates – drawing on the same UNGPs and OECD Guidelines noted earlier – with explicit, manager-facing expectations on disclosure and continuous improvement. These requirements are overseen through portfolio-wide stewardship governance (e.g. a stewardship or sustainability oversight committee), which sets escalation pathways – from engagement and proxy voting to index exclusion and divestment. In this way, operational discipline and incentives to reduce social externalities are woven into investment practice.

Crucially, to curb sustainability arbitrage while also mitigating structural trade-offs at the portfolio level, it is essential to design the environmental and social strands of UPC as a single, integrated framework and operationalize it through aligned asset-allocation and investment-policy criteria.

**Practical Challenges in Guardrail Design and Use:** Guardrails come in several layers and their adoption is spreading, but challenges remain.

## Social Guardrails and the TISFD

In environmental externalities, universal and comparable indicators – most notably GHG emissions – make it relatively straightforward for investors to align engagement policies and measure progress. By contrast, there is no single global metric for social externalities comparable to GHGs. Instead, investors must contend with diverse issues – poverty reduction, workplace safety, education access, gender equality – whose standards vary by region and culture. This makes it harder to harmonize priorities and milestones among investors and often leaves companies uncertain about which benchmarks they should align with.

Against this backdrop, quantitative and comparable indicators such as the share of workers paid a living wage or the implementation rate of human rights due diligence could serve as breakthroughs – a kind of "Scope 3" for social issues. Looking ahead, the final recommendations of the Taskforce on Inequality and Social-related Financial Disclosures (TISFD), expected in late 2027, will likely mark a turning point. TISFD is anticipated to provide a common disclosure framework for assessing inequality and social risks at both the entity and system levels. Such a framework would enable investors to set clearer social guardrails, promote more consistent corporate responses, and ultimately help reduce system-level risks.

## Proactive Integrated Guardrails

Minimum, integrated guardrails can close obvious arbitrage channels across environmental and social dimensions and thereby deter increases in externalities. Yet even where such floors are met at both the entity- and portfolio-levels, system-level spillovers can still arise unintentionally. As decarbonization advances, for example, internalizing externality costs can generate economy-wide inflationary pressure ("greenflation"), eroding the real incomes of vulnerable households and exacerbating inequality. This is not arbitrage; it is an aggregation effect – a fallacy of composition – where individually sound actions, taken in isolation, cumulatively create adverse macro-outcomes.

To manage these unintended, system-level effects, simply setting minimum floors is not enough. What is needed are proactive integrated guardrails. These go beyond floor enforcement by incorporating more ambitious criteria designed to achieve multiple objectives simultaneously. One approach is to establish composite KPIs at the portfolio level – for example, combining climate metrics (such as GHG reduction rates) with social outcomes (such as progress toward living-wage coverage, zero severe human rights violations, retraining progress, supply chain audit coverage). This enables investors to monitor whether decarbonization progress imposes disproportionate burdens on vulnerable groups and, if necessary, to adjust capital allocation.

Many investors already set portfolio-wide net-zero targets for climate, but there is no equivalent, universally agreed goal for social issues. Here, proactive guardrails serve not to enforce a single social "endpoint" but rather to ensure that transitions unfold in ways that progressively expand inclusion and reduce harms. In this sense, they provide an anticipatory overlay on top of UPC, complementing floors with forward-looking, multi-objective discipline and thereby strengthening resilience to macro shocks such as unexpected inflationary pressure.

## UPC and the Challenge of Capital Allocation

While the design of UPC frameworks has advanced rapidly in recent years, translating these into actual changes in capital allocation remains limited. Frictions arise from multiple sources: tracking-error constraints, fiduciary mandates, model uncertainty, divergence from legacy benchmarks, as well as cultural factors like short-term evaluation horizons and career risk.

Several measures can help ease these frictions. For tracking error constraints and divergence from legacy benchmarks, phased adoption – for example, piloting PABs or CTBs before widening coverage – and explicit tracking error management (pre-defined bands) help manage performance uncertainty during the shift. For fiduciary and mandate constraints, contractual clarity – by writing into investment management agreements (and related mandate documentation) requirements such as disclosure of transition plans, quantitative targets, data-submission frequency and format, and pre-defined triggers for reallocation and escalation – reduces disputes over interpretation and modeling assumptions and helps establish clear decision rights. To address short-term evaluation horizons and career risk, staged target-setting (e.g. the Net-Zero Asset Owner Alliance's Target Setting Protocol, which separates short-, medium-, and long-term goals and checkpoints) provides a common evaluation horizon and lowers pressures to backslide. Finally, recalibrating incentives – placing more weight on medium-to long-term KPIs and extending review periods – helps align asset-allocation and stewardship with UPC.

Ultimately, these measures depend on governance structures – such as investment committees and oversight mechanisms – to embed UPC alignment into capital-allocation decisions.

## Standard-Shaping: Raising the Bar Across Markets

While guardrails translate the principles articulated through norm-setting into internal operating boundaries, standard-shaping opens those same principles outward. It extends beyond the investor's own operations to influence peers, companies, regulators, and market practices, with the goal of raising the bar for rules and norms across the system.

In this outward-facing dimension, what distinguishes system-level investing from traditional ESG integration is a shift in emphasis – from changing behavior at individual companies to reshaping the rules and structures of markets and institutions.

271

**Dimensions of Standard-Shaping:** Three dimensions of standard-shaping: *field-building, developing common frameworks,* and *system-level stewardship* each have different foci, but taken together, they span the spectrum from mobilizing coalitions of investors, to creating shared metrics and disclosure frameworks, to influencing the institutional rules that govern markets.

While in practice some accounts treat *system-level stewardship* as the overar-ching concept –encompassing field-building, the development of common frameworks, and policy engagement –others adopt the reverse view, placing *field-building* as the broader category under which policy engagement and other standard-shaping activities are situated. To avoid confusion and to provide greater clarity on the specific mechanisms through which investors can raise standards across markets and institutions, this chapter adopts an analytical distinction: It treats these three functions as complementary dimensions of standard-shaping.

These three dimensions are not meant to be followed in a rigid sequence. There are multiple entry points. For instance, one pathway might be-gin with developing a common framework, then scale adoption through field-building, and ultimately connect it to regulation via system-level stewardship. Another might start directly with system-level stewardship – for example, through policy engagement – which then creates the mo-mentum for developing common frameworks and broader field-building.

*Field-Building: Investor Collaboration to Expand the Common Ground*

For norm-setting to carry real weight, it cannot remain a declaration of belief or policy alone. It requires allies who share the same vision and the creation of a shared foundation across market participants. This process of expanding the common ground is field-building. Specifically, this means enlarging the circle of investors and stakeholders who share common goals, and aligning them around shared expectations, common metrics, engage-ment practices, and support infrastructure – such as joint statements, templates, knowledge-sharing platforms, networks, and capacity-building initiatives – so that market-wide norms can take root.

A classic example is the early stage of Climate Action 100+ (CA 100+). Investors coordinated around a common set of asks aligned with the Paris Agreement and TCFD, expanded the signatory base across regions, and later aligned engagement around a shared benchmark – the Net-Zero Company Benchmark – to evaluate progress on common criteria. This brought discipline to collaborative work, while strengthening capacity and widening the coalition.

Similar field-building is now evident in areas beyond climate. In the area of nature and biodiversity, Nature Action 100 (NA100) has identified priority sectors, companies, and engagement themes to reverse biodiversity loss, presenting a collective engagement blueprint for achieving 2030 goals. On the social side, Platform Living Wage Financials (PLWF) mobilizes investors around a common approach to living-wage assessment, applying shared review cycles and engagement templates to support consistent, comparable dialogue with companies across global supply chains.

### Developing Common Frameworks: Integrating People and Planet

Transforming markets and institutions requires stakeholders to share a common language and yardsticks, enabling coordinated action. To achieve this, field-building expands coalitions and promotes alignment around existing approaches – such as established disclosure or engagement frameworks – while developing common frameworks, new principles, metrics, and disclosure systems that formally structure markets and institutions.

TCFD and TNFD illustrate this framework-development process: investors engaged in multiple public consultations to shape these disclosure frameworks, helping codify their own information needs as users. Similarly, the SDI Asset Owner Platform developed an SDG-aligned taxonomy under the leadership of asset owners, while the CA100+ Net-Zero Company Benchmark was co-designed by the investor community as a yardstick for decarbonization progress. Each function as a framework enabling cross-comparison.

Building on the precedents of recent disclosure frameworks, the development of the TISFD represents a critical next step: extending the framework approach from "planet-side" risks and opportunities to "people-side" ones. Like TCFD and TNFD, it is structured around four common pillars – governance, strategy, risk management, and metrics and targets – ensuring interoperability across frameworks. This shared architecture enables businesses and investors to consider People and Planet dimensions together. For system-level investors, such interoperability provides a powerful support: It allows both sustainability arbitrage and trade-offs across dimensions to be identified and addressed across these interoperable frameworks, reinforcing guardrails.

*System-level stewardship: Investor Action to Reshape Markets and Institutions*

System-level stewardship means that investors engage directly with rule makers as well as companies to reshape market institutions, operating frameworks, and infrastructure. At its core, this involves policy engagement – such as making policy proposals, holding dialogues with regulators, submitting public comments, and contributing views during legislative processes. But system-level stewardship also extends further: Investors may advocate with stock exchanges and standard-setters, press for changes in index and benchmark design, push for reforms to exchange rules or voting frameworks, bridge voluntary standards into regulatory adoption, or even employ strategic litigation and amicus briefs.

The concept is also referred to as *systemic stewardship*, *market-wide stewardship*, *macro stewardship*, or *beta stewardship*. Whatever the terminology, all share the same core idea: shifting the scope of stewardship from individual companies to markets and systems as a whole, and from entity-level performance to market stability and long-term value creation.

An example is CA100+ Phase 2 (from 2023 onward). Alongside entity-level (issuer-level) engagement, participating investors began advocacy with regulators and stock exchanges, supporting moves toward TCFD/ISSB-aligned disclosure and revisions to exchange rules setting expectations for companies to adopt credible transition plans. The Net-Zero Asset Owner Alliance (NZAOA) requires its members to set interim targets and has called on regulators and standard-setters to mandate/strengthen Scope 3 disclosure and to advance interoperable transition-plan requirements.

In the area of nature and biodiversity, the Investors Policy Dialogue on Deforestation (IPDD) has engaged directly with the governments of Brazil and Indonesia, pressing for Forest Code enforcement and other measures to curb deforestation. On the social side, the Human Capital Management Coalition (HCMC) – a coalition of U.S. institutional investors – petitioned the SEC in 2017 to require human-capital disclosure; their efforts contributed to the 2020 amendments to Regulation S-K, which added human-capital resources as a required principles-based disclosure topic.

**Challenges in Scaling and Embedding Standard-Shaping:** System-level risks transcend national borders, cutting across finance, climate, ecology, human rights, and public policy. They interact and compound as they manifest, leaving no investor immune. No single investor has the capacity to manage such complex, wide-ranging risks alone. This makes collaboration among investors, and the creation of shared frameworks through standard-shaping, indispensable. The more investors engage in standard-shaping, the more costs can be shared and the greater the collective influence on the system. Yet several obstacles hinder scaling and embedding standard-shaping across markets, including the free rider problem, proliferation of investor initiatives, and the balance between global foundations and local flexibility.

*Free Rider Problem*

Stewardship in general, as well as participation in collaborative engagements or in the development of common frameworks, inevitably entails costs for investors. However, the benefits extend to the entire market, including non-participants. In other words, a few committed investors bear the costs of standard-shaping, but the benefits are widely shared – a classic free-rider problem.

To mitigate this, asset owners can use their leverage. Specifically, they can require in investment management agreements that managers contribute to collaborative efforts or embed "alignment with international standards" as a criterion in stewardship policies. Cascading such institutional incentives down the investment chain spreads responsibility and cost of standard-shaping beyond first movers. Additionally, collaboration itself minimizes, but does not remove, the free rider problem, as it reduces costs to any participant compared to what it would bear if it undertook the broad stewardship efforts and standard shaping on its own.

Meanwhile, some investor initiatives have introduced accountability mechanisms to encourage active engagement among their signatories. For example, the PRI (Principles for Responsible Investment) is a voluntary organization that requires signatories to submit annual reports and publicly disclose their activities, thereby creating a system where superficial commitment results in reputational risk. The UK Stewardship Code, established and administered by the Financial Reporting Council, is not an investor initiative like the PRI; it is a governmental initiative. However, signing is voluntary, and institutions that fail to meet reporting standards may be removed from the list of signatories. These mechanisms – whether through voluntary reporting requirements or public accountability – make it difficult for investors to remain inactive after signing. This, in turn, reinforces the credibility of the initiative, thereby exerting reputational pressure on non-signatories – particularly as the number of signatories continues to grow. Today, PRI has more than 5,000 signatories, representing over

USD 120 trillion in assets under management. In this context, investors that remain outside face scrutiny to explain their distance from what has become the global standard for responsible investment – an implicit deterrent against free-riding.

## Proliferation of Investor Initiatives

In recent years, a growing number of investor initiatives have emerged, raising concerns among investors about "initiative fatigue" and stretched resources, as joining too many initiatives risks spreading their efforts too thin and achieving little impact.

Faced with initiative fatigue, investors are becoming increasingly selective about where to commit their limited capacity. A prevalent response is to adopt explicit participation criteria, weighing each initiative's objectives, cost-effectiveness, and degree of independence – particularly whether involvement might compromise their judgment or align them too closely with the agenda of dominant actors. On this basis, some investors have withdrawn from broad coalitions once the perceived value diminished, while others have consolidated their efforts into proprietary frameworks to reduce dependence on multiple external platforms and avoid duplication. These strategies do not signal disengagement but rather a disciplined reallocation of resources, aimed at keeping participation both focused and credible.

For initiative organizers, a key design challenge is to prevent duplication and ensure complementarity among initiatives. For example, NA100 and PRI's Spring are both collaborative engagement platforms on biodiversity, but with different focuses: The former leads a benchmark-driven engagement targeting biodiversity while the latter has a narrower focus on deforestation and land degradation. They both combine investor dialogue with policy advocacy. PRI has clarified Spring's complementary scope vis-à-vis NA100 and CA100+, offering a practical example of coordination across initiatives. With clearly divided, complementary roles, investors can deploy scarce resources more effectively, while platforms gain credibility and influence.

## Balancing Global Foundations with Local Flexibility

On global challenges such as climate change, it would be ideal for governments to set shared goals and provide a supportive policy environment for investors. In reality, divergences abound. In the United States, political pushback against ESG has intensified and timelines for achieving net zero move at different paces between advanced and emerging economies. On social issues such as inequality, the divergence is even more pronounced. While inequality is a global theme, its root causes are often linked to differences among countries' public institutions and social systems – education, healthcare, welfare, labor markets, and tax regimes.

For investors, this means that while the goal of standard-shaping should be to foster global common foundations, it must also accommodate local institutional and policy contexts. In practice, this global–local tension manifests as a trade-off between interoperability – to ensure consistency and comparability across global frameworks – and flexibility – to allow adaptation to national circumstances. The ongoing design of the TISFD illustrates this challenge in its effort to align with global disclosure frameworks such as ISSB and GRI, while recognizing that the drivers of inequality vary significantly across countries. To navigate this trade-off, one option would be a tiered approach: establish a set of core global indicators, while allowing supplementary indicators that reflect national circumstances to be selected and applied as appropriate.

Without sufficient flexibility to reflect local realities, global frameworks will fail to gain traction. Yet excessive flexibility risks creating fragmentation of approaches, ultimately increasing burdens for companies and investors alike and undermining adoption. Striking the right balance between interoperability and flexibility is therefore the central challenge in making global frameworks both effective and scalable.

## Guardrails and Standard-Shaping Through the Lens of Fiduciary Duty

Designing and operating guardrails and engaging in standard-shaping must be firmly aligned with fiduciary duty. In practice, this means demonstrating that adopting guardrails and standards to mitigate system-level risks represents a reasonable judgment consistent with the best long-term interests of beneficiaries .

A key challenge is how to make the outcomes of system-level investing visible. Gains in market-wide stability – contributions to beta – are harder to measure and attribute than the alpha (excess returns) targeted by entity-level ESG strategies. This calls for alternative evidence. One approach is to quantify the environmental and social impacts of the entire portfolio, offering a first step toward tracking system change. Several organizations, including GIIN and IFC, have developed methodologies for portfolio-level impact measurement.

Qualitative evidence also matters. Signs of behavioral change among companies through engagement, or early signals of institutional reform resulting from policy advocacy, can serve as interim KPIs. Since no single metric can establish causality between these indicators and system improvements, investors should build a "bundle of evidence" across multiple indicators and case examples, crafting a persuasive narrative for stakeholders.

Ideally, the guardrails themselves should be structured to function as outcome frameworks. If positioned not merely as constraints but as guardrails designed around the sustainability outcomes to be achieved, they can serve as investors' own benchmarks for measuring progress. For example, setting a guardrail such as "reducing portfolio carbon intensity below a defined threshold by 2030" not only constrains investment decisions but also becomes a concrete outcome target aligned with market decarbonization.

On the standard-shaping side, collaborative engagements can benefit from common outcome KPIs. Agreeing on shared benchmarks for measuring success helps close perception gaps, enabling investors to align around what counts as progress even when beta contributions are hard to express numerically. This, in turn, makes it easier to situate investor actions socially, and to gain understanding and trust from stakeholders. Moreover, aligning guardrails with recognized standards provides a ready rationale: They conform to market best practice.

In this way, by making system-level influence as visible as possible, investors can strengthen accountability to beneficiaries and earn their trust.

## Conclusion: Managing the Balance with Pragmatism

To conclude, it is important to recall the complementarity between guard-rails and standard-shaping emphasized throughout this chapter. Guardrails embed emerging standards into day-to-day investment processes, while standard-shaping channels practical lessons from those guardrails back into market norms. Together, they strengthen the institutional capacity to address system-level risks.

This complementarity becomes even clearer when viewed through the lens of scope – the range within which investors can act on their own – and agency – the capacity to execute those actions. Guardrails represent the internal or self-governing dimension of this lens: within an institution's own remit – its mandates, benchmarks, and stewardship policies – each investor embeds discipline, consistency, and accountability within its own processes. In contrast, standard-shaping extends that scope outward through collective agency: across issuers, sectors, and jurisdictions, in-vestors coordinate coalitions, policy dialogues, and standard-setting to shape market rules and norms. The alignment of scope (from firm-level to market-wide) and agency (from self-governing to collective) – each reinforcing the other – lies at the heart of this complementarity.

At the same time, such complementarity does not imply a static balance. The relative emphasis between the two may shift with external and internal conditions.

Externally, headwinds against ESG in the United States and concerns about antitrust have made collaboration among investors more difficult. In addition, for some participants, collectively defined methods or interim targets have become harder to reconcile with their own stewardship approaches. Together with the growing burden of regulatory and disclosure requirements, these pressures can make continued participation in specific voluntary initiatives challenging. These realities are amplified by free-rider dynamics as well as by resource constraints, initiative proliferation, and uneven regulatory landscapes that create friction in scaling collective efforts. In such circumstances, a more pragmatic course would be to narrow external commitments to essential initiatives and redirect resources toward reinforcing internal guardrails that can be directly embedded in investment practice.

Internally, the balance depends on organizational capacity and the maturity of the issues at hand. Where capacity in specific themes is still limited, investing in field-building – such as peer learning to share knowledge and practices – can prove effective. As organizational expertise grows, however, it becomes more appropriate to reduce the emphasis on standard-shaping and focus scarce resources on embedding and refining guardrails. Once internal guardrails have demonstrated their effectiveness and credibility, investors may shift outward again, turning those guardrails into market-wide norms – treating them as quasi-public goods that can be codified, shared, and scaled across peers to reduce coordination costs and promote broader adoption.

Ultimately, the balance between guardrails and standard-shaping is best managed with pragmatism – reviewed over time and adjusted in response to external context and issue maturity, so that investors can remain effective in addressing system-level risks. It is a dynamic process. Such pragmatism is not a form of compromise, but rather a strategic posture – one that seeks to achieve enduring change through collaboration.

Section IV:

# System-level Governance and Accountability

Chapter 16:

# Applying Fiduciary Duties to System-level Investing

## By Susan Gary, Keith Johnson & Tiffany Reeves[159]

## Introduction

While system-level investment practices have been used for years, their growing adoption as a recognized investment approach for improving returns and managing risk is relatively recent. Consequently, like other new investment practices, system-level investing may be viewed by some investment practitioners and lawyers as suspect.

---

[159] Susan Gary is Professor Emerita at the University of Oregon Law School. She previously served on the University of Oregon Board of Trustees and as a Regent of the American College of Trust and Estate Counsel. Keith Johnson is a Director of the Externalities Investment Research Network and former Co-Chair of the Institutional Investor Services Team at Reinhart Boerner Van Deuren s.c. He also served as Chief Legal Counsel for the State of Wisconsin Investment Board, President of the National Association of Public Pension Attorneys and Co-Editor of the Cambridge Handbook of Institutional Investment and Fiduciary Duty. Tiffany Reeves is a partner at Faegre Drinker, where she focuses on advising public pension funds on private investment, fiduciary, governance, legislative and general fund administration matters. She previously served as Chief Legal Officer and Deputy Executive Director at a $12 billion public pension fund in the United States,

Therefore, in certain jurisdictions, fiduciaries still likely need assurance that system-level investing is consistent with their fiduciary duties. This chapter provides an analysis of investor fiduciary duty principles intended as a resource for investors and their legal counsel seeking to understand how fiduciary duty principles interface with system-level investing. Our legal analysis is built on the *Handbook's* demonstration that system-level investing can generate improved long-term investment performance and offer risk management benefits that far exceed those associated with strategies limited to the capture of benchmark-relative alpha (added returns).

This chapter provides an overview of fundamental investor fiduciary duties from a United States practitioner perspective. Nevertheless, the legal principles on which we focus are similar in other key jurisdictions.[160]

In this chapter we focus on the following established legal principles essential in applying fiduciary duties to system-level investing:

- The dynamic nature of the prudent standard of care which requires that fiduciaries use a forward-looking perspective and adapt to changes in markets, knowledge and circumstances;
- The fiduciary obligation to investigate facts that are relevant to management of fund assets; and
- Even-handed application of the duty of loyalty to provide impartial treatment of different fund beneficiary groups that have conflicting

---

[160] See Freshfields Bruckhaus Deringer, *A Legal Framework for Impact*, (July 20212); https://public.unpri.org/download?ac=13902. Freshfields presents a legal analysis of fiduciary duties in 11 countries, including the European Union, United Kingdom, Australia, Canada, China and the United States; ("System-wide risks are the sort of risks that cannot be mitigated simply by diversifying the investments in a portfolio. They threaten the functioning of the economic, financial and wider systems on which investment performance relies. If risks of this sort materialized, they would therefore damage the performance of a portfolio as a whole and all portfolios exposed to those systems... There is no doubt that Asset Owners and investment managers have a duty to understand sustainability risks relevant to their ability to achieve the financial goals they are required to pursue and to take these into account as appropriate in their investment process. We consider that this would be accepted as the position in all the jurisdictions surveyed.") Pages 27 and 88.

interests, such as separate generations with varying investment time horizons and risk tolerance levels.

For broadly diversified institutional investors, systemic broad market exposures are often financially material; they can be responsible for more than 75 percent of long-term fund returns.[161] As a result, investor fiduciary duties, when properly understood, encourage investigation of system-level management practices and support adoption of related asset management practices. For funds where systemic risks present exposure to material financial losses that cannot be diversified away, fiduciary duties may even require that the asset owner adopt systemic risk management practices.[162]

This chapter makes it clear that an investor fiduciary's duty to act as a prudent investor evolves in response to new knowledge about markets, including evolving risk exposures and investment strategy developments. Market context is critical for any investor fiduciary, and this *Handbook* demonstrates that general market systemic risks have been found to increasingly drive portfolio-wide performance. Therefore, to fulfill the duties of care, loyalty, and impartiality, investor fiduciaries have an affirmative duty to develop an understanding of systemic risks and evolving investing practices, as well as to integrate system-level approaches into investment strategies when needed to protect delivery on fund obligations and serve beneficiaries' financial interests.

## Fiduciary Duty Context

Investor fiduciary duties have recently become a politically divisive issue in some jurisdictions, particularly the United States, with conflicting characterizations being promoted by different sides of highly partisan

---

[161] Ibbotson, Roger G., Perspectives: The Importance of Asset Allocation (April 16, 2010). Financial Analysts Journal, Vol. 66, No. 2, 2010, Available at SSRN: https://ssrn.com/abstract=1591170

[162] *Supra,* note 2.

debates. However, much of this debate has overlooked established fiduciary duty principles that have important implications for sustainable and system-level investing. An understanding of the full range of fiduciary duty principles (and their nuanced considerations) is essential for the accurate application of investor legal duties to current risk exposures, real-world circumstances and use of the current knowledge base. This holistic approach has particular importance for legal analysis of emerging approaches like system-level investing.

While the fiduciary duties of prudence and loyalty provide foundational guardrails for investment fiduciaries and receive the most attention, they are more complex and multi-faceted than often portrayed. Unfortunately, fundamental aspects of fiduciary principles are often not mentioned, particularly by commentators without an in-depth understanding of the complexity of fiduciary duties and the evolving investment context.

---

### Primary Investor Fiduciary Duties

- *Prudent Standard of Care (including duty to adapt to changes & act as a Prudent Investor)*
- *Duty of Loyalty to Fund Purpose & Beneficiaries (including duty of impartiality)*
- *Obligation to Investigate Relevant Facts*
- *Diversify to Reduce Losses from Diversifiable Risks (unless imprudent to do so)*
- *Reasonably Manage Costs*
- *Comply with Applicable Laws and Governing Documents*

---

In addition, understanding the different perspectives of asset owners (who are the fund's governing fiduciary body) and investment managers (who are typically delegated responsibility for only a portion of the fund) is essential for accuracy of any fiduciary duty analysis. Commentators often automatically adopt the perspective of investment managers (who tend to be more visible and vocal) without recognizing that the asset owner has overall responsibility for fund construction and investment strategy. Failure to take the asset owner perspective into account can result in use of an incomplete picture that skews analysis of fiduciary duties. Accordingly, this chapter is written from the perspective of a legal advisor to a fund asset owner.

## Dynamic Nature of the Prudent Standard of Care

The trust law standard of care requires a trustee to administer a trust as a prudent person would and includes the duty to act as a prudent investor.[163] For example, the Employee Retirement Income Security Act (ERISA), which governs U.S. private pension funds, instructs fiduciaries to act as a prudent investor *"with the care, skill, prudence, and **diligence under the circumstances then prevailing** that a prudent man acting in a like capacity and familiar with such matters would use in the conduct of an enterprise of a like character and with like aims...."*[164] *(Emphasis added.)*

*The duty of care is intended to protect fund participants, beneficiaries, and endowments held by charities from negligence and incompetence on the part of the fiduciaries who manage the assets. Such protection is important for any fund and may pose particular concern for pension plans, given that the assets represent participants' accumulated life savings. The duty of care broadly encompasses all aspects of managing assets in a fiduciary capacity, and one important component of the duty of care is the duty to act as a prudent investor — but it gets more complicated.*

---

[163] Restatement (Third) of Trusts § 77(1) (Am. L. Inst. 2007). *See also* Unif. Prudent Investor Act § 2(c) (Unif. Law Comm'n 1994) (A trustee shall invest and manage trust assets as a prudent investor would, by considering the purposes, terms, distribution requirements, and other circumstances of the trust. In satisfying this standard, the trustee shall exercise reasonable care, skill, and caution.")

[164] Section 404(a)(1)(B) of the Employee Retirement Income Security Act of 1974.

*The duty to act as a prudent investor is process-oriented and forward-looking. Investor fiduciaries must evaluate investments in the context of how they fit into the overall circumstances and strategies of their fund.*[165] *Specific investments are not evaluated on a standalone basis.*[166] *When exercising fiduciary duties, this focus on process can result in fiduciaries at different funds with dissimilar characteristics or circumstances using the same basic processes but reaching divergent results.*[167] In addition, prudence is not a static concept; rather, it is a dynamic standard that evolves over time as knowledge and circumstances change.

In the first half of the 20th century trustees invested to avoid risk and protect the principal.[168] Trustees were often limited to "legal lists" of allowed investments which analyzed risk on an individual asset basis, and sought preservation of the principal as the paramount goal.[169] As modern portfolio theory developed in the mid-20th century, private investors began to adopt the theory, which analyzed risk across the portfolio and used diversification to minimize risk.[170] This evolution of investment theory made its way into trust law, with adoption by the American Law Institute in 1990[171] and the promulgation of the Uniform Prudent Investor Act at the state law

---

[165] Unif. Prudent Investor Act § 2(c) (Unif. Law Comm'n 1994) (listing circumstances the fiduciary should consider).

[166] *Id.* at §2(b). The requirement to evaluate investments in the context of the portfolio and not in isolation is listed in the Prefatory Note to UPIA as one of the "five fundamental alterations in the former criteria for prudent investing."

[167] For example, variations between funds can also influence system-level investment analysis outcomes due to differences in size, liability time horizons, stakeholder or regulatory limitations, diversification, governing body expertise, etc.

[168] *Supra*, note 8.

[169] For concerns about the pre-UPIA prudence standard, see Bevis Longstreth, Modern Investment Management And The Prudent Man Rule, Oxford University Press (1986).

[170] For a more extensive history of evolution in the application of fiduciary duties, see Paul G. Haskell, *The Prudent Person Rule for Trustee Investment and Modern Portfolio Theory*, 69 N.C. L. Rev. 87 (1990).

[171] The American Law Institute adopted the prudent investor rule in 1990 and published the rule as §§ 227–229 of the Restatement (Third) of Trusts in 1992. The prudent investor rule was renumbered and now appears as §§ 90–92. See Restatement (Third) of Trusts ch. 17, forenote (Am. L. Inst. 2007).

level in 1994.[172] States now apply concepts of modern portfolio theory and the prudent investor standard to all fiduciaries, either through case law or by statute.

This 20th century shift in investment practice took place over several decades, leaving fiduciaries caught between two seemingly inconsistent investment approaches. One 1988 commentator described the tension during that transition, explaining that outdated rules held back investor fiduciaries:

> "A fiduciary cannot behave as a careful, wise, discreet, judicious and prudent man if he acts within the strictures of a prudent man rule that forces him to behave imprudently in the contemporary economic marketplace."[173]

The Third Restatement of Trusts was updated in 1992 to incorporate modern portfolio theory into the prudent investor standard applicable to fiduciaries. The Restatement drafters wanted to capture lessons learned from the difficult transition period, recognizing that as changes in investment industry knowledge and practice continue to evolve over time, the prudent investor standard should also continue to evolve. They added the following provisions to the Restatement:

> "There are no universally accepted and enduring theories of financial markets or prescriptions for investment that can provide clear and specific guidance to trustees and courts."[174]

> "Trust investment law should reflect and accommodate current knowledge and concepts. It should avoid repeating the mistake of freezing its rules against future learning and developments."[175]

---

[172] Unif. Prudent Investor Act (Unif. L. Comm'n 1994).
[173] Lynn Nichols, *Review of Modern Investment Management and the Prudent Man Rule*, 43 Bus. Lawyer 779 (Feb. 1988).
[174] Restatement (Third) of Trusts §227, Comment. f.
[175] *Id.* at § 227, Introduction.

The drafters understood that investor knowledge and investment strategies would continue to evolve, so they tried to make clear that the fiduciary standards should not be interpreted to block adjustments to continued learning. The dynamic nature of the standard of care is particularly relevant to consideration of newly evolving investment strategies like system-level approaches.

It appears that the investment industry and world economy are now in the midst of another period of transition.[176] The risks faced by investors in 2025 have evolved since the 20th century, continue to change, and have grown more interconnected.[177] For example, climate change impacts now increase market risks for companies across market sectors, accelerating uninsurable risks and raising tax burdens.[178] Growing income inequality has depressed consumer demand and GDP while increasing polarization, making it harder to address other problems and could potentially lead to economic recessions or crises.[179]

On the institutional investor side, when modern portfolio theory developed in the middle of the 20th century, institutional investors owned only 8 percent of the U.S. equity market; however, by 2017 they owned more than 78 percent of that market.[180] At the end of 2021, the biggest three institutional investors (BlackRock, Vanguard and State Street) collectively held a median stake of 21.9 percent in S&P 500 companies.[181] Investors

---

[176] Genevieve Hayman, Raymond Ka-Kay Pang, *Reframing Financial Markets as Complex Systems,* CFA Institute Research & Policy Center (October 2025).

[177] Mark Elsner, Grace Atkinson, Saadia Zahidi, *Global Risks Report 2025,* World Economic Forum (January 15, 2025).

[178] Ben Cushing, *The Long Term Will Be Decided Now,* Sierra Club (June 2025).

[179] Anshu Siripurapu, *The U.S. Inequality Debate,* Council on Foreign Relations (April 20, 2022); Pascal Paul, *Historical Patterns of Inequality and Productivity Around Financial Crises,* Federal Reserve Bank of San Francisco (March 1, 2022).

[180] Jon Lukomnik & James P. Hawley, Moving Beyond Modern Portfolio Theory (2021); *see also* Jim Hawley & Jon Lukomnik, *The Long and Short of It: Are We Asking the Right Questions?,* 41 Seattle U. L. Rev. 449 (2018).

[181] Lucian A. Bebchuk and Scott Hirst, *Big Three Power, and Why it Matters* 102 Boston Univ. L. Rev., 1547 (2022).

now are not only impacted by systemic risks but also have influence over systemic market factors that they did not have in the 1970s. These trends created a material paradigm shift that has influenced the viability of system-level investment as a strategy.

Change is inevitable, and fiduciaries have a duty to implement processes that identify, evaluate, and adapt to relevant changing circumstances and knowledge. ERISA uses the phrase "**under the circumstances then prevailing**" (emphasis added) to describe the prudent standard of care as a mandate for fiduciaries to pay attention to investment industry changes and improvements in peer practices, as well as evolution of the knowledge base and real-world circumstances that could create investment risks or opportunities over relevant time horizons. For pension funds and most other funds, this includes the long-term.

Peer practices can serve as a reference point for evaluating the prudence of fiduciary conduct. However, prudence is not a "lemming" standard . Differences in funding status, time horizon, risk tolerance, stakeholders, statutory provisions and other factors preclude application of a one-size-fits-all approach. In addition, prudence is not intended to serve as a roadblock to the adoption of improved practices or to prevent consideration of evolving knowledge and circumstances. In fact, prudence is inherently forward-looking. The word "prudent" comes from the Latin word meaning "to act with or show care and thought for the future."[182] Investors with future long-term liabilities simply cannot satisfy the duty of prudence by considering only short-term returns and ignoring long-term systemic financial risks.

Policymakers, legal advisors and courts should recognize adapting to evolving circumstances is a core investor fiduciary duty.[183] Inflexible statutory

---

[182] *See* Prudent, Oxford English Dictionary (3rd Ed. 2007).

[183] For a more extensive history of evolution in the application of the prudent investor rule, see Paul G. Haskell, *The Prudent Person Rule for Trustee Investment and Modern Portfolio Theory*, 69 N.C. L. Rev. 87 (1990); John H. Langbein, *The Uniform Prudent Investor Act and the Future of Trust Investing*, 81 Iowa L. Rev. 641, 643-35 (1996).

investment mandates, once enacted, can be difficult to revise timely, and can prevent investor fiduciaries from responding to market changes for decades. As discovered in the late 20th century, this can result in unwanted retention of risky holdings while blocking access to new and emerging opportunities. Given the relevance of system-level risks and opportunities described in other chapters of this *Handbook*, the dynamic nature of prudence generally requires investor fiduciaries to evaluate and consider system-level investing benefits in the context of their fund's characteristics.

## Duty to Investigate Relevant Facts

The prudent investor standard includes a requirement that investor fiduciaries investigate and verify facts that are relevant to investment decisions. The Uniform Prudent Investor Act (UPIA) states, as part of its standard of care: "A trustee shall make a reasonable effort to verify facts relevant to the investment and management of trust assets."[184] The Uniform Prudent Management of Institutional Funds Act (UPMIFA), applicable primarily to charities organized as nonprofit corporations, tracks language of UPIA,[185] and the official UPMIFA Comment explains:

> "This subsection incorporates the traditional fiduciary duty to investigate... The subsection requires persons who make investment and management decisions to investigate the accuracy of the information used in making decisions."

Documentation of fact finding and decision making is also important as a means of demonstrating compliance with fiduciary standards. Investor fiduciaries are judged by the care they have taken in their decision-making processes and not on the ultimate outcome of an investment decision.[186]

---

[184] Unif. Prudent Investor Act § 2(d) (Unif. L. Comm'n 1994).

[185] Unif. Prudent Mgmt. of Inst. Funds Act § 3(c) (Unif. L. Comm'n 2006).

[186] Unif. Prudent Investor Act § 8 (Unif. L. Comm'n 1994) ("Compliance with the prudent investor rule is determined in light of the facts and circumstances existing at the time of a trustee's decision or action and not by hindsight.").

For institutional investors with long-term obligations, this duty to investigate includes investigation of facts relevant to both short- and long-horizon investment management decisions. It also contemplates consideration of how fund investment practices at portfolios in one asset class might affect risk and return in other fund asset class portfolios – for example, how short-term risk and return strategies in public equities could affect long-term risk exposure to things like rating downgrades and bankruptcy that can end up being borne by long-term bonds in the fund's fixed income portfolios.

This fact-finding obligation also precludes fiduciaries from jumping to conclusions or blindly accepting assertions about facts. The duty contemplates use of a reasonable, good faith process of inquiry to inform decisions. The scope of this inquiry can be broader than the corporate concept of "materiality," because it extends to determination of what could be relevant to each specific institutional investor. This duty to investigate is central to informed decision-making and contemplates creation of documents that show the basis for fiduciary decisions.

The imposition by courts, advisors, or policymakers of an inflexible short-term approach that ignores long-horizon obligations and fails to encourage forward-looking processes that investigate all relevant facts is unlikely to end up impartially serving the best interests of all fund participants. Investor fiduciaries and portfolio companies both need the ability to plan for and adapt to inevitable future changes in markets, knowledge, and circumstances.

## The Duties of Loyalty and Impartiality

The duty of loyalty is intended to protect fund participants, beneficiaries, or charitable organizations' funds from theft or misappropriation by the investor fiduciaries, from favoritism (toward groups of participants or beneficiaries), or from diversion of trust fund assets to third parties or causes favored by the fiduciaries.[187] In particular, a fiduciary cannot sacrifice investment return or accept additional risk for purposes unrelated to the interests of the beneficiaries or to the purposes of a charitable organization's fund.[188]

While decisions based on personal favoritism do not comply with the duty of loyalty, an investor fiduciary must be able to make decisions based on improving financial returns. New investment strategies that consider reliable information beyond traditional metrics may lead to better financial results, and access to a wide range of strategies and funds may yield better opportunities or present options for lower risk.[189] If the investor fiduciary determines that an approach offers competitive investment opportunities that fit within the risk/return profile of a particular fund, the investor fiduciary should not feel constrained by unfounded presumptions or political arguments about the investment strategy. The fiduciary can choose investments that make financial sense, even if one side – or in some cases, both sides – in the ongoing culture wars misunderstands (or is committed to misunderstanding) the investment strategy. While this may be difficult

---

[187] Restatement (Third) of Trusts § 79, comment. b (Am. L. Inst. 2007) ("Conduct in administering a trust cannot be influenced by a trustee's personal favoritism . . . ").

[188] Fiduciaries for large funds may find ascertaining common interests beyond financial ones difficult, so this discussion focuses on decision-making for financial return. Fiduciaries of a charitable investment fund owe the duty of loyalty to the charity's purposes, and the duty of impartiality may apply to endowments, private foundations, or other funds established for long-term or perpetual existence. Fiduciaries for a charity can consider its purpose in making investment decisions and can accept concessionary returns for purpose-related goals.

[189] For example, use of Bloomberg ESG Scores as part of the investment process has been found to improve long-term investment results. Zarvan Khambatta, Michael Zhang & Didier Darricau, *Are ESG Scores Relevant for Portfolio Returns?*, Bloomberg Professional Services (June 23, 2025), https://www.bloomberg.com/professional/insights/sustainable-finance/are-esg-scores-relevant-for-portfolio-returns/ ("We see evidence of outperformance resulting from the use of the Bloomberg ESG Scores to construct portfolios. . . Investors, whether explicitly focused on ESG criteria or not, may benefit from studying and incorporating these signals into their investment processes. Furthermore, the performance differentials are not fully explained by traditional risk factors, suggesting that the Scores may contain under-utilized information.")

in situations where misinterpretation and politicized attacks from all sides are common, impartial adherence to fiduciary standards is mandatory. As a result, it is especially important that investor fiduciaries document their processes and analyses in the context of the full range of their fiduciary duties, in order to demonstrate compliance with legal obligations.

The duty of loyalty includes a duty of impartiality. This duty of impartiality imposes an obligation to identify, consider and make a good faith effort to balance competing interests between and among different groups of beneficiaries.[190] For example, pension fund fiduciaries manage assets for participants who are already receiving benefits and for those who will not receive distributions for several decades. These different generations of fund participants are likely to have different risk tolerance levels and time horizons. The presence of both 25- and 75-year-olds among fund participants raises the potential for uncompensated transfer of risks and returns between different generations. Investor fiduciaries must protect the long-term viability of the fund and generate sufficient growth in value to pay future inflation-adjusted distributions, while also having funds available to make distributions to participants who are approaching or are already in retirement.

Corporate directors have a similar obligation to manage their companies so as to include a focus on creation of sustainable value for the providers of long-term capital.[191] Exclusive focus on only short-term investment strategies can create serious risks for the equitable delivery of a future retirement benefit for younger participants and for the future competitive positioning of portfolio companies.[192] These are system-level concerns that can cut across asset classes, industries and portfolio holdings.

---

[190] Restatement (Third) of Trusts § 79 (Am. L. Inst. 2007).

[191] Kenneth McNeil & Keith Johnson, *The Elephant in the Room: Helping Delaware Courts Develop Law to End Systemic Short-Term Bias in Corporate Decision-Making*, 8 Mich. Bus. & Entrepreneurial L. Rev. 1 (2018).Available at: https://repository.law.umich.edu/mbelr/vol8/iss1/2.

[192] Companies managed with a long-term orientation tend to outperform their short-term peers over the long term. See *Measuring the Economic Impact of Short-termism*, McKinsey Quarterly 2017, Number 2, at page 57.

Indeed, in 1996, the United States Supreme Court recognized that investor fiduciary duties under ERISA include the duty of impartiality.[193] When interpreting §§404 and 409 of ERISA, the Supreme Court applied common law principles from trust law as part of the foundation for its holding: "The common law of trusts recognizes the need to preserve assets to satisfy future, as well as present, claims and requires a trustee to take impartial account of the interests of all beneficiaries. See Restatement (Second) of Trusts § 183 (discussing duty of impartiality); id., § 232 (same)."[194]

Fiduciary investors for perpetual charitable organizations also must manage assets across different time horizons. A charity's current needs may require distributions or use of charitable funds, while future needs require investment strategies that build long-term wealth to ensure long-term viability. Charities refer to the need for investments that preserve both short-term and long-term capacity as the need to protect intergenerational equity.[195] Universities should be particularly concerned about intergenerational equity as a goal for their endowments, given that common stated mission goals include things like educating future generations of students and solving society's problems.[196]

Investor fiduciaries typically manage assets across multiple generations of participants or beneficiaries or for an entity with perpetual existence. The duty of impartiality mandates careful consideration and good faith efforts to balance risk tolerance and time horizon conflicts between beneficiary generations. Fiduciaries investing a long-term fund, for example a pension fund or an endowment, usually must manage assets to address both short- and long-term obligations. These investor fiduciaries should not be

---

[193] Varity v. Howe, 516 U.S. 489, at 514 (1996).

[194] *Id.*

[195] Economics Professor James Tobin explained, "The trustees of endowed institutions are the guardians of the future against the claims of the present. Their task in managing the endowment is to preserve equity among generations." James Tobin, *What Is Permanent Endowment Income?* Am. Econ. Rev. 64 No. 2 (1974).

[196] For example, see the University of Oregon Mission Statement at https://www.uoregon.edu/mission-statement/.

artificially limited to focusing only on improving short-term returns.[197] System-level investment approaches can be a particularly effective way to bring this kind of time horizon balance into management of system-level risks and opportunities, especially for diversified funds with long-term obligations.[198]

Outside of the United States, legal advisors in the United Kingdom and elsewhere have begun to interpret pension law as allowing fiduciaries at large diversified investors with potential influence on market practices to consider plan members' future standard of living in retirement as a relevant fiduciary financial factor.[199] This has been explicitly applied to allow adoption of a system-level investment approach which uses the principles of universal ownership and collective action to manage long-term system-level financial risks. Given similarity of trust law fiduciary duty between the United Kingdom and United States, there is reason to believe that this analysis could be influential over time in the United States regarding impartial management of intergenerational conflicts of interest.[200]

## Implementation

Investor fiduciaries who might benefit from exploring management of systemic risk exposures should consider adoption of a process for the undertaking. While scope and complexity of the review could vary between funds with different investment portfolio characteristics, steps in the process might include:

---

[197] Withers v. Teachers' Retirement System, 447 F. Supp. 1248 (S.D. N.Y. 1978); Barry Salkin, *The Duty of Impartiality,* 36 Benefits L. J. (Spr. 2023).

[198] See McKinsey, *supra,* note 34, for research finding that companies managed for the long term tend to outperform.

[199] Pensions Age, *Groundbreaking Legal Opinion Provides Further Clarity on Fiduciary Duty Rules* (June 3, 2025).

[200] For example, the Uniform Prudent Investor Act in § 2 includes inflation and deflation as factors that must be considered by fiduciaries when investing fund assets, which appears to make beneficiaries' future standard of living a relevant consideration.

- Engage with knowledgeable experts who can bring trustees and senior staff up-to-speed;

- Learn from other investors who have been through a similar process;

- Identify an advisor (or the right personnel at a current advisor) with the expertise to guide the fund's fiduciaries through the process;

- Conduct an evaluation of systemic risks and opportunities to which the fund is exposed;

- Obtain an analysis of available system-level practices and options that fit the fund's circumstances;

- Consider performance and implementation experiences of peers that have adopted similar practices;

- Take the time to make an informed and prudent decision;

- Adopt (as needed) related investment policies, proxy voting guidelines, asset allocations, reporting protocols, performance expectations and oversight procedures for implementation; and

- Evaluate program success periodically and consider improvements or other needed changes.

## Conclusion

Investor fiduciary duties set guardrails for actions by delegated agents who manage assets of third parties. However, application of only a portion of the full range of fiduciary duty principles can result in mischaracterization of the delegated agents' fiduciary obligations. When new investment best practices emerge, it is not unusual for it to take time for legal and investment advisors to understand how fiduciary duties relate to the new practices. Nevertheless, knowledge, markets, and other circumstances change; the failure to timely adapt to the evolving environment in which investors must operate may result in unwanted exposure to changing financial risks or loss of returns from outdated practices or missed new opportunities. This includes systemic risks and opportunities which can have large impacts on long-term investment performance.

Several fiduciary duty principles can reduce exposure to these effects. They include understanding the dynamic nature of the standard of care, which evolves in response to changes; the duty to investigate relevant facts, which requires that fiduciaries undertake a reasonable inquiry to identify and understand changes (including advances in knowledge) that could impact investment activities; and the duties of loyalty and impartiality, which impose an obligation to identify and manage conflicts of interest between different fund beneficiary groups, including intergenerational conflicts associated with different investment horizons and risk tolerance levels.

These fiduciary duties have implications for system-level investment practices. Informed application of the full range of fiduciary duty principles allows (and in some instances, may require) consideration and application of system-level investment practices, especially at diversified, universal investors. The analysis provided in this chapter should assist investment fiduciaries and their advisors in understanding how fiduciary duties apply to management of systemic risks and opportunities.

# Chapter 17:

# Data and Information Flow for System-level Investors

## By Roger Urwin[201]

## The Data Journey – From Raw Data to Strategic Insight

What problem does data try to solve? All investors have data and information flow (and narrative) as an element in the value chain. The most significant use case is turning data into decision-useful intelligence as part of portfolio management. Data also plays its part in the reporting, accounting and accountabilities of the organization. For the system-level investor, there exist great challenges for the data to capture the essence of the sustainability impacts.

Most think first of 'hard data' but the data explosion currently before us brings much more 'soft data' to the coal face – data that may lack objectivity and reliability, but can prove critical because of the quality of its relevance and materiality. It certainly can add to the narrative. And a lot of ESG and sustainability data is soft.

---

[201] Roger Urwin is Global Head of Investment Content at Willis Towers Watson.

Data is the new oil is an accurate metaphor. Just as oil fuelled the industrial revolution and became the backbone of the 20th-century economy, data is now seen as the key resource driving the digital economy, innovation, and competitive advantage. Its presence in the investors' value chain is hard to overestimate. And like crude oil, raw data has no inherent value. It must be collected, refined, analyzed and processed to extract insights and create value.

The system-level investor, in a nutshell, has distinct objectives, deals with feedback loops, addresses systemic risks, intentionally influences real-world outcomes, and aims to build resilience. This makes any such investor uniquely dependent on data to build the intelligence on the system (with the ultimate goal of value creation which may be "alpha") and to support their system interventions (with the ultimate goal of improving system health).

System-level investors find themselves particularly reliant on a structured data journey that transforms raw inputs into strategic insights. This journey begins with data acquisition – both structured and unstructured – followed by parsing for materiality and quality. The scope and accuracy of sustainability data from companies is in a long phase of improvement to meet the requirements of investors and other stakeholders. The expected standards are rising under the watch of the ISSB and other standard setters and regulators.

**At the time of writing the state of company data provides only limited support to the system-level investor**. The issues are of company-to-company consistency, assurance, contested materiality and how to track and measure sustainability impact. Data on climate has improved substantially to a borderline pass in many sectors. Data relating to other sustainability sectors has much further to travel to reach that level.

But the picture is far from bleak. The system contains a lot of relevant data and information; and the growing influence of AI (artificial intelligence) methods adding to the value of that data has the potential to be transformational.

Figure 1 is a schematic of the 'Intelligence Stack' that the investor draws from in their investment process and portfolio construction. In its previous form, the "People Stack" combines with the "Tech Stack" to blend existing knowledge and beliefs with new data and context to reach decision-useful intelligence. This has been the investment process in a nutshell for a very long time. But we genuinely have a new version – the 'HI x AI Stack'. This in its advanced form integrates Human Intelligence (HI) and Artificial Intelligence (AI) to enhance decision-making.

The emerging proposition is that HI contributes context understanding, ethical judgment, and strategic foresight, while AI provides pattern recognition, automation, and predictive analytics. Together, they promise the nirvana of high-velocity, high-accuracy decisions to support the high returns and positive sustainability impacts that system-level investors aim for, within the level-setting of fiduciary duty and intergenerational fairness.

**The Intelligence Stack built from the People, Process & Tech Stacks**

All data, analysis and decision-making exists within the Intelligence Stack
And the HI x AI combination raises the accuracy, depth and velocity of that intelligence.

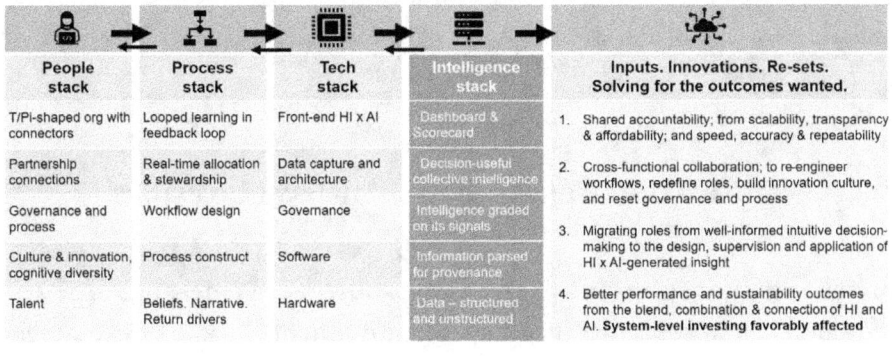

| People stack | Process stack | Tech stack | Intelligence stack | Inputs. Innovations. Re-sets. Solving for the outcomes wanted. |
|---|---|---|---|---|
| T/Pi-shaped org with connectors | Looped learning in feedback loop | Front-end HI x AI | Dashboard & Scorecard | 1. Shared accountability; from scalability, transparency & affordability; and speed, accuracy & repeatability |
| Partnership connections | Real-time allocation & stewardship | Data capture and architecture | Decision-useful collective intelligence | 2. Cross-functional collaboration; to re-engineer workflows, redefine roles, build innovation culture, and reset governance and process |
| Governance and process | Workflow design | Governance | Intelligence graded on its signals | 3. Migrating roles from well-informed intuitive decision-making to the design, supervision and application of HI x AI-generated insight |
| Culture & innovation, cognitive diversity | Process construct | Software | Information parsed for provenance | |
| Talent | Beliefs. Narrative. Return drivers | Hardware | Data – structured and unstructured | 4. Better performance and sustainability outcomes from the blend, combination & connection of HI and AI. **System-level investing favorably affected** |

**Thinking Ahead** Institute
An innovation network founded by WTW

Data systems of course fall well short of this nirvana at present. They lack the interoperability in data – the ability of different systems, platforms, and organizations to exchange, interpret, and use data seamlessly. They lack the basic data necessity of a single easy-to-use view of all their holdings and related risks that is accurate, real-time and affordable. The aggregation of data needed at total portfolio level is the 'CRADLE' basket of **C**onsolidation (all assets), **R**eal-time data, **A**nalytics (risk, by asset and at total portfolio level), **D**ecision-useful, **L**anguage friendly and at an **E**conomic cost.

The biggest demand for this Elysian data mix comes from TPA investors (Total Portfolio Approach). The TPA framework and methodology is often defined as what it is not. It is not subject to benchmark pressures, being designed to align with goals, attract best ideas and marry appropriately long-time horizons with shorter-term dynamism. TPA investors tend to be the most discerning in their data quest. They see the portfolio challenge as a competition for capital and perceive accurate thinking and nimble action as a huge performance edge.

In the author's frequent interactions with asset owners transitioning to TPA, the overwhelming majority observe that the weak link in the Intelligence Stack is currently the data and its limited inferential quality. They are all trying to solve for a much stronger 'CRADLE' score to build their sustainable edge in alpha.

## The Distinctiveness of System-level Investors

**So what sort of solutions to the data problem are emerging?** The system-level investor sees that their target returns can only come from a system that works. They see certain growing vulnerabilities in that dependence, and they seek better resilience to cope with the systemic risks lurking out there. The system they depend on is primarily an economic one, but also environmental and social. We increasingly need to recognise inter-connectedness, which is an accelerating force within our world ecosystem. To mitigate the economic, environmental and social systemic risks, the system-level investor has the incentive to contribute to the security of the system, via sustainability and real-world impact strategies like net-zero investing.

The simpler aspect of sustainability is financial materiality that focuses on how environmental and social issues affect the company's financial performance. This, put simply, is ESG integration, or outside-in materiality. For example, climate change impacts supply chains, leading to increased costs or reduced revenues.

The more complex issue is impact (or inside-out) materiality, with its focus on how the company's activities impact the environment, society and the economy. The timescales involved can extend much longer, and the measures are 'softer'. The classic example is a company's carbon emissions that contribute to global warming, affecting ecosystems, communities and companies. The investors' opportunity here is to try to achieve a positive impact on the system through real-world decarbonisation. But this comes with the significant associated need for data and narrative to measure what is being managed and what impacts emerge.

The regulatory environment in many jurisdictions encourages and, in some cases, mandates robust data architecture and governance to ensure transparency, accountability, and strategic alignment. For example, the TCFD framework is widely used among larger asset owners to disclose their climate risk exposures in a systematic and consistent way. The disclosed metrics to assess climate-related risks and opportunities include Scope 1, 2, and 3 greenhouse gas (GHG) emissions, carbon intensity, water and energy usage, waste management; and also, internal carbon pricing policies, practices and implications. This data brings focus and some clarity to the growing transition risks and physical risks associated with climate change.

System-level investors increasingly rely on soft and alternative data sources to capture a broader spectrum of insights across multiple sustainability fields. These lists often include five segments: climate change and renewable energy; biodiversity and nature; human rights and inequality; human capital and diversity; and healthcare and anti-microbial resistance (AMR). Each segment can be fitted into a matrix of investment opportunities. The horizontal axis looks generically at five distinctive sustainability strategies: exclusions, stewardship voting and engagement; public market tilting; private market targeted impact investments; operations in privately owned assets; and systemic engagement.

There are opportunities in each segment, but it will be the quality of the data that may well dictate the scale of the investment strategy pursued. Sustainability rightsizing reflects opportunities as much as mindset and skillset. The climate area in current times supports the biggest effort.

The intentionality involved also means that certain types of sustainability data may become a crucial part of reporting. For example, PGGM has healthcare impacts as a key part of its system-level (3D investing) strategy and reports to stakeholders on its related social impacts.

Joined-up thinking and narrative across governance, investment, and measurement functions are required to build a coherent data framework for reporting, particularly in the case of asset owners. Balanced scorecards alongside Key Performance Indicators (KPIs) and Key Risk Indicators (KRIs) have become increasingly common responses to this hunger for good data that has rich inferential quality. This shifts a singular focus on benchmark outperformance to multi-dimensional reporting and accountability with coverage of both process and outcomes.

While scorecards look backward, dashboards look forward. Where multi-asset portfolios previously had a simple focus on risk and return expectations, now the challenge is to codify the multiple measures that capture optimally configured portfolios. Figure 2 has an example of one such dashboard.

## Use of portfolio quality scorecard
Illustration of scorecard for a multi-asset XYZ fund (using TPA)
Robustness and resilience key additions to the line-up of factors

| | Dimension | Metric | XYZ | SAA illustration | TPA illustration |
|---|---|---|---|---|---|
| Prime factors | Return | Expected return vs cash (% pa) | 4.6% | Most SAA Models based principally on these 5 factors | The TPA Model is based on more factors |
| | Risk | Volatility (% pa) | 7.3% | | |
| | Efficiency | Sharpe ratio | 0.63 | | |
| | Relative risk | SAA/TPA relative risk | 3% - 5% | | |
| | Low cost | MER | 0.54% | | |
| Ancillary factors | Sustainability | ESG risk exposure (/100) | 23 | | |
| | Climate | Implied Temperature Rise | 2.5°C | | |
| | Flexibility | % daily liquid | 26% | | |
| | Access to skill | % contribution from skill | 31% | | |
| | Governance | Oversight complexity | 3/5 | | |
| Robustness & Resilience factors | Diversity | Equity beta | 0.37 | | |
| | Tail risk | Expected tail risk (% TCE) | 18% | | |
| | Systemic risk factor | Systemic tail risk – 10Y % TCE | x | | |
| | Climate risk factor | Climate tail risk – 10Y % TCE | x | | |
| | Systems-stewardship | Systems-stewardship spend (%) | x | | |

**Thinking Ahead** Institute
An innovation network founded by WTW

2

To summarize, system-level investors, by operating under mandates or beliefs that extend beyond backward-looking financial returns to include real-world impacts, have significantly elevated the complexity of their system, the underlying value chain and their dependence on data. But with new methods and innovations with respect to data and measurement, they emerge as better investors.

# The Role of Data in Stewardship

While stewardship alone cannot solve looming systemic risks, with policy and regulatory change essential in this regard, investor stewardship is one of the most important activities that investors can carry out. It helps to address the drivers of these systemic risks, mitigate them, and secure better long-term value as a result.

I commonly invoke the principle of "what get measured gets managed." But with stewardship and its impacts, there is a limit to the amount of data we see, and its relative quality and relevance.

The issues with data in stewardship come up most in measuring impact and resourcing. And it remains a persistent challenge to get robust, comparable, and decision-useful data.

Stewardship's effectiveness is inherently difficult to quantify. The impacts of engagement, voting, and policy advocacy often manifest over long time horizons and are influenced by multiple actors and externalities. Measuring the impact of stewardship on investment results is difficult, as most available data relies on estimates and qualitative reports rather than standardized metrics. Moreover, systemic stewardship is, by definition, designed to affect the entire marketplace or at least broad swaths of it, so even when it accomplishes its goals, there is no "control group" or counterfactual against which to measure.

The data difficulty contributes to the strong consensus that stewardship is under-resourced across the industry. Yet, the absence of clear guidance or requirements for measuring and reporting stewardship resources means that organizations have rarely disclosed how much time, money, or expertise is devoted to stewardship activities.

In this area there has been recent progress. In a PRI-sponsored initiative[202], a discussion paper prepared by Thinking Ahead Institute (part of Willis Towers Watson) examining the measurement issues suggested adopting standardized frameworks for measuring and reporting stewardship resources, to enable benchmarking and accountability.

The report supported a structured measurement approach, in a Stewardship Resources Assessment Framework. This framework encourages organizations to estimate stewardship resources using Full-Time Equivalent metrics, adjusted for seniority and including third-party costs. The aim is to enable comparability across organizations and support more productive conversations between asset owners and managers about stewardship ambition and resource adequacy.

---

[202] Putting resources where stewardship ambitions are. *Structured measurement to empower asset owner-asset manager conversations* | Thinking Ahead Institute thought leadership, commissioned by PRI (2024)

The industry's current average allocation of internal costs to stewardship is estimated at around 5 percent of total investment resources (considering the investment process costs alone). The report suggested that this should approximately double to meet rising demands, value-adding opportunities and threats from systemic risks. With greater resources more attention can be given to improving the measurement of impacts. And more focus can be given to systemic stewardship that is less focused on the risks and returns of individual holdings in isolation, but more on addressing systemic issues – climate change and others – with regulators and policymakers so as to protect and preserve the critical systems that impact broader portfolio returns. Engagement activities with a system-level lens protect and enhance the value of investors' assets over time by identifying and responding to market-wide risks to create long-term value while allowing individual companies to compete within the same social and environmental guardrails that limit externalities.

Systemic stewardship is most effective through collective action. Fostering dialogue between asset owners and managers, by using data as a basis for setting expectations and aligning stewardship practices with systemic risk management goals (like the proportion of resources dedicated to collaborative and system-level activities) is one concrete example of this.

In summary, data on stewardship is inherently and systemically weak. But all the signs are that it can get better if the resources and mindsets shift to see stewardship as strategically critical to system-level investing.

## The Role of Data Specialists: Navigating the ESG Data Ecosystem

System-level investors, with their expanded framing of the investment ecosystem, depend critically on accessing and processing highly specialized data. This will often be expedited by engaging data specialists.

As the volume and complexity of sustainability data have grown, the role of data specialists – firms such as MSCI, Sustainalytics, S&P Global, and others – has become increasingly pivotal. These organizations act as the critical interface between the raw data supplied by external providers and the decision-useful intelligence required by portfolio managers, steward-ship teams, and senior leadership.

These providers carry a heavy responsibility to be the translators and quality controllers of the sustainability and governance data ecosystem by applying accurate, fair and ethical practices. That highlights the importance of their methodologies and transparency.

These sustainability data providers have responsibilities that begin with sourcing and evaluating data from a rapidly expanding universe. Each provider brings its own methodologies, coverage, influences and biases. For example, MSCI and Sustainalytics both provide widely used ESG ratings, but their approaches to materiality, controversy assessment, and sector weighting can differ significantly. S&P Global, ISS ESG, Moody's, and a host of other providers add further to this landscape. The ecosystem is hyper-complicated as a result.

The first challenge for data specialists is to assess the provenance, reliabil-ity, and relevance of each data stream. This involves understanding the underlying methodologies, the frequency and transparency of updates, and the degree to which the data aligns with the organization's own sus-tainability priorities and regulatory obligations. Data specialists must be vigilant for inconsistencies, gaps, and methodological changes that could affect comparability over time or across portfolios.

Following data acquisition, the next step is integration and harmonization. Data specialists are responsible for mapping disparate data sets onto internal systems, ensuring interoperability, and resolving conflicts between sources. This often requires the development of bespoke taxonomies and translation layers, particularly when dealing with non-standardized or "soft" data such as qualitative assessments, controversy flags, or forward-looking scenario analyses.

A key part of the data specialist's role is engagement with data providers. This is not a passive relationship. Leading investment organizations actively challenge data sources on data quality, request clarifications, and advocate for improvements or customizations. Data specialists participate in industry working groups and collaborative initiatives with a precise intention to gain greater transparency and standardization across the sustainability and governance data ecosystem.

Data specialists also play a crucial role in supporting stewardship and reporting. They curate and validate the data that underpins engagement strategies, voting decisions, and regulatory disclosures. As stewardship activities become more sophisticated – moving from simple voting records to nuanced, impact-oriented engagement – data specialists try to ensure that the information flow is robust, timely, and fit for purpose.

The rise of artificial intelligence and advanced analytics further elevates the importance of data specialists. They are increasingly called upon to work alongside data scientists, leveraging machine learning to extract insights from unstructured data, identify patterns, and anticipate emerging risks. This requires a blend of AI sophistication, technical acumen, domain expertise, and critical thinking.

Finally, data specialists are stewards of data ethics and governance. They must navigate issues of data privacy, intellectual property, and the responsible use of AI-generated insights. Their work underpins the credibility of the organization's sustainability claims and the trust of clients, regulators, and other stakeholders.
The ecosystem has another branch of data and technology specialists that are vendors of integrated software providers in the chain. Organizations like SimCorp, Aladdin (BlackRock), Barra (MSCI), Charles River (State Street), Jacobi, Addepar and others are part of a big expansion of the software transition to platforms and away from legacy systems heavily

reliant on spreadsheets. They aim for front-to-back solutions for port-folio management, trading, risk, compliance, accounting, and reporting putting investors into a more mature and streamlined position than they can achieve in their normal tech transitions. These organizations are increasingly widely used by leading asset owners in their technology stack to evolve the intelligence stack.

In conclusion, data specialists of various types are critical ecosystem contributors to ultimate data success for the modern investment organization. And that particularly applies to the system-level investors that have a much more complex, data-savvy mandate, including the TPA investors that are among the most discerning data consumers.

## The Increasing Role of AI in Data Flow

Use cases of AI vary widely and reflect its general-purpose status. A strong majority of the world's largest asset managers see AI becoming a growing force in operational efficiency, investment reporting, portfolio construction, and processing and using sustainability data[203]

The biggest quest is to see what it can add to the investment process and to performance. And the system-level investor would be particularly minded to use it to support their goals in understanding and addressing system health, and developing strategic intelligence for portfolio strategy and construction.

A particularly interesting example here is AI-driven strategic intelligence working on foresight applications, particularly scenario analysis using AI tools to navigate geopolitical, environmental, and technological disruptions.

The system-level investor sees performance in multi-faceted terms. Risk-adjusted returns are central to the goals, but sustainability factors sit alongside, and investors seek measurable contributions to real-world impact as data dynamically emerges and evolves over time.

---

[203] P&I Thinking Ahead Asset Manager 500. (2025)

Of course, there has been considerable and prolonged slicing and dicing of ESG data to address alpha appetites. This data mining will naturally deepen within an AI-focused system-level investor environment.

The technology future will see increasing harnessing of advanced GPUs and parallel processing, and the likely presence of quantum computing may also become transformational in time. New algorithms emerge that leverage neural networks, deep learning, and large language models. These all learn from data, but the question becomes exactly *what* data. It feels like at present we may be drowning in a vast data lake (or swamp?). It's a case of "data, data everywhere but not a lot to think." The critical question is where the alpha signals are lurking, but this has not yet been answered.

To summarize, let's return to the Intelligence Stack as a layered framework that transforms data into decision-useful and actionable intelligence. The next steps in the data journey will involve material improvements made in the HI x AI stack which should quickly out-run the HI-alone stack. This phase is relatively straightforward. Investors apply critical thinking at the top of the stack to the data visualization that HI x AI produces to ensure decisions are as accurate as possible; that includes being contextually sound and ethically grounded. The stack in ideal circumstances builds collective intelligence into an exciting high-velocity "flow" combining human judgment with computational, systemic and data efficiency.

## The Future – Strategic Evolution and Organizational Readiness

Here are a generalized set of takeaways applicable to most investors. First, the future of system-level investing is shaped by data, via technological acceleration, geopolitical shifts, and sustainability imperatives. International accounting standards are evolving to strengthen sustainability metrics. Investors are evolving to a more strategic focus in their sustainability thinking. AI will play a substantial role in enhancing data processing and decision-making.

Organizational readiness with AI involves integrated thinking, joined-up leadership, and a shared vision across stakeholders, a balanced commitment weighing wider considerations, notably the externalities carried by accelerating energy consumption.

Ultimately, the quality of data and technology will be judged by the depth and validity of the inferences they support, and how these enable excellent risk-adjusted performance and resilient and sustainable investment outcomes.

The costs and benefits of data quality need to be assessed on joined–up terms. That involves adopting a complete picture on data and its place in the value chain. Most data users evaluate benefits of a given level of data quality too narrowly – they often over-emphasize the simple facets of data quality like objectivity, accuracy and timeliness. They see the problems with subjectivity, hysteresis, uncertainty and estimation in a relatively poor light. They do not give sufficient regard to data quality, in terms of the crucial reliability and relevance trade-off (also seen as provenance versus materiality) and the natural scarcity of good quality data in complex systems with correlations present but causalities very scarce.

Of course, most of our present realities with data concern the difficulties from legacy systems, over-running projects, too much data (not too little) and weak interfaces where users find front-end systems clunky but don't find it easy to articulate what would be better.

The challenges for investors don't really get any larger. Technology crosses investors' skills boundaries but there should be no unbridgeable gap across disciplines and functions, or turf wars about recognition and attention, for great data to emerge.

And for a real 'flow' in intelligence we need a culture of putting the story with the data. The investment industry often falls short by favoring the measured ahead of the meaningful. We need the story to add meaning to the data with good theory making up the triad.

## Summary

System-level investors face complex challenges in transforming raw sustainability data into strategic insights for portfolio management and impact measurement, particularly on interoperability and consistency.

- Data journey importance: Investors rely on structured processes to refine raw data, especially soft ESG data, into decision-useful intelligence, though company data quality varies widely across sustainability sectors and jurisdictions.

- System-level investor distinctiveness: These investors prioritize system resilience and sustainability impact beyond financial returns, addressing both financial and impact materiality over long time horizons.

- Regulatory and data frameworks: Frameworks like TCFD support transparency in climate-related risks, while sustainability data spans multiple fields including climate, biodiversity, human rights, and health.

- Investment strategies and data quality: Investment opportunities depend heavily on data quality, with climate-related efforts currently receiving the greatest focus among sustainability strategies.

- Stewardship challenges: Measuring stewardship impact and resources remains difficult due to limited, inconsistent data, though initiatives advocate for standardized resource measurement to improve accountability and effectiveness.

- Role of data specialists: Data specialists (like MSCI, Sustainalytics and others) bridge raw ESG data and decision-making by assessing data provenance, harmonizing datasets, engaging with providers, and supporting stewardship and reporting.

- Role of software specialists: Integrated software providers accelerate the pathways to the consolidation of portfolio data into a single easy-to-use view of all their holdings and related risks that is accurate, real-time and affordable.

- AI integration: Artificial intelligence enhances data processing and investment analysis, especially within the combined human intelligence and AI 'Intelligence Stack,' though there are challenges in identifying signals amid data noise.

- Future outlook: Technological advances, evolving standards, and organizational readiness will shape system-level investing's future, emphasizing the balance between data quality and sustainable performance outcomes.

Chapter 18:

# CalSTRS Case Study Stakeholder Communication and Management: How to Explain Why You Do What You Do

By William Burckart and Jon Lukomnik[204]

For a universal owner like the California State Teachers' Retirement System (CalSTRS), communication is not a cosmetic add-on to investing; it is part of the investment process itself. As the largest teachers' retirement system and the second-largest U.S. public pension fund (more than $382 billion as of September 2025), CalSTRS' portfolio performance depends not only on the fundamentals of individual holdings but also on the health of the financial systems and markets in which those holdings live. That scale and mandate create an obligation to explain why actions taken

---

[204] William Burckart and Jon Lukomnik are the editors of this *Handbook*. They both are Adjunct Professors of International and Public Affairs and Brandmeyer Fellows for Impact and Sustainable Investing at Columbia University.

and resources spent to protect system health are not only consistent with CalSTRS fiduciary duty, but necessary. It is just as important to do so in ways that earn legitimacy with members, policymakers, the press, peers, and markets. In practice, CalSTRS treats communication as strategy-enabling infrastructure. Communication is the governance-anchored architecture that translates complex, system-level analysis into decision-useful information for heterogeneous audiences and documents the throughline from intent → tool → effect across reporting, stewardship, and policy work.

This fiduciary orientation is not implied – it is codified. CalSTRS' Investment Committee first adopted a statement of investment responsivity in 1978 and added specific environmental, social and governance (ESG) risk factors in 2006. This provided a foundation for the Investment Committee's adoption of nine Investment Beliefs that guide all policies, procedures, and plans, and that explicitly recognize the materiality of system-level risks, with climate risk called out as financially material to the total fund. Those beliefs are then operationalized through the Investment Policy Statement (IPS), and the Sustainable Investment & Stewardship Strategies (SISS) Program and Portfolio Policy (Investment Beliefs; IPS; SISS Policy). These governing documents give trustees and staff a common, transparent script that links system conditions to capital allocation, engagement, escalation, and policy/standards activity.

Three features of that architecture are especially important for stakeholder communication:

- **A single narrative spine: Beliefs inform policy which determines action.** In accordance with CalSTRS fiduciary duty, the IPS embeds a long-term orientation and requires integration of material risk and opportunity considerations, including reference to CalSTRS' policies in active decisions, with expectations and escalation if policy is violated. These policies and Beliefs, approved after much research and analysis, make it possible for trustees and staff to explain any capital allocation, stewardship, or policy step as an implementation of board-approved fiduciary guidance, not a discretionary "preference."

- **Transparency.** To make that policy narrative legible externally, CalSTRS couples policy transparency with public disclosures – stewardship priorities, vote rationales, and issue-specific briefs – so observers can see the rules of the road ex ante rather than reconstructing them. This is particularly useful when there are controversial issues. The ex-ante disclosure of policy demonstrates that policy, not political whim, has determined CalSTRS' actions.

- **An explicit systems frame.** CalSTRS names the systems it seeks to influence – climate stability, market integrity/transparency, and healthy workforce and communities – and ties them to total-fund outcomes. The SISS Policy and related materials convey that the success of CalSTRS' investments is linked to the health of the broader systems; this systems framing underlies both strategy and external communications including reports, engagements, coalition work, and policy submissions. The same fiduciary logic is consistently expressed no matter the audience.

From this foundation, CalSTRS treats communication as strategy-enabling infrastructure. Several channels matter:

- **Member-facing** explanations emphasize pension security. System risks like climate change are non-diversifiable, so fiduciaries must manage them across the whole fund. To maintain accountability, CalSTRS pairs plain-language explanatory content with board-level updates and accessible metrics (e.g. progress toward the interim climate target).

- **Policymaker/regulator engagement** is discussed as market plumbing. High-quality, comparable disclosure and global standards are preconditions for accurate pricing and a stable cost of capital. CalSTRS publishes comment letters and testimonies and leverages leadership roles (e.g. the former CIO was on the International Sustainability Standards Board Investor Advisory Group) to connect standards design to market efficiency.

- **Peer-facing leadership** through investor groups such as Ceres, the Council of Institutional Investors, and Climate Action 100+ allows CalSTRS to amplify and normalize the fiduciary frame within the industry.

- **Public storytelling** uses concrete cases (e.g. lobbying alignment at Phillips 66) to show how stewardship protects system-wide value for diversified owners. Each vignette links an investment tool (proposal, vote, dialogue) to a system condition (policy alignment) and then to portfolio-wide risk/return.

Because the audience is heterogeneous – members, legislators, corporate management teams, regulators, and media – CalSTRS varies rhetoric and depth without deviating from the core fiduciary message. The result is a communications practice that is nonpartisan, data-driven, consistent and focused on fiduciary considerations. CalSTRS' expectations of corporate action and disclosure (e.g. TCFD-aligned reporting, board diversity thresholds) and vote rationales are published so that observers can see the financial logic. This minimizes the risk of it being relabeled as "political." This pre-emptive transparency is deliberately designed to maintain legitimacy in contested environments. CalSTRS also issues periodic "Engagements in Action" updates that link active stewardship to targeted system outcomes, thereby enhancing transparency, relevance and currency.

Finally, CalSTRS pairs narrative with measurement and accountability so stakeholders can see the throughline from intent → tool → effect. For example, regarding climate risk, CalSTRS' net-zero by 2050 target is disclosed alongside MSCI Climate Value-at-Risk analytics, low-carbon index reallocation figures (e.g. 20 percent of public equities; $28.9 billion as of 12/31/2024), and governance mechanisms, for annual review. This transforms a potentially abstract pledge into a disciplined, total-fund program. Portfolio-wide monitoring, semi-annual investment reporting, and technology infrastructure (e.g. enterprise risk platforms) allow CalSTRS to communicate progress credibly and course-correct as conditions evolve.

Why begin a stakeholder communication chapter here? Because legitimacy is an input to investing at CalSTRS' scale. Like it or not, being that large shines a spotlight on everything CalSTRS does. Members must trust that policies and actions are about their retirement security; policymakers must see a market-function rationale; peers need an understandable and replicable model. By embedding communication in governance, anchoring it to explicit beliefs and policies, and publishing the tools and measurements that link actions to system conditions, CalSTRS turns communication into a system-level instrument. And this strengthens the very conditions upon which its beneficiaries' long-term financial outcomes depend.

## The Problem: Why System-level Investing Stretches Traditional Communication

System-level investing requires a fundamentally different communication architecture from both MPT-only or impact investing frameworks. Where traditional reporting describes holdings, risk, return and some "market color", communications about system-level investing explains long, complex feedback loops of causality to show how fiduciary decisions made today influence the resilience of markets tomorrow.

CalSTRS operates within a severely heterogeneous communications environment. The audience includes members and beneficiaries, state and national policymakers, portfolio company executives, investment managers, peers, and global standard setters. Each brings its own perspective, and sometimes they conflict. As an example, consider the current disconnects between what different people think when the three letters "ESG" are mentioned. A single message therefore risks fragmenting on contact.

To address this, CalSTRS institutionalized an enterprise-wide three-year stakeholder-feedback and strategy cycle involving member surveys, board and investment committee reviews, and strategic-plan recalibrations. This cadence functions not only as consultation but as comprehension testing – an opportunity to assess what is understandable to various audiences and what resonates, allowing it to adjust tone and technical depth (for instance, plain-language member materials versus policymaker briefs), and align future communications with emerging priorities.

The communication risk is clear: If members recognize "ESG" only as exclusions (divestiture), and policymakers interpret ESG integration as ideological, then CalSTRS' system-level toolkit, cross-portfolio capital shifts, multi-year corporate engagements, and policy or standards work –can be misconstrued or politicized. To pre-empt this, the fund publishes its criteria in advance and corroborates claims with measurable progress indicators and public documentation, including comment files and vote rationales, thereby anchoring actions in a strong fiduciary frame.

## Explaining Non-Diversifiable, Systemic Risk

Risks to the environmental, social and financial systems can create systematic, or non-diversifiable, risks for investors, as well as cascading effects across economies and markets. Climate change, biodiversity loss, and social instability each pose portfolio-wide threats, obligating fiduciaries to mitigate them in the wider world as a matter of prudent duty since they cannot diversify them in the capital markets. Yet this legal-economic chain – systemic risk → fiduciary duty → portfolio-wide response – is conceptually dense and easily mischaracterized by outsiders unless consistently tied to risk-adjusted returns.

CalSTRS addresses the challenge by coupling narrative with analytics, translating abstract risk into tangible metrics. Scenario tools such as Climate Value-at-Risk (Climate VaR) and total-fund allocation levers make systemic exposure legible to non-specialist audiences. In doing so, the fund focuses on climate and stable company workforces not as moral aspirations but as financial conditions affecting every beneficiary's retirement security.

System-level outcomes rarely result from single action. CalSTRS' engagements typically target conditions within systems – policy alignment, sectoral transition, or disclosure norms – rather than immediate earnings metrics. Two examples illustrate this dynamic:

- **Phillips 66:** CalSTRS filed a shareholder proposal and mounted a public campaign that led the company, in October 2021, to publish a lobbying-activity report, aligning policy positions with Paris and emphasizing a lower-carbon focus.
- **Duke Energy:** After a filed proposal and sustained dialogue (supported by Climate Action 100+), Duke Energy committed to retire coal by 2035-2040, phase out older oil and gas units, and reach net-zero methane by 2030.

Neither engagement produces a neat, short-run payoff, which a traditional, non-system-level, MPT-focused investor would want in order to make a nice, neat story for its communications program. Yet each is fiduciarily relevant because it targets risk drivers at the system level. Narrating such indirect causality demands discipline, repetition, and transparent rationales – an evidence-based storytelling practice CalSTRS has embedded in its reporting cadence.

## Politicization and the ESG–Backlash Trap

In the U.S. context, stewardship tools – voting against unresponsive directors, applying board-diversity goals, or enforcing TCFD-aligned disclosure expectations – are sometimes reframed by non-investors as political acts. CalSTRS' published governance principles include expectations for climate disclosure and for board diversity as a baseline of good risk management. This consistent framing deters such criteria from being misrepresented by external entities with their own non-fiduciary objectives as social activism rather than fiduciary oversight.

To counter this, CalSTRS publishes its rationales, expectations and escalation pathways before proxy season, providing a transparent and fiduciary reason in advance for every vote or engagement. It issues periodic updates linking stewardship actions to systemic risk conditions – thereby correctly positioning what might appear as "politics" to others as wholly in the realm of prudent portfolio risk governance.

## Policy Engagement

At its core, investing is a process of data gathering and analysis. That makes every investor a key stakeholder in how information is collected, standardized, disclosed, and assured. Because reliable data moves markets, system-level investors necessarily engage with the policy and standard-setting processes that influence the quality, quantity and periodicity of data.

Such engagement is, in effect, a form of advocacy – but advocacy aimed at improving market efficiency, transparency, and risk management. Systemic risks are, by nature, matters of public interest, which can make investor participation in comment letters, testimony, or international frameworks both necessary and fraught, since such policy participation occurs in an arena where others engage for non-fiduciary reasons. CalSTRS addresses this by maintaining a consistent rationale: improved comparability, transparency, and rule consistency reduces information asymmetry and cost of capital, strengthening markets for all participants.

Whether through CalSTRS' former Chief Investment Officer's role on the ISSB Investor Advisory Group or in submissions to regulators, CalSTRS grounds every policy contribution in the same principle: Better data and clearer rules are essential infrastructure for efficient markets and long-term value creation.

## Making Internal Coherence Visible

Finally, credibility depends on visibly connecting beliefs to implementation. The more abstract the strategy, the more critical it becomes to show the beliefs → policy → action chain. CalSTRS' nine Investment Beliefs (updated 2020) explicitly recognize the financial materiality of various risks, including the significance of climate transition risks. These beliefs cascade into the Investment Policy Statement and the Sustainable Investment & Stewardship Strategies (SISS) Program and Portfolio Policy.

Internal coherence is built first, then translated into audience-specific, evidence-based messages delivered by trusted governance voices and corroborated through public artifacts such as board-approved policies, vote rationales, comment letters, and quantified progress reports. This architecture is reinforced by a reporting cadence, member-survey feedback loops, and a technology infrastructure that make adaptation visible, not merely progress.

## Communication in Practice: Case Vignettes

The effectiveness of system-level investing depends not only on what investors do but also on how they communicate their actions. Consistent, well-designed communications keep an investment organization aligned and focused on the risk/return impact of its investment actions, even when those impacts are at the end of a complex chain of influences and feedback loops and taking place in a real-world context dynamically over time. CalSTRS has several examples of how disciplined communication can translate complex investment strategies into public narratives that reinforce fiduciary legitimacy, accelerate policy learning, and shape the norms of the investment system:

- **Transparency featured prominently in the commitment.** CalSTRS framed measurement as part of the implementation process, disclosing indicators such as MSCI Climate Value-at-Risk, portfolio-emissions deltas, and the shares of portfolio allocation across climate-aligned and transition assets, alongside progress reports to the board and the public.

- **System-Level Engagement Campaigns.** CalSTRS is known for its stewardship campaigns, at least partially because clarity and transparency accompany its actions. The fund openly publishes expectations for corporate disclosure – such as minimum thresholds aligned with the Task Force on Climate-related Financial Disclosures (TCFD) – and defines escalation criteria for when dialogue advances to shareholder proposals or public advocacy.

Across all these engagements, CalSTRS consistently links stewardship to systemic risk management. Each campaign is framed as addressing a system condition – such as climate transition risk, policy misalignment, or social-cost externalization – that affects the performance of a diversified portfolio. By making that linkage explicit, the fund reinforces engagement as exercising fiduciary duty at scale.

## Lessons Learned

CalSTRS' experience demonstrates that treating communication as a strategic discipline rather than as compliance or superficial public relations can align an entire investment organization, clarify decision logic, create transparent expectations, impose accountability, provide guidance to peers, and make system-level investing complexities understood to both internal and external stakeholders. Effectively, such strategic communications become a governance mechanism. Each disclosure, report, and campaign serves a dual purpose: to document progress and to shape norms. By consistently making its strategies legible – quantifying progress, clarifying intent, and situating decisions within the broader market and policy context – CalSTRS turns information into influence and narrative into infrastructure.

This coherence across communication layers creates a positively reinforcing feedback loop. The credibility of portfolio commitments enhances CalSTRS' authority in corporate dialogues. The tangible outcomes of stewardship engagements validate its policy advocacy. Successful policy advocacy builds the enabling environment for future portfolio resilience. CalSTRS' communication architecture connects investment beliefs to policy, policy to practice, and practice back to those beliefs. The result is not a collection of announcements but a cumulative narrative that signals leadership, invites replication, and contributes to the overall health of the systems on which beneficiaries depend for their current and future pensions.

Several lessons emerge from CalSTRS' approach to system-level communication:

- **Make beliefs public and connect them to policy.** CalSTRS embeds its investment and stewardship beliefs directly into formal governance documents. By publishing the chain of reasoning – how beliefs inform strategy, and strategy informs action – the fund turns explanation into governance transparency.

- **Treat stakeholder input as strategic infrastructure.** A three-year cadence of member and stakeholder consultation through the enterprise-wide strategic plan process underwrites the legitimacy of allocative and stewardship priorities. This rhythm transforms consultation from reputation management into a feedback mechanism for adaptive strategy.

- **Publish the "rules of the road" before controversy arises.** By setting and disclosing engagement criteria, escalation pathways, and voting rationales in advance, the fund depoliticizes proxy season and builds consistency across cycles. Predictability becomes a hallmark of integrity.

- **Use storytelling to demonstrate system logic.** Through case-based communication – such as its engagements with Phillips 66 and Duke Energy – CalSTRS links instruments to system conditions and those conditions to portfolio risk in a way that all can understand. For CalSTRS, narrative is not anecdote but pedagogy that teaches markets how systemic stewardship works.

- **Frame policy and disclosure work as market plumbing.** By publishing regulatory submissions and using its leadership roles on standard-setting bodies to explain why standardized, assured data improves pricing and market function, CalSTRS reframes policy advocacy as a fiduciary necessity for efficient markets.

- **Communicate adaptation as deliberately as progress.** Regular reporting on what has changed – how new data, scenarios, or stakeholder insights have reshaped strategy–signals that the institution learns and adapts in real time. This dynamic transparency builds trust and reinforces CalSTRS' image as a dynamically adaptive, not reactive, investor.

www.ingramcontent.com/pod-product-compliance
Lightning Source LLC
Chambersburg PA
CBHW072012230526
45468CB00021B/1194